D1516006

SPOKEN IN DARKNESS

SPOKEN IN DARKNESS

SMALL-TOWN MURDER AND A FRIENDSHIP BEYOND DEATH

Ann E. Imbrie

HYPERION

New York

Library of Congress Cataloging-in-Publication Data

Imbrie, Ann E. (Ann Elizabeth)

Spoken in darkness/by Ann E. Imbrie.

p.   cm.

ISBN 1-56282-842-8

1. Serial murders—Michigan. 2. Snavely, Lee, 1950–1974.

3. Victims of crime—Ohio—Biography. I. Title.

HV6533.M5I42 1993

364.1'523'092—dc20

[B]   92-21434
                                                       CIP

Book design by Margaret M. Wagner

First Edition

10 9 8 7 6 5 4 3 2 1

To my mother and father

For there is nothing covered that shall not be revealed;
neither hid that shall not be known.
Therefore whatsoever ye have spoken in darkness
shall be heard in the light; and that which ye have spoken
in the ear in closets shall be proclaimed upon the housetops.

Luke 12:2–3

SPOKEN IN DARKNESS

P r e f a c e
1 9 7 5

Who murdered her was never the mystery. We might
have made a mystery out of it, wondered what became
of the doctor's daughter who, in the twenty years she
lived among us, had left town only briefly now and then.
But by 1975, no one whispered her name anymore over
kitchen counters, across backyard clotheslines. No hand
reached across a bridge table to touch another woman's
arm, to interrupt the photos of children and grandchildren, to pose the worried question. No flyers tacked up
on telephone poles counted the time. *Disappeared six
months ago. Missing now more than a year.* As it happened, and
hardly by accident, we shrugged her absence away, if we
noticed it at all. Then we discovered her missing and we
discovered her dead in the same moment, her name
linked with her killer's name on the same page of the
newspaper.

I was off in graduate school in another part of the
world when I heard the news from my mother, over a
cold telephone. I see myself standing in a dark hallway,
the telephone on a small table under recessed lights, a
chic design, up to the minute when the house I then
rented was new.

My mother hasn't called to tell me. She has called to
chat with the one daughter who, for a time, is also a
wife. We speak of wifely things. The weather turns
warm, the laundry piles up and starts over, the husband
works on the nerves. Where one path splits off from the
other, the talk crackles and puts us on edge.

"How's school?" my mother says.

"It's June already. The semester ended a month ago."

At my objection she withdraws the question. We are
still on trial with each other.

"So, how's the vacation?" she asks instead.

"I don't get one this year." I laugh. "I have comprehensives in the fall."

"Does that mean you won't make it home this summer?"

"I don't know, Mom." I want to tell her, *my life is more than an interruption of yours.*

Then she eases in, sheltering and uncertain. "You remember Lee Snavely?"

The casual mention of her name takes me back to the county in Ohio where Lee and I grew up. It is crisscrossed by railroad tracks and lonely country roads, the perfect setting for impossible accidents, disasters that cannot happen and do. Cars hurtle into each other at intersections, couples are obliterated at railroad tracks. Stretched taut and unwavering on all sides, the landscape explains the mystery to me. You misjudge distance, speed, shape, everything, across those open fields. Accustomed to seeing nothing for miles around, you won't see something when it's right on top of you, even if it's a train about to run you down.

Since I left home, I have lived among hills, near rivers, on the other side of mountains that focus the view. For the years before that, Lee Snavely, the doctor's dark-haired daughter, was the only difference I had to look at. Without her, I might have gone blind.

"She was my best friend," I say.

"That was a long time ago," my mother reminds me, as if to say, protective of me still, *who could Lee be to you now?*

The stranger I was taught to fear. My mother's daughter, I have long since stopped holding Lee in mind.

"Whatever happened to her?" I am ashamed to ask.

"The papers are full of it," my mother sighs.

She sketches the grim details: the small town in Michigan, the pieces of identifying jewelry, the man whose life drifted from trouble to trouble, the estranged wife who notified the authorities more than a year after the fact that her husband had buried several bodies in garbage bags under a bedroom window.

My mother shivers on the far end of the line. "It's awful," she says, and there is nothing else to say.

Later, in the other room, I draw back the drapes and stare blindly into the yard through the plate glass window. Without the curtains, the birds can't see the glass for the air. They misjudge distance and space, lose their bearings, and fling themselves against the startling glass. I find them later, hardly a trace of the collision in their bodies, except a ruffle about the neck and a dull quiet in the eyes. Now, my standing at the window warns them away.

A car rounds the corner, and honks its horn farther down the street. The woman across the way comes out for the mail, her cat on a leash. I stand there, watching, as late afternoon wears down to evening, until I can name the noise I do not quite hear.

The memory of Lee beats its wings in my heart.

My mind spins back to the fairgrounds, to the farm machines, to an August day, hot and humid and still, when I first met the dark-haired stranger from another church and another elementary school.

PART
ONE

We are in the dog days of August, Mexican season. Migrant workers, Mexicans who pass through town this time of year in huge open trucks, stoop over in the fields, crates stacked in front of them, or burlap bags slung over their shoulders. They come to pick tomatoes. Boys from the local high school lucky enough to land well-paying jobs at the one factory in town unload the fruit from giant flatbed trucks. T-shirts tied around their waists spill down over slim hips, and sweat glimmers across their shoulders in the sun. They pick over the tomatoes casually, posing, joking volubly as they work, and send the good ones along conveyor belts into the Heinz plant. At the end of the line, the fruit drops into steamy vats and cooks down into ketchup. There is no escaping the sweet weight of the smell that hovers over town.

At the fairgrounds just inside the town limits, the whole county comes together for the fair. In the merchants' building, a local insurance agent in suspenders talks up term policies with the passers-by. Next to his booth, an optometrist shows off the latest contraption for the testing of eyes, and beyond that, a kitchen knife salesman carves elaborate roses from radishes. Somewhere farther down, an out-of-towner who travels through the flatlands all summer from fair to fair leans against bags of weedkiller or fertilizer, a spray gun for pesticide at the ready. ONE FARMER FEEDS 76 AMERICANS, *his sign shouts in red, white, and blue.*

In the livestock building, a brood sow stretches out lazily in the mud, and a crowd of yammering piglets struggles to get at her. Cows, dumb-eyed and lonely, twitch their tails against flies. A bull the size of a small tractor, thick and muscular, looks up at a cluster of teenagers gathered at the fence, then lowers an indifferent head to pull at his feed. The girls gawk at the penis, whisper behind cupped palms, then race away in laughter for the safety of prizewinning quilts and needlepoint and jam.

Out on the midway, the gypsy wagons line up. In one, a cotton candy machine spins sugar into thick pink clouds. In another, syrup drools from a spigot over a cone of crushed ice, and thick, chewy pretzels glisten with salt. Across the way, the merry-go-round travels in tame circles, round and round and up and down, its mechanized music filling the summer night. A father or two stands beside a grinning horse, the protective hand resting against the small of his child's back. The fathers ride for free.

Beyond the carousel, the Tilt-a-Whirl swings out of control, and screaming bodies collide or skinny elbows jam into the padded seats. At the Ferris wheel in the center of the midway, a dark, tattooed arm reaches across a row of girls' laps to lock the restraining bar into place. Drawing back, the forearm grazes a breast, and under the thin cotton shirt a nipple springs involuntarily to life. A startled head drops, turns slowly, and the eyes, wide and uncertain, stare into the stranger's face. He wets his lip and winks, then stretches his arm toward the lever that starts the machine moving. When the wheel lurches forward into its upward spin, the man reaches for the seat, and pulls it back hard. "Here's to a hell of a ride," he laughs, and sets the car rocking on its way.

At the end of the week, the man disappears into another county, in Michigan to the north or Indiana to the west. The girl lies in the dark of her bedroom, her eyes fixed on the ceiling. Fingers, smooth and delicate, find their way to her breast. She touches herself there, turns her face into her pillow, and imagines the motion of the swaying car.

I know nothing of this yet. I am eleven years old, poised on the brink of loss and of knowing. The sign on the north edge of town reads BOWLING GREEN, COUNTY SEAT. POPULATION: 12,005. I imagine someone hired permanently by the town council to change the number every time a baby is born. It is 1962. The sign painter works well into the night to keep up with the babies.

Where the dust and the gravel of the midway give way to grass, farm machines loom up, more fun for a child than the merry-go-round. Extinct species displayed at the fair as if in a museum, by Allis Chalmers, Massey-Ferguson, John Deere. A green Brontosaurus spitting corn over its shoulder out a small mouth at the end of its neck. A red Tyrannosaurus rex designed to chew up earth. For a week every summer of my childhood, until I am tall enough for the Ferris wheel, I climb around on farm machines and imagine living moments before the Great Ice Age.

I meet Lee Snavely for the first time, those farm machines behind us, at the end of the midway of the Wood County Fair, this particular summer near the end of my childhood, the summer before the seventh grade.

1 9 6 2 – 1 9 6 4

Lee had a beauty mark on her cheek, like Elizabeth Taylor's. She was not like anyone I had ever seen before, exotically beautiful, her hair a dark circle around her face, her eyes dark as well, her eyebrows shadows against the light of her skin.

That day at the fair Lee wore blue knit shorts, and a white, short-sleeved top with a scalloped collar trimmed in pink. I stared, fascinated and alarmed, at her chest.

Like me, I thought, facing seventh grade, *she needs a bra and isn't wearing one.*

My father, innocent of the world, said Lee shouldn't have been at the fair at all that week, her own father buried less than a week before. My mother said it was no wonder, after a funeral like that.

Lee's father, the doctor with the big house in the country, wanted no mourners. At the committal a band played "Oh God Our Help in Ages Past" Dixieland style—saxophones, clarinets, trumpets, and one banjo. The people gathered in a half circle on a little rise near the back of the Oak Grove Cemetery. When the music started, one head turned to another, a question in the eyes. A nervous fan disturbed the air before a woman's face. A man, another doctor, shifted his weight, uncertain where to put his large, gentle hands. A child giggled at a squirrel that darted behind a headstone. No toe tapped. Cheerful syncopation bounced around the grave and the saints came marching in.

My father, a Presbyterian minister, shook his head over the whole business. No local preacher should have allowed such a thing, he said. People are helped by the sadness of funerals, sorrow is the order of the day. But Loyal Bishop, the Lutheran pastor, was new in town, and he agreed to the dying man's request. Maybe, fresh out of seminary, he was still young enough and handsome enough to think there were many ways to make a joyful noise unto the Lord.

The scandal of her father's funeral was the first thing I knew about Lee, before I'd even met her, and the information set me up right. As I came to know her, I figured the tough spin she gave everything spun right out of her genes.

Two weeks after the start of seventh grade, Cheryl, a popular eighth grader and out of my ken, asked three or four of us to meet her for lunch in the school cafeteria. Other small groups of my friends clustered around other eighth-grade girls seated at various points on the cool side of the lunchroom.

"About the dress code," Cheryl began.

The student handbook spelled that out: girls had to wear dresses or skirts and blouses to school. No pants, no cut-offs, no sloppy sneakers, no halter tops. They wanted us to look like girls without causing a distraction. It was a fine line to walk.

"When Miss Cook pulls the chairs into a circle," Cheryl continued, "keep your knees together at all times."

Miss Cook, young and blond and fresh out of college, taught American history. She announced on the first day of school that she didn't believe in lining up chairs in rows, no sooner a good idea than it turned dangerous.

Rule #1: Knees together.

"When you're changing classes," Cheryl said, "walk up the middle of the stairs. Along the railing, the boys on the next flight down will look up your skirt."

Rule #2: Middle of the stairs.

"Don't hang around with boys who wear white socks."

"Why not?" one of us asked, bravely. Most of the boys we knew wore white socks.

Cheryl rolled her eyes. "White socks are queer," she said.

Rule #3: No white socks. I was beginning to think I should take notes.

"Try to get to school fifteen minutes early, and check your locker before home room."

This rule I already understood. Cheryl's invitation had been written on notebook paper and stuck in the ventilator slits of my locker. I didn't know how she figured out which locker was mine. Eighth grade was full of mysteries, the next magical link in the chain of command that stretched all the way past the other side of high school to our mothers. We learned what we were to become, step by step.

"And you girls can't walk around holding hands anymore. That's sixth-grade stuff. You want people to think you're lesbians?"

We girls eyed each other suspiciously and shook our heads. Of course not, I thought, but I didn't have any idea what Cheryl was talking about.

"Tell your parents it's time you had your first boy-girl party," Cheryl added, conspiracy in her whispered tone.

An older girl named Linda came up behind Cheryl and tapped her on the shoulder.

"You about finished here yet?"

Cheryl rose from her chair and leaned on the long table to look at us sternly.

"If you guys have any questions," she said, "ask Mrs. Wynn or one of the other gym teachers. I don't want to get a reputation for hanging around with seventh graders."

Linda and Cheryl walked off together, their arms wrapped around their books.

Our town organized children under the age of twelve into five different elementary schools, all of them named for the streets they were built on. Those streets wandered past churches and shops and grocery stores with wide, clean aisles; past houses hidden behind rambling front porches, shaded by maples and dying elms in the center of town; past duplexes crowded together, separated by narrow, gravel driveways or paltry gardens; past brick houses farther out in the subdivisions, slung low to the ground, stretched out on green swaths of lawn. Eventually some of those streets wandered out to the country, where they turned into roads and cut wide strips between miles of soybeans and tomatoes and corn, farms with red barns and white silos. This was our Eden: at twelve, all of us converged on one junior high school, trailing our neighborhoods behind us, and we didn't know it yet.

The eighth-grade girls didn't ask Lee to join in those little talks. She grew up in the country, like a farm kid, although her father had run with the country club set. She didn't fit with the crowd, lived on the outside of the circle. The eighth-grade girls probably didn't know who she was. Lee, I thought, was safe to ask. From where she stood, she couldn't blab about how dumb I was to the whole school.

I met her at the bus stop at the end of the day, before I caught up with my real friends down at Rogers Drug where we bent our heads over *Seventeen*, played discreet transistors under the tables, and drank Coke out of shapely glasses. In mid-September, the maple trees along Grove Street where the buses waited in line to pick up their children had already started dropping leaves. Crimson and yellow swatches stuck to the sidewalk with the recent rain. I had a lot to learn in a hurry, and I wasn't going to learn it at Rogers Drug. I decided on the direct approach.

"She's a woman who loves other women instead of men," Lee said.

"You mean girls can be queer?"

Lee nodded. "It's like a medical word," she said. Lee wanted to be a doctor like her father had been, and she already had a head start on a technical vocabulary.

"So you've had the talk, huh?" she added.

I looked up at her, surprised at how word gets around, and scooted a maple leaf into the gutter with the toe of my saddle shoe.

"Pretty scary, isn't it," Lee said. "All those rules."

"Yeah," I said. Junior high was full of dangers I hadn't dreamed of.

The door of her bus jerked open, and, twirling her skirt in the air, Lee stepped into the doorway. She turned toward me, pulled her skirt up above her knee, and did a little can-can kick from the first step.

"What happens," she said, "when you *want* boys to look up your skirt?"

Then she disappeared down the dark corridor of the bus.

I hadn't thought of that possibility yet. All at once I saw how easily you could get trapped in the rules.

As it turned out, we didn't have to nag our mothers about the boy-girl party. They knew the rules, too.

They got on their telephones right away and planned a progressive dinner party for us, made in the image of the parties they had for themselves. They chose three houses, all with finished basements, all within a block of each other so we could progress easily from one stage of the party to the next, and they made up the guest list from among the children of the mothers they knew. Mrs. Snavely wasn't tapped into the network, but I asked my mother to add Lee's name to her guest list. We might not have had the party at all, if Lee hadn't tipped me off to how important it was.

At the first house, we played getting-to-know-you games like "Famous Couples." If you had "Juliet" pinned to your back, you had to wander around asking yes or no questions about yourself until you figured out who you were, and then you wandered around some more looking for "Romeo." He had to be your partner for the next game, Pass the Orange, or Winkum. Then, at the second stage, we had dinner (sloppy joes and potato salad) across the street. Finally, we got dessert and dancing at another house down the block.

The eighth-grade girls were right: this was advanced stuff, putting Johnny Mathis on the record player and dancing with Denny Weaver, my first true love. We didn't get it quite right. When I tried to teach him the steps to the only slow dance I knew, we stood a good twelve inches apart and stared at our feet, counting one-two-three-four. We didn't whisper yet that fall.

By May we knew that the best kind of slow dancing didn't have steps. You hung from his neck like a pendant. He circled your waist like a belt. You heard the music in your blood, you felt his heart in your chest, and then you just stood there and swayed.

Being friends with Lee caused me a little trouble at school. "Best" didn't mean "only," but you couldn't have two best friends. So when Lee came along, I pretty much had to throw over Maggie Howell, who'd been my best for as long as I could remember.

Those years with Mags had been filled with unusual tortures. When we were just kids and learning the spelling rules, she invented a game out of "when two vowels go walking, the first one does the talking." We played it at her house, marching around in a line of two. Maggie always got to be the first vowel. When I tried to object, that I was a guest, that I ought to have the honor sometimes, Maggie turned to me, one hand on her hip and a finger wagging my way. "Ah, ah, ah," she said, "the second vowel is always silent."

I was slow learning to hate this girl, who already had a mother's wagging finger down pat.

"You could have tried *wienerschnitzel*," Lee suggested, years later in junior high.

"Foreign words didn't count," I said.

"Then how about *steak?*" Lee said, right away.

I didn't hold it against Maggie any more, now that we were grown up and in junior high. But then came the cheerleading tryouts. In the spring of seventh grade, Maggie got me to try out for the eighth-grade squad.

I knew I couldn't make the team. I couldn't roller skate, and I couldn't bowl either all those times Maggie dragged me off to Pine's Roller Rink or Al-Mar Bowling for her birthday parties. Here she was, up to her old tricks, pushing my buttons, talking me into an even greater public embarrassment.

Come on, she said. *Everybody tries out.*

Practically every girl I knew was working on splits in her odd moments in gym class and memorizing the words to cheers in the halls between classes. Against my better judgment, I didn't want to be the exception to the rule.

We had practice one Saturday afternoon out at Maggie's house. Her older sister, Jean, a high school cheerleader, served as a technical adviser, passing down the lore. She helped me work out the moves for my tryout cheer. (*We've got the Bobcats on*—**clap**—*our team, and they're grrrreat,* **clap clap**.) Conveniently, the routine didn't call for a toe jump, but it was still a lost cause. Mrs. Wynn and the other judges would make us all do toe jumps and splits separately.

All afternoon at the practice session, Maggie was seductively encouraging.

"But Mags," I said, "what about the toe jumps?"

Maggie reminded me of the gym teacher's conviction. Anybody could be a cheerleader, she said. But Maggie had that wrong. It was every girl's right, perhaps, but the official privilege belonged to the athletic few.

The necessary poise, the charm, the personality I might have mustered, but I could complete a toe jump as easily as fly. I'd been clumsy since before I was born, taught by years of family jokes thereafter to match the awkward picture in somebody else's mind. Every stage of the movement seemed potential disaster to me—the running start (my tennis shoes would trip me up), the leap into uncertain air (who could trust it?), throwing my arms out to the world, spreading my legs into an intimate split, all that achieved and suspended in a crucial moment. A toe jump broke the rules of my gravity.

And then there were the rules of decorum. I'd have to do it in front of the whole school.

When the time came, we sat, sweaty-palmed and uncomfortable, trapped on folding chairs alongside the basketball court across from a bleacher full of boys who had come to gawk at the show. I kept my knees closed up tight (Rule #1), and inside I squirmed, waiting for the summons to the middle of the gym when suddenly a new set of rules nobody told you about would apply. On command I was supposed to open my legs wide for all to see.

The cheerleader rode on the team bus to the football games (no chaperone but the coach), breathing in the tense anticipation of the road trips away, and comforting or carousing with the boys on the way back. She patted the butts of the basketball players when they spilled out onto the gym floor one by one in their white uniforms, like Chiclets sliding from the box. And on a good toe jump, the ultimate lady and the ultimate tramp, she flashed her panties in front of everybody, not just by permission but by design. Toe jumps improved team spirit.

At sixteen, plenty of girls might have *killed* for the chance. The tryouts were almost that loaded, even at twelve.

I struggled through my tryout cheer, stiff arms and knee bends, but I balked at the toe jump. I returned to the locker room in defeat before they asked me to show off my splits.

"Why did you even bother?" Lee asked, when it was all over. "Cheer-leading isn't for you."

"I know," I said. "I don't know."

"It's that old Maggie Howell," Lee explained, "still trying to do all the talking. You shouldn't let her get to you like that."

My mother had been telling me that for years, but she meant to say, *be nice, bear it patiently, turn the other cheek.* It sounded different coming from Lee. She tried out too, and didn't make the team either, but she adjusted immediately. Some things, she told me, you just have to do for the kicks.

Maggie made captain of the squad. On game days all the way through high school, she wore the short red skirt with the white inset pleats and the ruffled red panties underneath. They were part of the uniform.

Lee and Maggie should have gotten along better. They had plenty in common: their fathers were both doctors, even if Lee's was dead. They both lived in big houses in the country, had German shepherds as pets, and both did pretty good toe jumps. But they were nothing alike. Lee knew what to do with her medical background.

The best Maggie could manage, even in junior high, was to show me a book of cartoons she had stolen from her father's study, drawings of fat-faced babies speaking from inside their mothers' bellies, making jokes about pregnancy from the baby's point of view. They were funny, but Maggie wanted me to think we were getting away with something looking at them.

Lee was a different story. She kept *Playboys* stashed under her bed. And once, when I was spending the night out at the farm, Lee brought out one of her father's medical books to show me detailed drawings of the parts of women's bodies.

"This is called the *mons veneris*," she said, pointing to the picture, "because of Venus, the goddess of love."

"You mean like in venereal disease?" I said.

My parents believed in foreign languages, and I was taking private lessons that year from the local Latin teacher recently retired from the schools. A lot of our sex words came from that ancient, sacred tongue.

"And you know what *pudendum* means?" I asked.

"Sure," Lee said. "That's the female genitals."

"But do you know what it *means* really? 'That which we must be ashamed of.' It's a passive periphrastic."

"Who says we have to be ashamed?"

"History, I guess," I said.

"History is a lot of shit," Lee said. She was good at her Anglo-Saxon. With that she started taking her clothes off.

"You, too," she said.

"You mean get undressed?" I asked.

"Don't be such a baby," she said. "Here's your mirror."

"Shouldn't we lock the door?" I asked.

Lee looked at me like I was crazy.

Our knees drawn up toward our chests, our shoulders barely touching where our backs pressed against a shared pillow, we lay on her bed, holding mirrors between our legs. The rumble of a car speeding down Napoleon Road grew louder as it passed, then faded away in the distance. A dog from the kennel outside barked once, twice, and was silent. We looked, and we touched. We compared our parts, soft and pink and knowing, with the pictures set out for us in ordinary black and white. From downstairs, the noise of Lee's stepmother absently shuffling papers in the den floated up through the heating vents and was lost in the sound of our breath.

I didn't like having friends over all night. My mother was always looking in on us, checking to make sure we were behaving ourselves. *What's up*, she'd say. *Having a good time?* Besides, our house didn't have a basement, or a rec room, or even a window equipped with a tree we could climb out to, in case there was someplace to go. The best I had to offer was a radio, and a refrigerator full of leftovers and cookie dough for sneaking late-night snacks. My mother refused to keep store-bought cookies on hand.

It was one of the rare occasions when I first knew Lee that she spent the night at *my* house. W-FM was running a special program on the Everly Brothers that spring night toward the end of seventh grade. Most of their songs were oldies already, classics, the DJ said. My mother had told us twice to turn the radio down. But when "Dream, Dream, Dream" came on, we turned the volume up anyway, and sang along. That song was the first 45 I'd ever bought, an oldie even then. It seemed years ago, way before fifth grade, and I still knew all the words. *Whenever I want you, all I have to do is dreeeeam, dream, dream.*

Then the DJ announced the next big hit. *What are we gonna tell our friends when they say oooh la la?*

"How could they spend the night in a movie theater and not get caught?" I said.

"Maybe they rolled off their seats," Lee said.

On the edge of the bed, she closed her eyes, dropped her head forward, and slowly slipped to the floor with a thud. In no time she was invisible under the bed. We were still little girls at my house.

We convulsed into giggles right at the moment my mother poked her head in the door.

"Little Suzie's going to have to wake up pretty early," my mother said. "Lights out."

Lee crawled out from under the bed, dust in her dark hair, and we scrambled under the covers.

"Mothers spoil everything," I said, before I caught myself. Lee didn't have a mother to look in on her.

In a moment, I heard the betrayal of my own mother's care in my adolescent complaint, and I knew it would hurt her feelings. But I needn't have worried about hurting Lee's. As it came to me, Lee's story was the saddest true story I knew. A lot of people had died in her family. She was used to it. She told the story straight, and I thought she was very brave.

Lee's mother died when she was a little kid, she told me, just like her grandmother, who died when Lee's father was six. Lee was the oldest of three children and the only daughter, and her daddy loved her best. He depended on her after her mother died because he was so busy as a pathologist working out of more than one hospital at once. His work kept him away from home for long stretches at a time, and Lee practically had to bring up her little brothers all by herself. But she adored her father, and she didn't mind. She would have done anything he asked.

She showed me his picture once. He was a big, handsome man with black hair, like hers. In fact, they looked a lot alike. He had been one of the Iron Men on Yale's football team, she said, way back in the 1930s. She wanted to be just like him when she grew up.

Then, two years before I met her, Lee's father found someone else and got married again. His new wife already had a daughter, an older girl, almost out of high school. They all moved in together in a big house in the country, Kaskaden Farms, they called it, where Dr. Snavely kept German shepherds in kennels. They trained them, to sell as guard dogs, not pets. They had a swimming pool on the farm. It was the only swimming pool in town.

Everything was going just fine, but the summer before seventh grade, Lee's father died suddenly of a heart attack after a golf game. It wasn't his fault he died, Lee said. But even though he didn't mean to, he still went off and left her and her brothers in the care of somebody they hardly knew. She was his wife, Lee said, but she was somebody else's mother. Lee didn't like her one bit.

We made a tent under the covers, and turned on the flashlight I'd hidden under the pillow. We kept the radio on low. *Hey bird dog, get away from my quail. Hey bird dog, you're on the wrong trail.*

"You must really miss your mother," I said.

"What's to miss?" Lee shrugged. "I hardly remember her."

I didn't know anybody who'd lost one parent, let alone two, and a stepmother was out of Cinderella.

"So where's the fairy godmother?" Lee said.

"If I had a fairy godmother, she'd let me shave my legs," I sighed.

It's a measure of how important I had made smooth, hairless legs that I thought Lee and I were complaining about the same thing.

Early fall in the eighth grade, just after school started, I helped Lee plan a pool party. We wanted that party to be perfect, and we spent a lot of time setting it up, picking out all the best slow songs, trying on different outfits. It was a good thing we worked so hard on it, because as it turned out, it was the only party Lee ever had.

The week before, I stayed over at her house, and we sat up late in her bedroom wearing shorty pajamas, writing and revising the guest list. We marked off two columns on a piece of paper, one labeled "Boys" and the other "Girls," and started by listing the couples. Tom and Lee. Ann and Sean. Jim and Maggie. The other Ann and the other Tom.

"They broke up last week," I said.

"But we can invite them both, don't you think. I mean, they'll be *civil*."

"Oh sure, they can be the extras."

"So, what about Mike?"

Lee was doubtful. "He wears white socks," she said.

"Yeah, but he's a good dancer. And cute, too. And there's Joel." I was running through the list of extras.

"And Carla," Lee added. "Wouldn't Carla and Joel make a good couple?"

"Oh, let's see."

I wrote their names down on a piece of paper, crossed out the letters their names had in common, and worked the lottery we used to determine our romantic futures: love, hate, friendship, marriage, one possibility for each uncrossed letter until you ran out of them, and the last uncrossed letter spoke the truth. This particular match up ended in "love," but if it hadn't, we would have added middle names and started over, a way of cheating fate. It was an odd little ritual, since both compatibility and incompatibility depended ultimately on what the names *didn't* have in common.

"We can change into our bathing suits if it's warm enough," Lee said.

"And we can dance out by the pool," I said. "Isn't that romantic?"

"Plenty of dark corners for interdigital contact and osculation," Lee said. "That's making out."

"What about your mother?" I could never have a make-out party at my house.

"She won't even notice," Lee said.

Once we had our plans in order and called everybody on the list, the mothers took care of their own plans. They hooked into the telephone network to figure out whose mothers would drop us off, in clumps, out of station wagons, and whose mothers would pick us up when the party was over. They'd learned their lesson the past summer, when my whole gang of girls spent our Saturday nights at the Little League park. We climbed out of the station wagon and told the mother driving that some other mother was bringing us home. Then we met up with the boys and rode home on the handlebars of their bicycles, our hair flying out in the wind.

After that summer, our mothers didn't leave the arrangements up to us.

By halfway through the party, things were going pretty much as we'd planned. About the time Joel and Carla started falling in love, Lee and I took a break, and slipped into the bathroom together to congratulate ourselves. The orchestra behind Bobby Vinton's "Blue on Blue" was swelling up, the sounds drifting in from poolside. I approached the mirror to put on my lipstick, smoothed a little of it into my cheeks for color. Lipstick came in flavors that year, and my flavor was Coca-Cola.

"I don't get this song," I said.

I often heard the words wrong, converting the real thing to the image of the world I had in my head. For years I thought Tammy Wynette fit right in with my social studies lessons, singing about some guy named Stan from New Orleans, "Stan, Bayou Man." *Guantanamera* sounded in my ears like *one ton of manna*. Biblical words seemed right at home on the Top Forty charts. Now I thought I heard Bobby Vinton singing about something from *Ephesians*.

Cool little 'Phesian. That's what it sounded like to me.

"That's *cruel little teasin',*" Lee said, and rolled her eyes.

Even after Lee set me straight on the words this time, I didn't get what Bobby Vinton was talking about. *Cruel little teasin'*? A tease was my big brother, tickling his little sisters until we almost suffocated. What could that possibly have to do with Bobby Vinton breaking up with his girlfriend and being blue on blue?

"I'll show you," Lee said. "You be the boy."

She made with her arms like she wanted to dance with me. I dutifully slipped my arm around her waist, and started leading her around the tiny bathroom. Right away, I noticed the difference. My knees didn't knock against hers once, the way they did when I danced with boys. She nestled up to me a little off center, our breasts alternating, and every step we took, her thigh pushed between my legs. When we stopped, she left me dizzy and aching and dumb.

"*That's* teasin'," Lee said.

I stepped back from her, barely recovered, relieved under the circumstances to have played the boy. "Some trick," I said, when I had my breath again.

"It's not such a useful skill," Lee shrugged, "when you're a one-man woman."

She turned quickly out of the bathroom, off in search of Tom and one of the big, comfortable chairs for making out in. I stared into my own face in the mirror, flushed with the lipstick on my cheeks, and pulled my hair back behind my ears. For a moment, I tried to imagine a boy's face looking back at me.

When I found Sean standing around with the cottonwood trees, I led him off to a darker place along the privacy fence around the pool. We danced close all the way through "What Will My Mary Say?" and "Be My Baby." We kissed while we danced. When I felt sure of the lesson I'd learned, I shifted my thigh into place. Sean's breath rippled through his shoulders.

"Hmmm," he whispered in my ear, and pulled me as close as he could. "I didn't know you were that kind of girl."

"I'll be whatever kind of girl I want," I said.

There were a couple of problems at that party, things we hadn't counted on and couldn't control. But brave and unchaperoned, we managed, I guess.

The two Toms started poking at each other from opposite sides of the pool with those long aluminum rods you scrape the bottom with, and one of them fell in with his clothes on. We thought it was funny—*splish, splash, he was taking a bath*—but then Tom came back up again, sputtering water, and mad. He thought the other Tom had done it on purpose, and was ready to punch him, but Sean broke it up and made them shake hands. You know how boys are: two of them do something to each other, and then they shake hands, as if everything were just fine, because they don't want you to think they're bad sports. You can tell they'd just as soon kill each other.

And at one point, Bonnie and Bob had some kind of fight. He was a little runt, but he had a bad temper and sometimes flew out of control. Bob kept telling Bonnie to stop whining at him, and when she wouldn't he hauled off and hit her in the face with the back of his hand. He was all over her apologizing, but she started to howl anyway, and when she started to howl, the dogs in the kennels around the pool started to bark, and the noise got all mixed up with "The Monster Mash," spinning loud on the record player. I thought that would bring Lee's mom out for sure. She was crazy about those dogs.

But she never did show up, as Lee had predicted. Usually, a mother wants to get a look at her kid's friends, checking to see that they don't have cigarettes rolled up in their T-shirt sleeves, or making mental notes about what they're wearing so she can complain to her friends on the phone the next day about what the other mothers sent their kids out in. Maybe Mrs. Snavely didn't have friends to complain to, living way out there in the country. She didn't look us over once.

"You'd think she would have at least been worried that Tom's parents might sue," Lee said after everybody else had gone home. Their boy might have hurt himself falling into that pool.

We wandered around the swimming pool, wadding up soggy crepe paper and throwing away paper plates. All of a sudden I understood why the only flurry of maternal activity I ever witnessed in Mrs. Snavely was the time Blusie, one of their German shepherds, not a breeder but a house pet, took a bite out of me and my favorite pair of wool bermudas. Mrs. Snavely, all nervous fuss and bother, rushed me to the emergency room for a tetanus shot and paid for everything.

"You mean," I said, "if I'd asked she would have bought me a new pair of shorts?"

"You could have made money on the deal," Lee said.

From the driveway my mother, come to take me home, tooted the horn. I shot one more bedraggled decoration in the trash, and scooted off for the car.

"Two points," Lee called out after me.

"See you Monday," I called back.

My mother was full of questions about the party. What did you do? Who did you dance with? What did she fix to eat? Some questions I didn't particularly want to answer, and I struggled against the pressure coming from behind the steering wheel.

"Come on, Mom," I said finally. "It was a party. You know."

She let it go at that. She wasn't after the details. When she came to the point she was driving at, I heard immediately the shift in her voice.

"How did you like Lee's mom?" she asked.

In conversations with my mother, I had learned to listen closely. A little test edged into her voice, and under the circumstances, a lie was out of the question.

"She wasn't around much," I said.

My mother figured it out before her phone started buzzing the next morning. Some of the other mothers gathered force over the wires that very night, even before some of us arrived home. The next time Lee tried to plan a party, it never got off the ground. None of our mothers would let us go.

A few weeks later, Lee asked me to sleep over on Saturday, and I told her sure before I asked my mom, who reminded me that I'd have church the next morning.

"Ask your father," she said.

I knew what that meant. He would say, Ask your mother, and I'd run back and forth from the kitchen to the living room until I got smart and figured out the answer was no.

"We'll see," my mother mused, and we both knew that meant no, too.

From years of practice, we were good at beating around the bush. My parents didn't raise their voices with me because they didn't have to. They let the words *lean* one way or another. Under the pressure of their subtle weight, I didn't act, I adjusted. To move too quickly, to breathe too heavily, to speak too loudly might bring the house of cards tumbling down around us all.

I tried a different tack, to shift in the prevailing wind.

"I already told her okay," I said.

It was a mild threat, and I thought it might work.

"Why don't you have Lee to our house," my mother suggested.

She needed to keep an eye on me. I loved my fun with Lee, and wanted to protect it. But I had to protect my mother, too, who worried about my wandering too far out of range, where something bad might happen to both of us. To have it both ways, my fun and my mother too, sometimes I had to lie.

"Some other time," I said, with hardly a wince in my heart. "It doesn't matter."

After that, I stopped talking about Lee at home, and I tried to see her whenever I could at school.

Mostly it was in the afternoons, when I found her in the middle of a bunch of girls from her English class, clustered around the frosted window in the girls' bathroom. She was taking bets on the teacher's bra.

That bra was a distraction and an opportunity. At the beginning of every class, the strap started slipping out from under her sleeve, down over her wobbly, old-lady arm. And before class started every day, Lee met up with a group of girls from the class, each of them taking a guess at the statistics. How far would that strap get before the teacher felt the thin, satin line against her skin? At what precise moment would she find an excuse to write on the blackboard, as if seized by the beauty of grammar, when really she was trying to jiggle her bra strap back up under her sleeve? Sometimes, she reached right into the front of her blouse and jerked the strap into place. Lee watched the clock all period, and then threw a paper wad at the girl whose guess came closest. Otherwise, she said, English class was boring.

Lee managed to avoid trouble for it herself. Donna, on the receiving end of some of those spit balls, got in trouble instead. At the parent-teacher meetings that winter, Donna's mother learned that her daughter was developing an "attitude," it interfered with her schoolwork, it kept her off the cheerleading squad, and the teacher suggested that the girl be encouraged to find other friends.

I couldn't have gotten away with it in my English class, even if I'd wanted to, even if Miss Gelvin hadn't been such an elegant lady, always meticulously dressed. At the first hint of an idle moment, Miss Gelvin had us all copy out our homework, the major spelling rules, or a poem by Robert Frost, or long lists of prepositions, on yellow tablet paper, marking across the top in big letters, CIM. "Copy in Ink and Memorize." Then we sat there, our hands cupped around our eyes (for the focus, she said), until somebody could stand up and repeat the whole page by heart. I had the most practiced memory in the class, and I might have to know someday why *preferred* has two r's and *offered* only one. There was no clock-watching or spit-balling in Miss Gelvin's class. She kept us in line with a ruler.

I inherited memory from my father. Late Saturday nights or early Sunday mornings, my father's voice came to my bedroom, from behind the study door across the hall or up from the kitchen. I didn't hear the words distinctly, only the sounds—the rise of a question, the slight pause after one of his little jokes, the rhythm of a phrase repeated when clarity most mattered. In the course of the week, he had written his sermon, an elaborate structure of ideas and illustrations, and the night or the morning before, when I was in bed, he rehearsed his words, making sure he had them all by heart. When he stood in the pulpit, my father delivered that whole sermon, and he never used notes.

Words of one syllable, or more than one syllable accented on the last, ending in a final consonant preceded by a single vowel, double the final consonant when adding a suffix beginning with a vowel. I believed in spelling, and remembering was in my genes.

From *her* dad, Lee inherited science.

One day at school, she met me at my locker first thing, all excited. "Did you bring your lunch today?" she asked.

"Of course I did."

"I've found a great place where you can eat it," she said.

When the lunch period came, Lee took me back to the alley behind the school building. All the hoods went back there to smoke cigarettes before school, and any other chance they got. Lee wasn't interested in smoking yet. She wanted to show me the biology shed.

They didn't teach biology to eighth or ninth graders, but the junior high used to be the high school. When the janitors moved the biology lab out to the new high school building on the north edge of town, they'd left behind a bunch of stuff in a little shed in the alley. For Lee, it was a find.

"Look at all this," she said, when she took me in.

All over the shelves I saw scrunched-up dead things in big glass jars, brains and frogs and foetal pigs, creatures taken from their mothers' bellies at different stages in their development.

"Who killed all those babies?" I wanted to know.

"They were dead before they were born," Lee said.

"That's sad," I said.

"That's science," Lee said. "Won't it be neat in biology, cutting up frogs?"

I was unconvinced.

A person who wants to go to medical school has to get used to that kind of thing, Lee said, cutting up frogs and looking at dead babies while she is eating her lunch. Lee walked around the shed, her tuna salad sandwich in hand, peered into each jar, traced a shape in the glass.

"Look at that," she said. "That's a brain."

I said wouldn't it be fun if she could take over Dr. Howell's general practice someday.

"And spend the rest of my life poking Popsicle sticks down kids' throats?" she said. "Not on your life. I'm going to be a pathologist like my dad."

I didn't know what pathologists did. Lee said they looked at blood and stuff under microscopes and most of their patients were dead.

"It's in the interest of science," Lee said, "and disease control."

"I still think plain ordinary babies aren't be so bad," I said. "Practically everybody has babies."

"Yeah," Lee said. "But absolutely everybody dies."

I couldn't argue with that.

"I hate babies," Lee said. "Babies are soft in the brain."

I shook my head, without meaning to, and looked at her worried. Maybe I hadn't heard her right. She'd been a baby herself once. All of us had.

My mother didn't let me spend the night at Lee's much anymore, but sometimes she relented about Saturday afternoons. I didn't get it. It seemed to me that a person could run into as much trouble in the daytime as after dark, especially at Lee's.

When I went to Lee's house on Saturday afternoons, we usually played out in the barn. It was a big empty shell of a building, with wooden ladders for climbing on and lofts for dangling your feet over. Barrels squatted here and there, old tools hung on the walls. All the animals had been sold off some time before, and a few others had invaded. Occasionally we saw a field mouse dart under a pile of old hay, and once a possum ambled lazily out from under a floorboard, in broad daylight, like she owned the place. Isn't that just like a mother, Lee said. That possum had a nest of babies under there.

The barn was full of lessons. In that barn, I found out about autopsies, and discovered a very disturbing fact about the dog food we fed our Misty at home. What did I think was in the can, Lee said, when the label just said "meat."

Most of Lee's father's patients, she told me, were dead *people*, but once, in the interests of science, he did an autopsy on a horse. Right out here in the barn. You can still see the stains on the cement floor, Lee said.

The horse had been something like a pet; all the kids were learning to ride on it. But then one day it fell over dead, with a thud, just like that, without any apparent reason. That made Dr. Snavely mad. He cut the dead horse open in the middle, and spilled its insides out on the floor in the barn. He was out here poking around for hours, Lee said, trying to find out what killed that horse.

I had seen my father gut fish we ate for dinner sometimes in the summer, and I imagined this picture on a much larger scale, in a phylum more like my own. The toe of a heavy rubber boot prodded the dark red kidney, pushed against the liver, dusty brown and spongy. The lungs, flat and pink on the outside, fibrous and tough inside. Yards of intestine, complicated, milky, warm still toward the center. Inadequate instruments, undersized and blunt, did their work.

"What did kill it?" I asked.

"It had a bad heart from the very beginning," Lee shrugged. "It was just waiting to pop."

There wasn't a thing he could do about it, the heart, engorged and on fire, pumping its way toward explosion. I squinted my eyes shut with the picture of it. Afterwards, Lee said, her father fed the horse meat to his favorite dogs.

Birds chattered in the rafters above us, and swooped around in the dusty air, unable to find their way outside again, even though the door stood wide open and the windows had no glass. I yelled at them, and waved my arms, *there, there, the window's over there,* and Lee laughed at me, because the birds didn't pay any attention. They fluttered and swooped and chattered in the frenzied air, and then one smashed into the wall by the door. It fell with a soft noise to the cement below, its feathers ruffled into a necklace along the line where the tiny bones had broken.

Lee and I were best friends for what seemed like a long time, most of seventh and all of eighth grade, first in the open and then in secret. We did all the things together that best friends are supposed to do. But then all of a sudden, for no apparent reason, she acted like she didn't want to see me anymore. In fact, she sort of disappeared. I didn't see her in the halls much, or in the girls' bathroom between classes, and she never called.

"I don't understand it," I said to my mother. "I don't think we had a fight."

"You've been spending a lot of time together," my mother said. "Maybe you have cabin fever."

My mother said it was a Navy term. Sailors got to feeling they were too big for the space they were in, stranded in the ocean in a boat. All they could think of was getting out, and they turned frantic about it.

"Is that why sailors have such a bad reputation? Like in *Mr. Roberts?*"

"They do have a wild time," my mother said, "when they're on liberty."

I wondered if it would ever come back to normal.

"It will be good for both of you," my mother said, "to take a rest from each other. Like shore leave."

She sounded relieved, and I tuned myself to her mood. I settled into her conviction. Lee and I had cabin fever, and needed a vacation from each other. Spring vacation, I thought, ought to do the trick.

It didn't. When you're twelve or thirteen and take a vacation from your best friend, the circle closes in to cover over the empty space. It has to be that way, because when you're twelve or thirteen, you can't go it alone. And maybe my mother knew that all along.

Eventually, I drifted back to my old gang, all of them cheerleaders, all of them daughters of my mother's friends. Once I'd learned from Lee Snavely that different people were meant for different things, Maggie didn't have so much power over me, and all the way through high school we were best friends again. I could sleep over at her house whenever I wanted.

I last saw Lee Snavely several years later, in 1971, on the other side
of high school. We passed each other going opposite directions on
Wooster Street, right next to the junior high where Lee and I had been
best friends. She waved cheerfully, and called out to me from across the
street.

"Is that *Lee?*" I shouted back.

I waited at the corner for the light to change, bouncing my eager heel
against the curb. From across the street, I felt happy to see her thick,
dark hair. Once I got closer, I changed my mind.

We exchanged facts for a few minutes on the corner. I was home from
college for the summer. She was on her lunch hour from work at the
drugstore on the east side of town. I shifted my weight, stared at my
sandal, then found an excuse to make my way further down Wooster
Street.

"Let's get together before you go back to school," Lee said. "Eric
would love to see you."

"Sounds great," I said.

For a moment it seemed that we were two old friends, two married
ladies trying to arrange a white wine lunch at the Pheasant Room, as our
mothers might have. I meant what I said, that I'd like to see them, spend
an evening with Lee and her husband Eric, whom I'd known in high
school, but I didn't make good on the promise.

I carried with me when I left a picture of what Lee was wearing, a blue
knit mini-skirt, and a white, sleeveless T-shirt, a more grown-up version
of what she'd had on at the fair, that day nearly ten years before. One
look at her outfit marked it in my memory. At her thighs, her upper
arms, her shoulders, her collarbone, huge purple bruises ran to gaudy
yellow, like jewelry dropping from her neck. We didn't share a circle
anymore, but in a small town, talk doesn't respect a circle. I had heard
at Christmas parties and backyard barbecues that Eric was hard on her.
And seeing it for myself, I thought when I left her that day on the street
that we weren't like two old friends at all. By that time, I had learned
my lessons well. In her place, I would have worn long pants, long sleeves.

Diminutives I never cared much about. A few people I've known have gotten away with calling me Annie, and to this day my father sometimes stretches his luck to Annie Banannie. When your name is a simple monosyllable, there isn't much you can do with it except try to make it cute.

I've never been particularly interested either in the names families come up with for kids—Bud, or Buzz, or Pip—nonsense words invented to distinguish them from their siblings or from a father with the same given name, names that are too private to have much appeal beyond the home, like endearments between lovers.

A genuine nickname is a gift bestowed on you by your friends, speaking both intimate knowledge and affection, apparently contradictory responses I despaired of getting in combination.

You have to be somebody *to* somebody to earn a really good nickname. Nicknames are a kind of power, or a sign of it.

In high school, some people didn't need nicknames because their real names gave them trouble enough all by themselves. Dick Small was Dick to everybody, even the teachers who insisted on reading the roll out loud at the beginning of the year, speaking the last names first. It took Dick's moving to New Mexico to escape his own name. Out there, they call him Richard.

Almost all the teachers had nicknames, little ironies perpetrated against their worst habits, or cruelties aimed at defects they couldn't help. Monkey Morse, Hog Hilton, Ivan the Terrible, bald-headed Curly Cook. The football coach, Carny Jack, was as tough and sleazy as a midway hustler, and somebody was always tootling a calliope tune whenever his name came up or he swaggered at a distance down the hall.

The only woman in school with a nickname was a teacher we all called "Horny" behind her back. She wore her skirts to her thighs and lectured from the front of the room, her hand resting on the shoulder of the most conveniently cute boy in the front row. She left school for a while, and then returned with a married name. It brought its own set of problems. Most people didn't believe she'd really married anybody, let alone an officer in the Vietnam War she claimed was shot down and killed shortly after their wedding day. But if she'd wanted a new name, she wouldn't have invented one so delicate to pronounce, not when she taught high school boys. Her new name was Mrs. Fluck. Motherflucker, the boys called her.

Centers of social interest, boys had a corner on nicknames, giving them and getting them. Nicknames spoke their bodies, Porky and Stretch, or punned on their real names, Dusty Rhodes, Dunebuggy June. For a while, some of the boys I knew called themselves by their fathers' names. One gave up a perfectly good name to be called Barney, and another asked to be called Claude—sixteen-year-old boys eager for their patrimony, wanting their fathers' names, no matter how goofy. Boys turned into men that way, taking on their fathers' names.

The nicknames I liked best implied stories, the kind of stories girls couldn't safely live or tell, some escapade or prank or habit that left a public legacy in a name, like a code. There was Krud and Failure and Cream Jeans. Most of the stories I never knew. I couldn't have figured out why the boys called one of their own "Boner," because it was years before I knew what the word meant, although my older brother let me understand it was something dirty.

And then, of course, there was Eric Fletcher, two years older than I. His walk spoke a natural rhythm, he danced like he was born to, he came from the wrong side of the tracks, he had a head full of kinky hair. A tall, handsome, muscular boy with all that hair. It was blond, of course, but he came as close as anybody to being black. All the older boys called Eric Fletcher "Coon."

Eric's younger brother, Mark, spent three years in our high school, long enough to establish an identity for himself. Mark was a hood. Everybody told stories about him, getting into some scrape or another down at Keeter's pool hall where he picked fights with the older boys. Mr. Fletcher had taught his sons to box, kept regulation gloves in different weights hanging on nails in his garage, and had marked off a place in the backyard where his boys could spar with each other, or with other boys who took unofficial lessons. Mark wanted to take on everybody.

Once, over a pool debt, he challenged Eddie, a football player nearly twice his size.

The other boys gathered in a protective circle around the two of them in the alley behind Keeter's, shielding them from interruption, and Mark went into his fancy footwork, dancing around the older boy, pesky and irritating, punching the air, wiping his wrists across the corners of his mouth. Eddie stood there, shaking his head.

"I'm not going to box with you," he said.

Eddie placed one giant foot toward Mark, took hold of his jacket, picked him up, and pushed him back against the brick wall behind them. Then he set him on the ground, gently, as if he were laying a suit out on the bed before folding it into the suitcase, and straddled Mark's chest. That was the end of that.

Eric spent only a year in our high school, and earned about half Mark's reputation. He didn't run from trouble if it came looking for him, but he didn't get into scraps like Mark because Eric didn't pick fights with people he knew. All Eric's trouble came from his not backing down to strangers.

He'd been a stranger himself too recently. Eric hadn't grown up with the rest of the boys, playing tetherball and Red Rover on school playgrounds with them, tormenting student teachers with them, rivaling them for the affections of the two most popular girls in the fifth grade, stopping off at Dirty Don's every afternoon with them for Coke in a bottle after a summer pick-up game in the park. Eric's family moved around a lot, trying to find a place where his father, an arc welder, could support them. Eric had lived in Bowling Green as a small boy, but he'd spent most of his growing up in Bryan, another small town to the west of Bowling Green, near the Indiana border, almost another state. He had played all his childhood games with another group of boys just like the ones he moved into when his family came back to Bowling Green in 1965.

Back then, we dimly recognized intelligent life elsewhere—we had relatives in Wasseon, we played against Otsego in football games, we rewrote our high school *alma mater* into words that made fun of Maumee. But a new kid in school might as well come from another planet. He had to prove that he didn't carry germs, didn't have plans for espionage, spoke English, before he would be accepted. One boy moved into town in the eighth grade. When he was a senior, we were still thinking of him as the new guy.

Where real differences did not exist, we invented them. Otherwise nobody felt important.

So maybe Coon Fletcher, the substitute nigger in a lily-white school, depended upon and resented both, picked his fights with strangers to prove what side he fought on now. Or maybe he was angry at having to fight his way in at all, and chose opponents who reminded him of himself. You could find enough strangers if you went looking for them. Like the time a few out-of-towners caused some trouble at a dance at the park the summer of 1965, before Eric was a senior, and the locals turned to him for help.

They came into the American Legion Hall to get him.

"There's something out here you'll want to take care of, Coon."

A bunch of rowdies had parked in a car along the circle drive. They were acting up, drinking, commenting on the girls who walked by, taunting the local boys by spitting insults at their girlfriends, legs, asses, tits, us.

"You littering in our park?" Eric said, a question first, polite.

"Who, me?" the driver said, tossing an empty out the window. It rattled to a stop near Eric's feet.

"Looks to me like *you're* the litter in our park," Eric said.

"That's telling him, Coon."

"You wanna make something of it, blondie?"

The driver got out of the car. He was larger, heavier than Eric, ready to make short work of the skinny guy with the blond curls. Eric teased him a little, traded a few quick fists with the other kid and then sent him sprawling on the asphalt drive.

Later at the Big Boy, where everybody hung out before Pagliai's opened pizza on the south side of town, one of the local toughs joined Eric's table. Brent hadn't been on the scene of the fight.

"What's that you spilled down your front, Coon?" he asked. "They didn't teach you manners where you came from?"

Someone else answered for Eric. "That's blood, Brent."

"You should have seen it," another boy volunteered. "Coon decked a guy. At the park. Some fool from Fremont Ross."

A guy like Eric could get lost in stories like that, trapped, as if he'd been told he couldn't do otherwise, even if he wanted to.

Eric didn't run with the pack. He didn't even travel much with a buddy, like the rest of them did. Mike and Failure. Boner and Chuck. My brother Greer and Eddie. Mark and Michael. They were practically couples, enmeshed in each other, rarely seen apart. Eric stayed clear of that; he traveled alone. He didn't say he was above it all, but he alienated them anyway. The other boys saw Eric with a mixture of envy and suspicion, the new kid, the rogue outlaw, who didn't need the protection and didn't want the company. He was the tough guy they all depended on to be what they were afraid to be themselves.

They might have boasted about knowing him at all, even vaguely, the way the residents of Clay County, Missouri, probably bragged on Jesse James, after they wandered past the family farm once or twice, saw the James boys working in the fields. At the same time, most of them felt surprised when Eric did anything well, anything right, because they didn't expect good out of him. They might have learned something if they'd just paid more attention to Eric himself. Actually, Eric did a lot of things well.

Take walking into a room, for example. Admittedly, the girls noticed that before the boys did, which may explain why the boys didn't seem to notice it at all. Eric had every inch of his body by heart, and he looked like an archangel, with a halo of curly blond hair, and big blue eyes. A boy like that didn't enter a room, he took charge of it, got all our attention without saying a word. At least, he got mine. Guys like Eric, I thought, had leather jackets and hearts of gold. "He's not really a hood," I said, "just sort of hoody."

This was my public statement. Privately, I didn't mind the noun. I liked the force, the potential danger of it. I thought of myself as living on the edge. Alone among my friends, I had seen the inside of Keeter's pool hall.

The boys hung out at Keeter's because they could smoke there, because Keeter served them beer illegally—or at least that was what we girls thought. The sign on the door said in crude, hand-painted letters, NO FEMALES ALLOWED. It didn't offer any explanation, but we all knew. Keeter's defined a man's world, where women aroused suspicion, caused trouble, or brought danger on themselves. Barring the door to women kept all kinds of trouble out and locked in the freedom of men on their own. This world spoke to me like a memory (*"You be the boy"*), and I imagined it with a mixture of fear and longing, a world noisy with foul talk, alive with movement and action, weighted with the smell of bodies jostling their way into a game or a fight.

It wasn't the same when a respectable businessman opened up the Cue and Cushion in an old appliance store, where he installed dusty rose carpet and fancy track lights, a nice place where most of the girls learned to play pool. That's what we called it, *playing* pool. We thought it was a game.

On a Saturday morning when I was fifteen, Lucy had just cut my hair at the Lion's Store Beauty Shop, and I walked past Keeter's on the way home. I glanced at the sign on the door, NO FEMALES ALLOWED, and the decision came to me. A girl might learn a lot by playing the boy. I worked it out first in my mind, then stepped in, casually, as if I were stopping by Rogers Drug for a candy bar. I made it to the middle of the room before anyone in there noticed me and I then realized I hadn't been thinking at all.

The place was practically empty. Pool tables stood in the center of the room, orange crates lined up against the walls for chairs. Vida, one of the local characters, a small-town version of street people, who dragged one leg behind him when he walked and spoke incoherently because of some physical damage to his mouth, sat on one of the crates with a spread-out deck of cards in front of his face. He pointed at them, one by one.

Pictures of nude women hung on the walls here and there, *Playboy* centerfolds, calendar photos detached from the line of days beneath them. There was a dartboard, and sure enough, a bar where Keeter, a small shrunken man with a bald head, wiped glasses with a cloth. Beyond the bar, the back door led out to the alley where pool games gone wrong spilled over into fist fights and loud arguments.

Another man in a T-shirt stood at the bar, his head bent over a beer, a jangle of keys hanging from his belt loop. The dark stain of a tattoo, a dragon's tail or a twisted briar, spilled down his arm from under his sleeve.

Keeter looked up from the glass in his hand to stare at me. "I don't allow no girls in here," he said.

I froze in the middle of the room, the front door behind me, the back door a long way off, on the other side of the bar.

The man at the bar waved his hand in Keeter's direction, as if to brush the objection away, then leaned over and mumbled something I couldn't hear. Keeter shrugged, and returned his attention to the glass. Then slowly the man turned his body in one arrogant movement to rest an elbow behind him against the bar. A large hand dangled from his wrist.

"How 'bout it, honey," he said evenly. "You want a drink?"

He laughed quietly and rapped a knuckle against the metal seat of the bar stool next to him. The sound reached me like an echo, distant, distorted, an invitation I might not safely refuse in this world I had wanted to enter. I knew it better now.

I started to back my way to the door, but a steady hand guided my elbow, moved me further into the room. Eric Fletcher had walked in behind me.

"She's with me, Keeter," he said.

Keeter looked Eric over, calmly, slowly, then nodded, and went back to his work. Eric draped his arm around my shoulder, and steered me past the bar to a pool table. The man went back to his beer and I breathed again.

"You know how to shoot pool?" Eric asked.

"I think I'd better go," I said.

"I'll show you," he said.

For twenty minutes, I forgot where I was, absorbed in watching Eric move from the end of the table to the side, stepping back to study his shots, leaning over to take aim. He showed me how to rack up, how to chalk a cue, and I watched him drop the balls, one by one, into the pockets he called. And then he offered me the cue stick.

"It's easy," he said.

"That's what you think," I said.

"No, really," he said. "You just swing your arm naturally, smooth, easy, like your elbow's a hinge."

I practiced swinging my arm in midair.

"That's it. Now you line the stick up, look right down the cue, and

imagine it's longer than it really is. Like there's a wire attached at the
other end. You want to think the cue pushes right through that ball and
hits this one on the side, here, where I'm pointing."

Eric had left me on my own, standing there watching my arm dangle
from my elbow. He had walked to the other side of the table and rested
his finger alongside the ball nearest the corner pocket.

"Concentrate now," he said.

I squinted down the length of the stick, aiming for Eric's finger. The
cue glided easily over my left hand on the table, poised on the tips of
my fingers for balance, and then slid off toward the ball. The ball
knocked against the seven just as Eric drew his finger away. I heard the
unmistakable sounds: wood on wood, wood on felt, wood slipping into
the leather pocket in the corner.

"Pretty straight shooting," Eric said. "You're a real hustler."

"I can't believe it went in." I said.

"Sure," Eric said. "You're a natural."

When he escorted me to the door and said goodbye, he told me it
had been fun.

"We should do it again sometime," he said.

"Maybe at the Cue and Cushion," I said.

"Nah," Eric said. "You can come here with me any time."

Two years later, as a senior in high school, when I learned the word
"charisma" in comparative government, I called up a picture of Eric
Fletcher right away, even though he'd already graduated by then. I saw
him walking into a room, any room, but particularly that one, divinely
gifted, rare, recognized for his authority by Keeter himself.

He had his own charisma, but my mind may also have borrowed some
from Mark Antony and loaned it to Eric. That was something else he
could do well, against all the odds an outsider in another way still. The
renegade, the boxer, the tough kid from the wrong side of the tracks
played Shakespeare.

It wasn't the usual drama students Mrs. Leonard had assembled for
her cast, but an assortment of roughnecks, troublemakers, and goofoffs
from her speech class, which most of them took because it meant so
little work. They formed the crew to play a series of scenes from
Shakespeare over one weekend in the fall of their senior year. It was an
opportunity, she said, to try on the buskins, to give secret actors a chance

to come out, to show talent hidden in unlikely places. Mrs. Leonard had truly democratic instincts, I suppose, but most of the boys probably preferred the closet, and thought this Shakespeare stuff a little too fancy.

Mrs. Leonard had chosen scenes from *Julius Caesar* as the centerpiece of the performance. It was taught in many of the English classes, it had a lot of good parts for boys, a tragedy full of setpiece dialogues and seductions and soliloquies, but was more easily excerpted and more appropriate to the range of high school players than *King Lear* or *Macbeth*.

The rehearsals made the whole thing look like a sure-to-be fiasco.

"Why can't we do this thing in regular clothes?" one of them asked. "I don't want to be seen in public wearing a sheet."

"A toga will give you a feel for the character."

"It's a big diaper, Mrs. Leonard."

"Yon Cassius has a lean and hungry look," Julius Caesar said, bouncing his eyebrows around like Groucho Marx.

"I'm after your girl," Cassius shouted.

"Et tu, you brute?" Caesar said, and then laughed.

"Friends, Romans, countrymen, lend me your ears," Mark Antony said.

"What's wrong with your own, Coon?"

Mrs. Leonard, determined for success, tried everything. She played records of British actors rolling their r's and broadening their a's. But midwesterners tend to flatten all their vowels, in imitation of the landscape, I guess, and all those British tones made everyone completely self-conscious. No one would do it straight. So she showed a film, all American actors, a very young Charlton Heston as Mark Antony, running through the streets of Rome in a loincloth and grainy black and white. That didn't help much either.

"Hey. That really is a diaper. You gonna wear a diaper Friday night, Coon?"

So Mrs. Leonard wrung her hands and crossed her fingers, probably prayed a lot, figured you can't really ruin Shakespeare, or thought that people would prefer comedy anyway. She might have been smarter to have depended more on Eric Fletcher.

He actually listened to the records, and watched the film, and practiced at home, coached by his mother, who had wanted to teach English and Latin herself.

"Never mind all the phoney stuff," she said. "Talk it like you understand it."

That's what he did. He made clear that he understood what he was speaking, offered all that blank verse with elegant clarity, as if the lines had been written for him. He made the costumes, the gestures, the whole stage his own.

I sat back in the fifth row, and I could feel it from there. I had come to see my brother play Brutus, the tortured, prosaic hero, but that wasn't where I was looking. The sheet hung open loosely at Eric's neck, and belted at his waist, fell in soft folds over his hips to the middle of his thighs. Leather straps wound their way from his sandals to his knees. In the definite gesture of Roman greeting, he brought his right fist to his left shoulder, marking a V across his chest, and walked calmly, forcefully through all his scenes. Ten minutes into the performance, I was ready to kill the conspirators, too, before they'd even committed the bloody deed.

By the time I heard Mark Antony's efforts to bury Caesar without praising him, I understood that Eric had convinced the rest, whipped them into shape without articulating a single explicit argument, just by being who he was. If Coon Fletcher could walk around in a diaper and make me believe him a man, surely the rest of them could. The performance went without a hitch.

In many ways it was a perfect piece of casting, Eric Fletcher as Mark Antony. Although Eric had a kind of candid charm, and not the dubious ability to twist his words and manipulate a crowd, he certainly had Antony's physical grace and athletic prowess, for which even mighty Caesar admired and loved him.

If Eric's mother took a special pride in her son's talent for drama, his father, himself a boxer and a physical man, must have had pleasure in Eric's other skill. Eric was a natural athlete, good at everything he tried without really trying at all. He didn't even go out for football until he was a senior, a new kid on the team, a trainee, completely inexperienced. And if he had to work at that, it wasn't because he wasn't good. It was only because coaches were just teachers really, and came to recognizing talent with the same prejudices against certain kinds of boys that teachers had.

At first Eric didn't see much action, and it frustrated him. One game, early that fall, he sat on the bench most of the first half, longing to get some grass stains on his uniform. He asked politely at first to be sent into the game. The coach, Carny Jack, didn't pay much attention, and at the half, in the locker room, Eric took him aside.

"I'm not going to play anymore, Coach," he said.

"You not feeling well, boy?"

"No, I mean, if you don't play me, I'll quit."

"You threatening me?"

The coach, a bantam, tough and tight and muscular, slammed Eric, a good five inches taller, against a row of lockers.

"Back off, man," Eric said, low and steady.

He was trying to be careful, to keep himself in check. The coach was somebody he knew.

"You're not quitting this game, and you're not quitting the team, either," the man said. "You'll play when I tell you to. Coon."

A dig, a jeer, a reminder, and Eric was ready for it.

"So tell me to. Carny."

The rest of the team wasn't sure who won in the battle of nicknames, or how the standoff had turned out. In the second half, the coach sent Eric into the game. And before the end of the season, Eric quit the team.

Maybe he had bigger plans than he had tenacity, maybe he wrangled too much with the coach. I figured Eric probably had something to prove, and once he proved it, he didn't need to keep going. Besides, he needed the energy for track season.

No coach, however dimmed by prejudice, however cornered by the kid's attitude, could have failed to see Eric's running. He was a long-distance runner on the track team, both in individual races and team relays. And he could sprint, too, finishing the quarter mile in forty-five seconds.

When I think of Eric even now, I see his physical beauty first. But then, even before the Shakespeare, which might otherwise mean more to me, this is what I see: a photograph, catching him in mid-stride, neither foot actually touching the ground, his chest thrust out and about to break the finish tape, his head thrown back, his eyes closed, his hair wetted down by sweat around his face, but those long blond curls released behind him in the wind. I may have seen such a photograph, in the high school yearbook, perhaps, but even if I did, the picture in my mind came first.

If things had been different for Eric, if he'd been born in a different year, on a different street, in a different town, had a different coach, almost any difference could matter, Eric's running might have bought him a ticket on another train, out of his neighborhood, away from all the stories and on to a college scholarship and success. But college scholarships, even for sports, required resources, not so much money as know-how, and parents who could work the system, who knew what forms to file and where to get them. Eric's parents knew how to get him into the Golden Gloves tournament, but they didn't know how to get him into college. And maybe Eric himself didn't want to go enough. But whatever he lacked, the resources or the will, the school counselors didn't put themselves out, either. And although Eric made some noises about taking courses at the university the next fall, nobody really expected him to do it.

He graduated and went to work at one of the few small industries around town, Rex Manufacturing, makers of folding chairs, work that was the lifetime equivalent of twiddling one's thumbs. Most of the old gang had gone off to school by the fall of 1966, but a few were still around, enough for company on a drive to Bryan in his '65 Mustang, red, middle of the night, for the odd breakfast at the twenty-four-hour pancake house there. And his days turned to labor, not so much mindless as physical work, a pleasure of its own kind for a man who knew every inch of his body by heart. And the nights turned to a beer or two with his buddies, none of them too close, a trip now and then in the red Mustang, none of them too far because there was always work the next day, and the day after that.

The time passed slowly, until one day, spring of 1967, he got to talking with his friend Matt, who wasn't doing much more himself than hanging around.

"We could enlist," Matt said.

"They'll get us soon enough anyway," Eric said.

"Enlisting means we have to go for three years."

"If we volunteer for the draft, it's only two."

"So, what are you doing tomorrow?" Matt said, half serious.

"The Ides of March?" Eric said.

"Bad luck, huh?" Matt said.

"For Caesar."

They waited a day anyway, so as not to tempt fate. They hadn't been out of high school a year yet, and on March 16, they went to the draft board to volunteer, a second-story office in a storefront around the corner from the police station on Wooster Street. It had all been as casual as that, because they had nothing better to do. A few days later, Eric and Matt were on the bus to Columbus for induction.

They were going as buddies, two friends for the trouble of one. Eric was fine, an athlete, a healthy, vigorous man. But once they got there, something went wrong with Matt, his blood pressure shot up, and despite information from his family physician that he would be all right, that this was a fluke, a case of nerves probably, the Army wouldn't take him, and Eric, himself again, the rogue outlaw, the renegade, went on alone.

Six weeks of boot camp, where Eric distinguished himself, winning the physical training award, the greatest number of points in the company, scored for all those jumpings over, runnings through, climbings off, slidings under on whatever obstacle course the Army could devise. Then on to airborne infantry training, the spots reserved for the best physical specimens in the bunch. The next stop was Vietnam. He was there by November 1967, having turned nineteen a month before, just in time for the Tet Offensive.

In 1967, total American troop strength in Vietnam stood at half a million, swelled by one hundred thousand boys like Eric who arrived that year alone, at the rate of nearly ten thousand a month toward the end of the year. These were not a few new recruits mixed in with sturdy combat veterans. They were green boys, as likely to kill each other in their ignorance and confusion as to kill the enemy, whoever that was. The rotation policy for deploying troops ensured a short stay for most of them, just one lonely year as individual replacements sent to join groups of other transients already in the field, to be given on-the-job training for a kind of war in which training didn't count for much.

Vietnam was a war against strangers, made to feel that way by the napalm and the scatter bombs, by ground cover defoliation and pacification of the native element, by forced urbanization and surgical raids, by body counts and relocation strategies, by constant reminders that the enemy was so different, so foreign, so strange as not to be human, not animal even, but gook. And there was Eric Fletcher, the tough kid from the wrong side of the tracks, all of whose trouble, his friends said, came from his not backing down to strangers, who never picked fights with people he knew. You'd think it would have been Eric Fletcher's war.

1 9 6 5 — 1 9 6 8

Lee wasn't around when I started high school in 1965, and the rest of our lives kept right on track without her. Tom moved on to a new girlfriend, a senior about to graduate and go to college. Maggie Howell captained the cheerleading squad, learned about sororities from her big sister, took to calling the kettle black and all of her friends "fakey." Carrie Holden dyed her hair blonde, and cracked her gum in class. Donna stayed beautiful, and pretended not to be smart. I made friends with the first hippie in school, and shook my head over the Beat poets, who didn't write rhymes and said dirty words in print.

We all kept busy practicing for our PSATs and trying to raise money for the junior prom. We learned the D. C. Shuffle, and the Monkey and the Jerk. We listened to the Beatles and the Rolling Stones, and argued in the cafeteria over which group was better. That was a major line of demarcation between us, the line between the Beatles and the Stones.

As for Lee's absence for the first part of that year, all our good breeding sensed in it something unsavory. Privately, we speculated, and whispered the mystery into a scandal in the school cafeteria.

"She told me she was moving." Tom shrugged.

"Then how come you don't have her new address?" Maggie asked, accusingly.

My boyfriend had just moved to California, and he certainly told me where he was going.

"We said goodbye already," Tom said. "She wanted to make a clean break of it."

"But she wouldn't have moved without telling her girlfriends," I said.

Nobody I knew would have done such a thing.

Tom had been Lee's boyfriend the year before. He

probably knew the truth, but under the circumstances we suspected, we didn't think he'd tell it.

"She's going to Anthony Wayne High School this year," he insisted.

After Tom headed off for French class, Maggie motioned for us to come closer, and we leaned over the table. She voiced our suspicions in a whisper.

"There's a home in Toledo for wayward girls. They find people to adopt the babies when they're born."

The thought spooked me. I knew how much Lee hated babies, all soft in the brain. I imagined a group of welfare workers or nuns in some home for unwed mothers, snatching the baby from Lee right away, so it could be adopted undamaged.

"I don't think she wanted a baby," I said.

"Jeezopeet," Maggie said. "She didn't get pregnant on purpose."

"But her father was a doctor."

"Accidents do happen," Maggie said.

We all knew they did, but we weren't quite sure how. Learning about sex was a little bit like learning grammar. Every teacher you had assumed some other teacher taught you the year before, or the year before that, as if none of them wanted to talk about it, as if grammar was a bunch of dirty words. A massive silence surrounded dangling participles and infinitive clauses, and you learned to fear making mistakes you didn't know how to avoid.

In the same way, our mothers' vigilant silence on the subject of sex had announced their fear without articulating it, and recreated the fear in us without assuring our protection from it.

In high school, the boy behind the counter in the concession stand over the lunch hour sold candy and called all the girls "sweet tarts." One day, I brought the word home, called my little sister a sweet tart. My mother hit the roof. Don't call your sister a tart, she said. I tried to tell her it was a kind of candy, but she wouldn't let me say it at home. Wait until you're older, she said. You'll understand. My brother had given me the sound track from *Hair* for Christmas, and it stayed put in its sleeve until I took it away to college. I had little sisters at home, my mother reminded me, and one of those singers clearly said "masturbation" out loud. I couldn't tell the difference, even then, between the power of sex and the power of words.

But Lee was better educated than all of us. She had that medical vocabulary. She studied pictures of women's bodies. She heard clearly all the words to "Louie, Louie," and passed them on to her friends.

"Lee would have known how not to get pregnant," I said.

"So what if she had a baby," Carrie Holden said. "It's not the end of the world."

Heads, bent low over the lunch table, bobbed up in surprise. Legs shifted under the chairs. Carrie didn't speak out of turn, exactly, but everything she said came out a little too loud. Babies meant only one thing to the rest of us, and we talked about them in whispers.

But for Carrie, babies were the beginning of the world. They had so many of them at her house.

I didn't socialize with Carrie Holden much anymore, but we'd gone to Sunday School together for years, her family Presbyterian for generations like mine. As a child, I loved to play at the Holden's house, a clamor and havoc of children, screen doors banging shut with all their comings and going, kids climbing all over the kitchen counters, Holden kids and the friends of Holden kids, shouting at each other over the blare of the radio, answering the telephone like pros. "Holden's morgue," they said. "You kill 'em, we chill 'em. You stab 'em, we slab 'em." In all that commotion, it was hard to tell how many children they *had*, five, six, maybe even seven, most of them girls who never learned to be ladylike.

I vaguely remember Mrs. Holden from those days, a thin, elegant woman, a pillar of calm, a foghorn in that sea of confusion. When the noise got too much for her, she shouted back as loud as she needed to—"Okay, everybody out!" Screen doors banged all around her, ten pairs of shoes clumped out of the house, and Mrs. Holden took a long drink from her iced tea. Somehow, no matter how big her voice, she never sounded cross.

A guest at the bridge club, a stranger meeting Mrs. Holden for the first time, hearing her rehearse the names of all her children, might have asked politely was she Catholic, and she would have played happily into the local joke. *Oh no*, she probably said, waving a spangled wrist in the direction of the question. *We're oversexed Protestants.*

Across that particular bridge table, Mrs. Holden's line might have sounded crude. But her household wasn't about sex, not really. It was about kids. The Holdens loved babies, whatever age they were. They wanted a lot of them, and they loved the life into every one they brought into the world.

Carrie took after her mother.

The last I'd seen Lee, the year before when we were still in junior high, she'd been living on the farm after her father's death with her stepmother and her two brothers. When she returned to school at the end of our sophomore year, she was living with a foster family in town. The very idea of it gave me the shivers.

It was every kid's nightmare, that one day you'd push your parents too far, and they'd up and boot you out on the street. That nightmare, though forgotten by morning, dictated the adolescent mood, set all of the tests we devised into motion. We wouldn't have tested our parents' love if we didn't need the proof, and we wouldn't need the proof if we didn't doubt it just a little.

I wanted to know how that could happen, but I was too polite or too scared to ask Lee. I turned instead to my old friend Jim, whose father was a judge, and the only elected Democrat in town. I figured he ought to know.

"If she kept running away from home," he started to explain.

"I heard she hitchhiked to Cleveland all by herself," Maggie volunteered.

"Her stepmother could have her declared wild and incorrigible," Jim continued.

"Can somebody do that?" I asked. "To their own children?"

"It happens all the time," Jim shrugged. "In court."

"Well," Maggie said. "That woman isn't Lee's real mother."

"You don't have to talk like it's contagious," Carrie Holden said.

But we might as well have thought it was. If in our hearts we feared abandonment ourselves, we should have been more sympathetic with Lee's plight. Instead, we attached our fear to her, and our judgment as well, as if it were her fault (*she was wild and incorrigible*), as if we couldn't admit that the people in charge, our parents, our teachers, could make such disastrous mistakes (*no real mother would allow it to happen*). It was too scary to imagine. The line between Lee and the rest of us seemed so narrow, we couldn't stand to look over it.

Or maybe that line seemed so wide, we could barely see her at all on the other side of it, orphaned, stepmothered, farmed out to foster care. Our mothers stayed home, set curfews, fixed dinner. Our fathers, who never had much to say to us, were nonetheless *there*, silent and comforting presences at the fringes of our lives. All of our families looked so much alike that inconsequential differences were magnified into the real thing, and real differences obliterated, squeezed out, silenced, or ignored. An oddity was a Democrat among the Republicans, an Episcopalian among the Methodists and Presbyterians, a mother who bleached her hair, a father who tended his yard instead of playing golf. The narrow borders of our lives protected us, to be sure. But those borders also created limits beyond which we couldn't imagine, kept questions out, kept secrets in, and confined us to spaces so small that we rarely had to speak above a ladylike whisper.

Unless, of course, you were Carrie Holden, living proof that you could be noisy and safe at the same time.

Lee kept to herself mostly, went her own way, the only girl in the Science Club, the only girl hanging out between classes with the Vo-Ag boys at the far end of the hall in the west wing. I used to see her there, blowing smoke from her cigarette out the door so she wouldn't have to stand outside, laughing and flirting with a bunch of boys wearing grease-stained overalls, or denim jackets and muddy boots.

She was already past the break-your-heart stage. By then, most of the rest of us were growing our hair long, to our shoulders and beyond. If we bothered at all, we set it at night on orange juice cans or huge brush rollers, hoping for that soft loopy flip at the ends. At the cutting edge of fashion, some girls were *ironing* their hair before they left for school in the morning. Lee wore hers short, with clip curls at the ears, the hair teased high into a bouffant at the crown of her head. She looked out of place, like Connie Francis among the hippies, and out of time, like the original Philadelphia girls from *American Bandstand*, hard-luck beauties with complicated last names.

On my way out of Latin class, shunted off to that end of the building because so few of us studied it, I waved in her direction and she turned away. Eventually I stopped waving, and told myself she wanted it like that. The eager chatter, the clumsy, curious questions of my earlier friendship with Lee turned to whispered comment. Before too long, the whispers acquiesced into the silence that surrounded whatever difference, for whatever reason, I had learned to fear.

Our high school didn't have a track system that organized classes by the students' abilities. Despite the fact that ours was a university town, and we were fed teachers straight from the Department of Education, the local schools lagged behind current educational theory. The school authorities claimed that not having a track system was more democratic, and educationally sound. Students learned more from their peers anyway, and the weaker students would benefit from associating with the brighter ones.

It was a big lie. The way it worked out amounted to a track system, and lots of kids didn't get a fair shake. The guidance counsellors had ways of rigging the classes and pushing certain teachers and electives, so the college prep students stayed pretty much together, to provide the proper intellectual stimulation for each other in the classroom. Lee was certainly plenty stimulating, but somebody must have decided she wasn't college material, a kid who'd maybe run away from home, caused somebody a lot of trouble, or had a baby. She and I shared only one class: Mr. Warren's American Literature class our junior year.

Mr. Warren coached the sophomore football team, and assisted Carny Jack with the varsity players. Unlike most of the coaches, Mr. Warren was smart, with a master's degree from the university, so he got to teach junior English. But even in Mr. Warren's class, I learned more from my peers than from my teacher, just like the official word said. Mr. Warren was always telling us it wasn't a matter of right and wrong, but of "appropriate" and "inappropriate" readings, and we caught on to him real quick. I learned what I remember best about American Literature from Lee.

She sat at the back of the classroom where the troublemakers arranged themselves. She didn't get involved much in the discussions. But near the end of the period, when Mr. Warren asked one day if we had any questions, she came up with something that threw everybody for a loop.

"I don't get this stuff at the end of *Billy Budd,*" she announced.

"What 'stuff'?" Mr. Warren said.

"This stuff about how he's hanging from the yardarm and nothing's moving."

Mr. Warren looked at his text a moment, coming up with his answer.

"Well, when it's all over and Billy's dead, we're left with an image of ominous quiet. Don't you think that's appropriate?"

"But the purser and the surgeon have a long talk in the next chapter about how Billy didn't have an erection when he died."

Mr. Warren looked up and then down again. "Where do you find that?"

"It's in the book," Lee sighed. "Isn't that what 'spasmodic movement' means? A man has an erection when he dies by hanging."

"Let me see your book," Mr. Warren said. He thought Lee was making it up.

The teacher marched down the aisle to the back of the room, picked up Lee's copy, held it toward the window to see it better in the light of day. He read silently for a minute or two, and finally recovered himself when he found something that fit in with his theory that Billy was a Christ figure.

"Right here," Mr. Warren said, "on page 124, the purser says it's a testimony to Billy's incredible willpower. It's a sign from God. Billy is the sacrificial lamb."

"And then the surgeon says that's not scientific," Lee said.

"It doesn't have to be scientific," Mr. Warren said. "It's *thematic.*"

"Christ figure or not," Lee said, "Billy Budd had an erection like everyone else."

Lee had picked a pretty good seat at the back of the class. From there, she could confuse everybody about who were the troublemakers and who were the smart kids.

It was an easy confusion to make. In my high school, we had three ways to achieve fame: sports, school, and trouble. They weren't mutually exclusive activities. It helped, in fact, if you scored in two out of three categories.

Sports and school took special talents, but trouble and school came to almost anyone who wanted the combination. To get yourself attended to, to earn a reputation as a troublemaker, you only had to pull off a practical joke on a teacher. That sometimes took a little ingenuity, but otherwise, it was a quick accomplishment because most of our teachers didn't have senses of humor.

One boy achieved hero status among his friends for faking a faint during some experiment in the chemistry lab. He was lying out cold at the back of the room, surrounded by a bunch of boys faking panic, and he frightened the teacher nearly to death. That happened before I even got to high school, and the kids were still talking about it.

Another group of boys got a paddling in the principal's office for throwing a bunch of corn husks at Mr. Hilton, the principal, when he was leading cheers in his red and white letter sweater at a pep rally. They didn't hit him, weren't even trying to. Mr. Hilton knew all the kids called him "Hog," and I guess he resented it because he suspected the truth of what we all thought: he looked like a 4-H prize pig, with his round face and turned-up nose, and those dark little eyes, so close together. When they threw corn husks at him, they might as well have called him a pig in front of the whole school.

On your own time, just plain trouble created the opportunity for another category of behavior altogether. It happened somewhere off school property, in cars or at home when your parents weren't. School and trouble amused your friends. Trouble on your own frightened your parents. Trouble at school was safe; independent trouble happened in the world, and sometimes involved the law.

It also differed by gender. Boys could be wild—running with a pack, hanging out at the pool hall, cutting up convertible tops or cutting school—without being sexual. Some of the wildest boys in school were just car crazy. That wasn't true for girls. To be wild and a girl meant having a reputation. Wildness in girls established the difference between causing trouble and being in it. When a girl said, "I'm in trouble," she didn't mean she was on her way to the principal's office for detention.

The definitions were clear and rigid, intended to keep us in line, and it was the rare kid, boy or girl, who stepped outside them. Lee Snavely, I came to understand, did. Her wildness may not have had anything to do with sex. Lee's trouble was more like the trouble of boys.

When I was a junior, I was the first in my crowd to have a date for the prom. Tom, Lee's old boyfriend, asked me in February for the dance in May. He had been my friend since Mrs. Van Winkle's nursery school. We'd taken bridge lessons together and dancing lessons, and we'd never gone out on a date. We were buddies, and he already had a girlfriend, so I wouldn't have to worry about the usual boy-girl stuff.

But boys will be boys. I spent the next three months fending him off in the front seat of a Ford. At first it was easy, casual, sweet, making out a little with somebody I knew so well. But as the weeks passed, Tom grew more insistent, and I began to feel trapped between possible reputations. Being known for a goody-goody created a social disaster as bad in its own way as the moral compromise that speed implied. A girl had to play her part right and carefully, steaming up the windshield without fogging up her brain. A few weeks before the prom, Tom finally exploded at me with the truth.

He'd heard from the other boys that I did it already.

I assured him the other boys had me wrong.

"Well, not quite," he said. He marked an X in the tic-tac-toe board I'd doodled in the fog we'd made on the windshield.

I had to laugh a little. "You caught me," I said, and we were back to being friends again.

Tom explained the whole story to me. He felt a responsibility. His girlfriend was older, in college already, and she'd expect him to know what he was doing when the time came. He had wanted to make himself needy and generous at the same time.

"I thought since we were friends and all, and like I really need the experience, well, I wanted you to be my first."

"You and Lee didn't do it?" I asked.

"No," he said.

"You mean she didn't get pregnant?"

"Not by me she didn't."

"So where was she last year? Did they send her off to foster parents somewhere else, like she's got now?"

"I don't know," Tom said. "I thought she moved."

Under the circumstances, I was sure he was telling the truth.

"Does this mean the prom is off?" I said.

And then it was Saturday morning, the day of the prom. I had my outfits laid out on the bed at home, and a boutonniere for Tom's tuxedo sat in the refrigerator.

We had divided into committees, the Brick Road Committee, the Up, Up and Away Committee, the Toto Too Committee, and we were working very hard making the high school gym look like the Land of Oz. Lee hadn't volunteered for a committee, but she showed up anyway.

By Friday night a yellow brick road had started meandering around the edges of the dance floor. A Tin Man, a Lion, and a Scarecrow now guarded the door. Before much longer, the Emerald City in all its glory would rise from behind the bandstand, where later that night and into Sunday morning, an orchestra would play "Over the Rainbow."

Lee came screeching into the gym that Saturday morning, sliding across the wooden floor in her stocking feet, and stopped just short of half a *papier-mâché* head of the Great and Terrible Oz.

She dropped into a puddle in the middle of the gym floor, as if she'd melted. She came back up, batting her eyes, a little girl from Kansas, singing in a nasal voice about bluebirds and lemon drops.

The top steps of ladders creaked. Whole rolls of crepe paper bounced down the bleachers. Eyes looked up from the paper cloths being smoothed out on cardtable tops. It was funny and we wanted to catch the act.

None of us was prepared for the shock, and it took us a while to catch on. Slowly, the silence gave way to awkward giggles, then to curious whispers that passed the questions around the gym. Had she been out all night, we wondered. Maybe she'd driven across the border into West Virginia. Or had she walked in someplace in town, made up and dressed to the nines, so sure she wouldn't raise doubts that nobody asked her for proof?

Lee was as drunk as a boy, and it couldn't have been past ten in the morning.

"Get a load of that," some guy said. "Hey, Frank, you still need a date for the prom?"

"I don't know," Frank answered. "She might take advantage of me."

"That's the point, knucklebrain."

The scene started out funny, like a good joke on the grown-ups, passed quickly through scandal and something like fear, then suddenly turned ugly right before our eyes. We heard ourselves breathing again when the chaperoning teacher stepped in and took over.

"Okay, everybody," he shouted. "Back to work. Chop, chop."

Then he took Lee's arm, gently enough, and hustled her out of the gym.

"Where are you taking her?" Carrie Holden shouted, and she clambered down the bleachers after them.

He took her into the hall where the phone booths were.

"Here's a dime," he said. "Call your folks to come get you."

"You forget," Lee said. "I don't have folks."

"I'll call my dad," Carrie Holden said.

"Who should I call, then?" the teacher asked Lee.

"How about Auntie Em?" she said.

"Don't get smart with me."

"Call the county. They own me."

And that's what he did. The welfare office, juvenile division, had had these calls before. They came and got her, but they didn't take her back to her foster parents, or to her stepmother either. They took her to the county jail.

"You just sit there and think about where you're heading," they told her, and pushed the cell door shut.

Lee missed the prom that year, because she spent the night in jail, right there next to the county courthouse on Prospect Street.

And the next morning, having heard about the incident from Carrie, John Holden skipped church and went down to the jailhouse instead. No kid could be that much trouble, he said. He had a bunch of them at home, and he ought to know. Besides, he was a lawyer, and recognized criminal behavior when he saw it. Release her to me, he said, I'll be responsible. And they did, and he was, and it came pretty close to a good thing, too.

Eventually, most of us discover the disaster. No bond lives unconditionally, if only because somebody has to die in the end. But by the time we discover it, some of us, at least, are equipped to handle it, because somewhere along the line, somebody loved us enough.

The Holdens loved their kids that way, and they tried to love Lee that way, too. They took her into their noisy circle and did their best to set limits for her, to love her as their own. But maybe by then Lee was already beyond limits. Maybe she was beyond the circle of love itself.

For kids coming from such a household as the Holdens', lively and loving, the eventual disaster may not feel like an earthquake, the most devastating of disasters, the ground crumbling beneath you. But for others, like Lee perhaps, discovering that you've lost everything with the loss of that bond, or that you can't lose what you never had in the first place, turns into freedom. Then recklessness means something different, not so much a test as an adventure, or a test of oneself, the kind of daring that comes with believing there's nobody in this but you. Maybe Lee was already to that point. Maybe, at sixteen, she was ahead of her time.

Not that it matters much, whatever the reasons. Lee wasn't dealing her own hand, and neither were the Holdens. It was a temporary situation from the beginning, the welfare office had said, and before the end of our senior year they found an official place for Lee, who finished high school in a little town just over the border in Michigan, where she was sent to live with some other family.

Eventually the Holdens remodeled the carriage house in their backyard, wired it for sound, and turned it over to the kids to get them out of their hair. About the time the oldest boys went off to college, the rest of the family moved out of town to a posh new development up near the river where some entrepreneur was building a group of huge colonial houses in the woods around a man-made lake. And the Holden kids turned out just fine. They're all grown up now, with kids of their own, and I like to imagine troops of Holden grandchildren shouting at each other across that lake, driving all the rich neighbors nuts.

Not too long after she left, Lee returned to Bowling Green, the only town she'd ever called home. And there, briefly on her own, she met up with Eric Fletcher, just back from Vietnam, living on nothingness, and looking for somebody just like her.

PART
TWO

The entire summer passes without rain. Soybeans shrivel in the fields, the topsoil cracked and dusty. Tomatoes drop from their vines without ripening, or rot through from the blossom end. The corn barely reaches the farmer's belt buckle by the Fourth of July. Airplanes drone overhead, seeding the clouds. Later, half the county turns out for a prayer meeting, a circle of hands, a binding of hymns, in a corn field in the next town over. In August, when all else has failed, a group of farmers pool their meager lot and import a band of Indians from the northern states. It is 1986. In Ohio, we do not yet say "Native American."

Ceremonial feathers tremble in the dance, but they do not coax water from the sky. Then, from the south, where the weather is better, other farmers load a convoy of flatbed trucks and send us corn to keep our cows alive. Drought is a shared disaster.

By midsummer, the weather has set the county on edge, made us all expectant. A woman, driving home from work, glances nervously at a water tower. She squints, rubs her eyes, shakes the image from her head. When she looks again, it's still there, etched in the corroded metal tank that stands on stilts above Fostoria: the face of Christ emerges from the rust, as plain as day. By the end of the week, he appears full figure, suffering a little child to come unto him, drawing a child into the sheltering folds of his robe.

People come from all over to take the image in. Cars clog the highways and the exit ramps; they overheat, run short on gas. A priest, reluctant to distress the faithful in a dry season, delivers a short sermon on the local news. Asked for his professional opinion, he tells the microphone in front of him we would all do better to find the mark of Christ in each other, in our brothers and sisters, in our children.

Still, someone prints up T-shirts and sells them, car to sweltering car.

All the while I do my work. Some days it's all I can manage to sit in my mother's house, stripped down, before the fan. In the afternoons, stretched out on her living room floor, I write letters to people I never knew. In the evenings, I telephone strangers, or people I haven't seen in twenty years, asking my questions, collecting information. But I can't put it off forever. Eventually I have to go out in the heat. In the mornings, I venture out to the coolest places I can find, the police station, the courthouse, the library, where I sit under a lazy ceiling fan, turning the crank on an old-fashioned microfilm reader. I am thirty-five years old.

By midsummer I have filled in the gaps, carried Lee's story on from where my memories of her left off. I have postponed this particular item, the end of Lee's story, the last newspaper article I have to find. I've never seen the clipping, and now I have to search for it. I don't remember when it first appeared.

Summer 1986

A long drive through the center of Pennsylvania brought me here, to Ohio, for the summer. I thought I knew why I was going home.

You must be so relieved, my friends had said from their distant lives, when the tenure decision came, and my place was suddenly secure. Most of my academic colleagues knew better than to congratulate me, having been through it all themselves, having learned what I knew, too. You can't let yourself ask whether you want it, because you're too busy trying to get it, and when you have it, tenure comes not as a relief but as a sinking thought. *Oh no, this is my life for the rest of it.*

A buoy bobs up in the water nearby when you tell yourself, *But now I can do what I want.* Then the question hits you like a wave, and you go under again. *Yes, but what is that?* Your own life on hold all those years, paying your dues, frozen by the control someone else has over you, you lose track of what matters to you. No wonder they say it's a woman's profession.

I passed along Route 80, through the mountains, watching my speed (the fines were heavy there), talking out loud to myself. I developed the dangerous habit early in childhood, when I discovered I could count on myself to listen. My own voice came in handy there, kept me company between the Susquehanna and the Allegheny rivers, where the radio grated on my nerves with its country twang, or crackled with static.

Stuck in a lane of traffic narrowed by road construction, the engine idling in front of me, I hung on to a defiant conviction. I'd seen it happen too many times. Anxiety keeps the edge on, security is soporific, and a mind is a terrible thing to waste. I spoke it out loud: *I will not go dead in the head.* Teach yourself a new skill, I told myself. Bend the skills you have to a new task. Otherwise it's all too much like talking out loud to yourself.

I thought it was my greatest fear, giving my mind over to dull habit, letting it go stale in the same old place it had been.

To protect myself from that, somewhere between Wilkes-Barre and Milton, Pennsylvania, I settled on Lee's story as my subject, the most interesting story I knew. The puzzle of it appealed to me, the distance between where she started and where she ended, the jigsaw gap between what I remembered and what I thought I knew. I had always been skilled at puzzles, and the exercise of this one would keep my mind alive. The decision was cool, like the mountain air around me. It conformed to me like the bucket seat of my car.

So, thirty-five years old, divorced, settled into a tenured position, I groped my way along Route 80, talking to myself, and not even I was listening. The dulling interstate, so familiar I hardly saw it, stretched out ahead of me, from exit to exit. I passed the occasional distraction. At Dubois, a black Converse hightop sat in the middle of the road—there's something creepy about one empty shoe along the highway, and I saw it in time to swerve. Near the stop for Snow Shoe, a dead deer lay crumpled along the berm, the audacious crows at their work, too committed to be disturbed by my car as it passed.

Eventually, Interstate 80 runs into the Ohio Turnpike, and I was almost there, on my way to my mother's empty house for the summer, to do myself a favor unawares.

I sit now, escaping the late summer heat in the Wood County Public Library on Main Street, a block away from the building on North Church Street where, as a child, I borrowed books that were too old for me. The new building, clean, well lighted, has a modern design. Colorful pennants and silk banners announcing Children's Story Hour and National Book Week flap like kites in the breeze created by the air conditioning above me. I'd never been in this library before the summer began, but I find my way around easily. I know the floor plan of a library in my bones, the way some women know the layout of each new grocery store they enter, walk straight to the produce, find the vanilla without looking, distribute the experience of many grocery stores over each new particular.

Doing this kind of research in a small-town paper (no index, of course) stretches my arithmetic and my patience. I add and subtract, counting forward and back from the dates I know for certain. In a darkened hallway in a house in North Carolina, I first heard the news of Lee's death from my mother. I left that house in 1979, moved into it in 1973. *Terminus ad quem. Terminus a quo.*

They must have found Lee's body in the middle seventies.

It will be a warm month, I think now, the snow melted, the ground thawed, if they're digging around in somebody's front yard for bodies, what's left of them. In this part of the country, that can't mean March, it might not even mean April. I ask the librarian for the spool dated May 1975, guessing on both month and year, getting my patience ready for a long session at the microfilm reader with the *Daily Sentinel Tribune.*

I can't call it great detective work, more like luck, really, and a long acquaintance with local weather. I haven't turned the crank twenty minutes—my grisly mathematics brings me that close—when the headline I want appears on the screen: BODY FOUND IN MICHIGAN MAY BE MISSING BG WOMAN. The date, May 23, my little sister's birthday, 1975.

The story runs for three days on the front page, and ends with Lee's obituary. The details I gather in my scan of the pages accord with everything I've known all along, everything I remember from my mother's having told me years before.

I pause only twice. First, to do some quick arithmetic. Lee was last seen alive in March 1974. March to March, twelve months, March to May, fourteen. Then I puzzle for a moment over the last paragraph of the last article, where I'm sure I've found a mistake. Lee is survived by her mother, the paper says. They mean her stepmother. Lee's real mother, who would have been looking for her all those months, was dead herself by then. I don't know the details, how her mother died or when, because nobody seems to remember her. And the obituary file in the public library doesn't begin until 1960.

I jot the questions in my notebook, *mother's death, how, when.* I'm keeping track of the things I want to ask Eric.

The last I had news of Eric before this summer, he was in prison. The way his life had gotten him there, I thought by now he might be dead. But I found him earlier in the summer, alive, and I found him by accident. I was at the library then, too, trying to pin my memories of Eric down to history. I mentioned his name casually to the librarian, not asking for help, just making conversation. Eric, she reminded me, used to drive the library's Bookmobile, years ago, before he got in all that trouble. Small towns have large memories.

But it's odd you should ask about him, she told me. He came up in the paper again, just a few days ago.

Sure enough, July 2, 1986, a little notice about Eric Fletcher in the *Daily Sentinel Tribune*. Despite everything, Eric turned out all right, was making straight A's at the University of Akron where he won a scholarship. He asked his mother, probably, to place the item in the home-town paper because he wanted people to know. *See, it's not what you think you remember. I didn't kill her.* Eric himself survived it all, was thriving, a remarkable achievement, really, though I made the cynical note at the time. Well, yes, remarkable, but then, Eric *is* a man. Most of the dead people in this story are women.

I guessed at an address for him in the Akron phone book, told him I was writing Lee's story from what I remembered and what I could learn. I asked if he'd help me.

I waited several weeks before he called me. He asked a lot of questions, doubtful at first, then said he guessed he could talk to me. He'd be in town, he said, at the end of the summer. I had meant to get together with them, Lee and Eric, fifteen years before, that summer I passed Lee on the street, and now, I was making good on my promise.

On August 16, Eric comes to the house, and sits in the living room with me, the ex-con, the hood from the pool hall, invited into my mother's living room, the most public room in the house. Every house I knew as a child had one. A room for entertaining guests and opening Christmas presents, called "the living room," although we all did more living somewhere else. Everyone gets along in the living room.

In all the houses I know, the living room is stiffer than the family room, the den, the paneled basements, where you rest your feet on coffee tables strewn with magazines and junk mail.

In my mother's living room, Eric drinks his coffee, smokes cigarettes, eats chocolate chip cookies, like any guest might. He isn't just any guest, of course. He is a character I have been creating all summer out of my memory and other people's, out of newspaper clippings and police files, a character who suddenly comes to life against my mother's cherry furniture.

"That's what you looked like the last time I saw you," he says, right away, pointing to a photograph of me on my mother's wall.

"I was fifteen," I say.

"And learning to shoot pool," he says.

All four of the children are there on the wall, captured by a professional photographer when we were still asleep in our own lives, my brother dark and intense, the three daughters dreamy and poetic, looking away from the camera at something we cannot name.

Eric doesn't say I've changed, but that's what he means. I hardly recognize myself from that photograph, my long hair still young and thick and blond then, the barrett keeping it off my face, no glasses. But Eric still looks exactly like himself—that is, exactly as I remember him. Tall, lean, muscular, a head full of beautiful blond hair. It's the first thing everybody says when I ask what they remember, that he was beautiful.

And here he is in the living room of my mother's house where I have been staying alone all summer, taking care of the place for my parents, surrounded by my own history. Here are the years of Christmas presents: opalescent paperweights, museum pieces hand-blown by a local artist; Royal Doulton figurines; Steuben glass handwarmers, all of them displayed proudly on tables not far from the corner where the Christmas tree stood. Here are the photographs, public and acknowledged. There is the desk whose drawers I do not open even now, because they are marked in my mind as private. I imagine them full of my mother's secrets. Every house I know, including my own, has a desk like that. Public rooms with private spaces. Tasteful decoration, messy drawers.

Now Eric paces at the edge of the Oriental rug, gesturing with his cookie, sweating a little as he makes polite conversation. He can't sit still for more than a few minutes at a time, he says, because of an injury to his back, and he limps just slightly as he walks around. His energy unbalances the living room.

I share a little history with him myself, a history that, however delicately, links Eric and Lee and me. I haven't seen Eric for twenty years, but it's the same now as it was then, the same as it might have been for Lee. I still can't take my eyes off him.

We chat for a few minutes, reminisce a bit, catch each other up on what we've been doing. At last, the scholar with a skill for taking notes, I pick up my notebook and ask the first question.

"How did Lee's mother die?"

Eric pauses, looks right at me, his eyes stunningly blue and clear. He squints them slightly into a puzzled look.

"She's not dead," he says.

"What do you mean, she's not dead?" I say.

Eric's body stiffens, pulls back into the air, and he raises his hands before him.

"Hold on," he says. "I'm just the messenger."

"Sorry."

"As far as I know," Eric shrugs a little, "Lee's mother is alive and well and living in Cleveland."

Something real and difficult has entered the living room with Eric's news and my anger at a betrayal I still cannot name. I am suddenly awake. I've been collecting information about Lee all summer, built up on the foundation of a lie. I know now I will have to start all over.

The Wood County Courthouse is a magnificent monster, one of the few surviving examples of the work of some Victorian architect whose name I can't remember, but who (we told ourselves as children) dived headlong off the roof of one of his own buildings when little towns like mine stopped buying his work. Shaggy gray stone, a local stone dug from the nearby quarry where to this day, occasionally, on a summer afternoon an unattended child drowns. Rough cut in the very beginning, and the rough places never made smooth, the building hulking and awkward even in the architect's imagination. Bronze trim now turquoise from years of weather, a terra-cotta roof on the spire that rises above everything in town, as long as you look at the building from the south, at least, so the contemporary high-rises at the university don't block your view.

Inside, wide marble stairs, cool and smooth, lead to the second floor, the offices circling the open space created by the stairwell, so that from the bottom step, I can look up to the arch of the ceiling above me, all of it stained glass. I remember coming here as a child with Maggie Howell to see an amazing exhibit, part of the permanent collection of local memory. It was in the showcase at the top of the stairs: three fingers cut off from the hand of the only man ever hanged in Wood County, barely recognizable as anything human, souvenirs preserved in a jar of formaldehyde. We stared into the glass, and our own reflections shimmered back at us. Then, exchanging glances that spoke one mind, we raced around the circle of offices at the top of the stairs, and chased each other down the wide marble steps, back out into the air and on to the grass beyond.

Now the showcase isn't there.

The office of the Probate Court, near the top of the stairs, keeps all the records of births, deaths, marriages. The other people who come by that office occasionally are older women mostly, country women, working out families in needlepoint, perhaps, for wedding presents. A clerk looks at me quizzically when I walk in. Tracing your family tree, she asks. I'm tracing somebody else's, I say, concerned that it's an act of trespass, and I might be denied. But the clerks let me come and go as I please, as if to say, good Protestants all of them, *marriage is of a public nature.* I can look at whatever I want.

Knowing from his obituary that Dr. Snavely remarried in 1960, knowing as well that a marriage license will include the record of any earlier marriages, I sit in the Wood County Courthouse, turning pages in a dusty book, indexed by hand but not alphabetized. The names of the men appear on the left page, the names of the women on the right, as if kept officially separate by public order until they had endured the ceremony itself.

Dr. Snavely's name is not recorded at all, an error, probably, on the part of the clerk writing all those S-names and skipping one by accident. But I know his new wife's name before she married him, Mason. There are fewer M's to sift through. That's how I find what I'm looking for, the old wife through the new wife. There, on Dr. Snavely's application for permission from the state to marry again, is Lee's mother's name, Lilyan Kovoch, the mother I always thought dead.

Divorces, I am told, are the work of another court, so I move to the records office across the building in the far corner. There I press buttons on a fancy microfilm reader, advancing the screen frame by frame, with each frame learning something I didn't know. I feel almost high with the information, the excitement of discovery, frantic with the effort to interleave these facts with my memories, matching up years as they appear on the screen in front of me with grades that organize my recollections: 1960, fifth grade; 1962, seventh grade. Occasionally I have to add or subtract in the margins of my notes to figure out how old she was when. I am looking for Lee in every number, in every interview, in every form, in every document I find. In each new piece of information I see her more clearly, a child I never knew because she invented a living room version of her life to tell her friends. But as I discover that child, something also drops away, not so much memory as belief or certainty, not so much affection as innocence.

As I read, a line forms to my left, people waiting to use the one machine in the office, midwesterners too polite to ask me how long I intend to sit there. I am reluctant at first to give up my seat to an elderly man trying to find out something about a stepdaughter whose husband had been in jail.

"I got no claim on her," he says. "Didn't even know her really, since she was gone before I married her mother. But I thought I might try to find her now my wife's dead. Thought this convict husband of hers might be able to help."

Here is another distorted family, a dead mother, a missing daughter, a husband in jail whose hint of information will send the man, searching, into the world. The irony makes me polite. I give up my place at the microfilm reader. But he sits there only a minute, then takes the cassette out of the machine before I have even walked away.

"Wrong case number," he says, and shrugs.

"I know," I say. "You run into a lot of mistakes."

I wish him luck before he wanders off to another office, to start all over. I know that even when he finds the facts, he may not know the story, because the facts can mask a tale as well as tell one.

These are the facts, cool to the touch, a matter of public record, in Wood County Court of Common Pleas Case #35885; Guardianship document, Juvenile Division, #5301; Land Records, Book 23, Center Township.

Lee's parents, John Geoffrey and Lilyan Kovoch Snavely, were married on October 6, 1945. One week before, in Reno, Nevada, Dr. Snavely, called Geoff, had secured a divorce, neat and expeditious, from his first wife, Betsy Duff Snavely, to whom he had been married for nine years. The first marriage produced four children, a daughter and three sons, the last of whom had been born earlier that same year.

Lee herself was born to the second wife on February 5, 1950, in Stamford, Connecticut. A few years and another child later, the family moved to Ohio, living first in Waterville, and then on the farm near

Bowling Green, purchased in 1955. By 1956, the family was complete: the doctor, his wife, and three children, Lee, her brother Geoff, and another brother, Bruce.

For a time, the family was expanded by one. William Greggory Snavely, called Bill, lived with them from 1954 to 1956. Until then, he had been living with his mother in Cleveland, where, at the age of fourteen, he was convicted of chronic disobedience and juvenile delinquency. A judge, rather than commit the boy to a juvenile detention center, had assigned him to his father's care. In 1956, he returned to his mother at his own request, and with his father's permission.

Lee's parents' divorce began in June 1960, when Lilyan Snavely issued a peace bond against her husband, a legal means of enforcing his distance from her on penalty of forfeiting $500. In August of that year, she filed for divorce, on the grounds that her husband repeatedly beat her. She petitioned the court for custody of Lee and the two boys. Her husband countersued, charging his wife with adultery. He also sought custody of the children.

On September 17, the divorce was granted. The charge of adultery against the wife had been withdrawn, and Lee's mother won custody of the children. She was also awarded alimony and child support, together with $400 a month, one of the family cars, and the household furnishings. The court stipulated that she must remain in Wood County.

In addition, the court required that the children, Lee, ten, Geoff, seven, and Bruce, four, be prevented from seeing their half brother, William Greggory Snavely, called Bill, now twenty years old.

In October 1960, Lilyan Snavely requested the court's permission to remove herself and her children to Cleveland, Cuyahoga County, where she had family, a job, a house waiting for her. She had been unable, she said, to find appropriate work in Bowling Green. The court responded by permitting her to live in Wood County, Lucas, Henry, Allen, Hancock, Sandusky, Seneca, or Erie counties, an enormous freedom stretching across northern Ohio, but restricted Cuyahoga County from the list of her options.

Instead, the court allowed her to remain in the former husband's house for several more months, paying nominal rent, until she could make other plans for herself. The husband, in addition, was instructed that he might not enter the property without her express permission. He could visit the children, twice weekly. Once the mother had moved on, he could claim the children for a month every summer, provided that when he saw them, the father was not accompanied by another woman, except his wife, should he remarry.

He did. On November 28, two months after his divorce, Dr. Snavely married Lillian Mason, same first name, spelled differently, the woman I knew as Lee's stepmother.

About a week after Dr. Snavely took his third wife, Lee's mother was admitted to St. Charles Hospital in Toledo, the psychiatric ward, her symptoms "anorexia, insomnia, lack of interest and depression." She received seven electroshock treatments, every other day for two weeks in early December. She had Christmas weekend off to spend with her children, a "spoiled" holiday, she told the doctor. Released from the hospital on New Year's Eve, she was no longer clinically depressed, the psychiatrist said, but still "manipulative." He gave her a prognosis of "fair." She then returned to her own family, to her father and sister Mary in Cleveland. During her hospitalization, and for a time thereafter, the children remained with their father and his new wife.

By April 1, 1961, the father had gained legal custody of the children. At that time, Lee was an eleven-year-old fifth grader at the South Main School.

There was, apparently, no more need for the court's intervention until a little more than a year later. Then, in August, 1962, Dr. Snavely died suddenly of a heart attack, living two hours after its onset, time enough to plan his own funeral as if he would hear the jazz himself. According to one witness, the attending physician and family friend, Dr. Snavely also requested that the children remain in the custody of his new wife, their stepmother for the past year.

Now everything started over. Lee's mother renewed her suit for custody of the children three weeks after Dr. Snavely's death. The stepmother also petitioned the court for their custody. The court-ordered investigation of the case lasted for seven months. It concluded with a dismissal of the stepmother's petition, and a provision that custody be granted to the children's natural mother.

On February 7, 1963, two days after her thirteenth birthday, Lee disappeared from junior high. Her mother, having won custody, removed the children to her house in Cleveland.

They didn't stay long. In early April of the same year, the mother returned them all to Wood County, to the county welfare office. On April 15, 1963, the welfare office accepted responsibility for their care. The children continued living temporarily in the large house on the farm, with their stepmother. The county administered their lives through disbursements from an account of $23,000 collected from the dead father's insurance policies.

In 1964, Lillian M. Snavely took the legal steps necessary to initiate the process of selling the farm—the property was still in probate—and shortly thereafter moved the children with her to Waterville, where Lee attended Anthony Wayne High School. By the time the farm was sold, in 1966, the stepmother had given the children over to the welfare office again, from which they were placed in separate foster homes. Bruce, the youngest, stayed on in Bowling Green. Geoff joined a family in Hershey, Pennsylvania. Lee, after several temporary placements, took up life and finished high school in Bay Village, Michigan.

In June 1974, representatives of the Wood County Welfare Office, Juvenile Division, petitioned the court to be released from the obligations of guardianship. That year, Bruce, the youngest of their wards, had been graduated from high school, and at eighteen had reached the age of consent.

By that time, when the official record comes to an end, Lee had disappeared. They found her, dead, and they found her by accident, over a year later, when nobody was looking for her anymore.

These are the documentary facts, names, dates, certainties, a matter of public record. The documents comprising Wood County Court of Common Pleas Case #35885 also contain a private record, much less legible, as if written by hand. Depositions, reports, summaries of conversation. They come at you from at least one personal point of view, and more frequently from two, the person speaking and the person taking note of the speech.

Here, for example, is a representative financial statement, a month's worth of expenses scrawled with a fountain pen in the doctor's hand. The cost of reprints of an article in a medical journal. Routine dental checkups for the children. Repairs on a thirteen-year-old Ford. Various expenses with the farm, having to do occasionally with the dogs, but mostly with sheep, Corridels, a registered breed. Alimony and child support to a first wife. Piano lessons for Lee. The cost of a subscription to *The New Yorker*.

The doctor's public life incurs expenses; he pays for things. His wife doesn't keep the family books, but she completes a form, too, responding to questions about financial matters. Her answers are full of gaps. Her estimate of the husband's income may be off by as much as $20,000. She doesn't know what's paid for and what isn't. But she estimates the value of their house at $60,000 and notes as well that the property, which must now be settled, includes another little house, set off on a distant edge of the farm, and valued at $8,000.

Here is the doctor again, completing a form, asked to provide the names and birthdates of the four children from his first marriage. He records their ages, but not their birthdays. He lists the male children first, although the form doesn't specify separation of the children by gender, and then the one girl two columns over on the page, as if she occupied a separate space in her father's mind.

In a similar way, he distinguishes the daughter from the second marriage as well. Now, a caseworker intervenes between the doctor and the information he provides. She works perfunctorily at her duties, is given to general descriptions like "pleasant," and "sincere." But she praises the father for his "sincere and earnest" interest in his children, remarking especially on his ability to individuate them. In her experience, it is, perhaps, a rare perception in fathers. He sets his daughter Lee off in a place of her own, praises her prodigious intelligence, comments upon her extraordinary dark beauty, considers her remarkably "well adjusted." He disparages the middle child, his namesake Geoff, as "too dependent," a mama's boy, clever at getting his own way. The other boy, only four at the time, is bright, healthy, aggressive.

At the time of the second custody hearings in 1962, between the mother and the stepmother, a host of witnesses is called. Among the voices recorded in these pages, I find some I know, or at least remember. Another local doctor, a local teacher. When I see their names, I call up their pictures readily. The doctor I remember as the father of handsome and rowdy sons, tall like their dad, who had enormous, gentle hands. The teacher, aristocratic, matronly, swept her gray hair back into a bun. She went to another church, taught at another elementary school, and

I don't even know how I remember her. If I did, what good would such a memory be to me now? I remember irrelevancies. The size of a man's hands. The color of a woman's hair.

And always, between the voices and the stories they tell I find the caseworker, another woman this time, who takes her job seriously, literally, who works at building a case. I can only guess at how good she is at her job.

Right away, she has trouble with the arithmetic of it all. She numbers the wives to keep them straight. Betsy Duff is Mrs. Snavely #1, barely a shadow here. Lilyan Kovoch is Mrs. Snavely #2. Lillian Mason is Mrs. Snavely #3, all of them taking their numbers in line from the name of the man they married. To me, it's simpler than that: Lee's father's first wife. Lee's mother. Lee's stepmother. Stranger, mother, stepmother.

The caseworker takes to judgment, both explicit and implicit, against Lee's mother. A "drinking problem" is hinted at. The woman appears "timid" and "uncooperative," a "martyr" who claims to have suffered "many abuses" at the hands of her former husband, none of them specified, who claims repeatedly that he must have done something to turn the children against her when she was in the hospital. The caseworker's record consistently undercuts the claim.

The caseworker reports as well that the house the natural mother has prepared for her children in Cleveland is adequately spacious and appropriately remodeled for a family of this constitution. Close to the local schools, in a nice, residential neighborhood. Several bedrooms, several baths, an attic refurbished as a playroom for the boys. But this house, she says, is "more a place to live than a home." "Sterile," she calls it.

In addition, Mrs. Snavely #2 openly criticizes her former husband's new wife as the rival for her children's affection. The caseworker hears the remark as a whine, as if it represented a clear fault, as if it suggested undignified or unladylike behavior, a feeling too raw to validate. Yet even the caseworker knows, and makes no allowance for the fact, that Lillian Mason, Lee's stepmother, had been the doctor's mistress for the last two years of his marriage. She lived, in fact, in the other little house on the property, the smaller dwelling whose value Lee's mother had estimated at $8,000.

At no point does the caseworker, or any other witness for that matter, mention the physical abuse, first made public in the wife's grounds for divorce, but now, it seems, too incredible or too messy to name.

The caseworker gives the stepmother a kind of nobility, interviewing her at length, noting that she is "relaxed and open," and refuses to speak unkindly of the children's mother. Nevertheless, Mrs. Snavely #3 reports extensively on the condition of the children when she first encountered them. They lacked any sense of "family cooperation," she says. They didn't make their own beds, and she had undertaken immediately to teach them some domestic skills. To teach Lee, for example, to cook, and to care for her own clothes.

Mrs. Banks, aristocratic and matronly, the sixth-grade teacher at the South Main School, remembers Lee as early as the fourth or fifth grade, when she was living first with both parents, and then, during the divorce proceedings, with her mother. A very bright child, "almost brilliant," Mrs. Banks says. When she was living with her mother, the child came to school looking like a ragamuffin, slovenly dressed. She remained aloof from the other children, didn't establish relationships easily, and the other children avoided her, suspicious, a bit fearful. "All this changed," Mrs. Banks says, "when the stepmother took over." As a sixth grader, Lee had been just as bright, but more cheerful, more careful of her appearance, not such a discipline problem.

The handsome Lutheran pastor who conducted the father's funeral remembers being at the farm, having promised the mother that he would check in, and seeing the children scatter to hiding places in the barn when their mother called from Cleveland. They clearly didn't want to talk to her, he says. A doctor, who frequently socialized with his friend and fellow doctor, remembers the children, particularly Lee, as ornery, difficult, "problem kids," when they were with their mother. And another troubling issue he feels he has to mention. The youngest boy, he says, was very slow in his development. Although otherwise a healthy and vigorous child, Bruce had been nearly four years old before he spoke one word. The doctor with the enormous, gentle hands implies, however hesitantly and reluctantly, that the child's failure to speak derived from an inadequacy in the mother.

Lee herself, interviewed as a seventh grader at the junior high, takes up against her mother, expressing in no uncertain terms a preference for living with her stepmother. Her mother, she says, "never liked her," was always criticizing her, told her to do something and then punished her when she did. Her mother went away a lot, wasn't there when the children came home from school. When that happened, they used to wander up to "Daddy's little house with Mom," where they'd find cookies, maybe, at least somebody at home. And the new house, the house her mother had in Cleveland, well, there was nothing much to do there, and the furniture was uncomfortable. Her aunt Mary, her mother's sister, who also lived there, was just a "bossy old school-teacher" who ordered everybody around, including her mother. Her mother didn't know what she was doing, and had to take direction from someone. Lee says she "doesn't like to think what would happen" if she were forced now to live with her mother in Cleveland.

Geoff, the second child, interviewed separately, repeats many of Lee's phrases, volunteers the same answers Lee had given, even when he is asked different questions. Little Bruce, six years old in 1962, isn't given the chance to speak for himself, but Geoffrey says Bruce wishes his mother was dead, so they wouldn't have to live with her anymore.

The caseworker admits that Lee did a "very good job" of coaching her little brother on what to say, perhaps even on rehearsing her own answers before the fact, practicing phrases she'd heard at home. The caseworker speculates that the mother was a "victim of a very carefully prepared plan of attack" by her former husband, still speaking his authority, having his own way, from the other side of the grave.

In all the gaps and silences created by the questions the caseworker is too polite to ask, one other person is given room to speak. William Greggory Snavely, called Bill, the mysterious half brother who shared a father with Lee, appears voluntarily at the social worker's office. A graduate of Yale, now a twenty-two-year-old master's candidate at Stanford, Bill Snavely has heard about the trouble, he says, and has come to help if he can. From the description of him on the page, I can almost see him, barging in.

He speaks nothing but contempt for his father, resisting that will, insisting that the children should live with their natural mother. The stepmother, he says, who "lived openly" with the father before the divorce, is not a fit parent. He claims that his father drank heavily, cheap liquor, a quart or more a day, that he had a violent temper, and that Mrs. Snavely #2 was innocent of adultery and alcoholism.

The caseworker who records his comments, still building a case, speaks freely and disparagingly of his character. She reminds her reader, for example, that "this boy" had once been convicted of chronic disobedience in juvenile court. And more recently, after the divorce, the court had not permitted the children any contact with him. Even now, his appearance, she notes, "leaves much to be desired," and he is "unrealistic in his living." No one else in the family, she remarks, seems willing to talk about Bill. Everyone avoids direct questions, glancing tellingly at each other, as if their eyes could whisper, whenever his name comes up.

Bill is here to speak for himself. At the time of the first custody hearing, he says, his father attempted to coerce him into testifying in court that he had slept with Lee's mother. When he refused to cooperate, the father accused him of being a homosexual—a charge, the son now says, "his own wife can dispute." And then his father booted him out of the house, sent him packing, a college sophomore, without so much as a ride to the bus station.

I make photocopies of everything before I leave the courthouse, the scholar's impulse to reconstruct a careful text. That impulse, too, is an irrelevancy, even for one who reads between the lines for a living. Still, I want these pages with me, to hold on to, as if I can get to the bottom of this, as if I can know the truth.

But what can this paper witness tell me? What can these human witnesses say, called to their accounting so many years before? What could they have seen? The effects, perhaps, distanced from their causes. The outermost ripples in distorting water, but not the stone itself that made them, dropping.

What matters most no one sees.

The clerks, good Protestants all, are wrong. Marriage is not of a public nature. Only the wedding is. What happened here, between man and wife, between mother and daughter, between father and son, happened in private, behind a closed door, in a locked room, in a buried heart that called no witness. Not in a living room, but in a family room, a bedroom, a paneled basement, a darkened hall. Not out on a tabletop for all to see, but hidden in a messy drawer.

I cannot know what happened, but I can guess at how it came to be. What we hide from public view careens unchecked to danger.

I step out from the courthouse, a cool tomb, into the August heat. Deck's Funeral Home, where Eric arranged Lee's funeral, where her stepmother arranged her father's funeral as well, is across the street from me. Behind me now the courthouse looms, hulking and awkward. I pause a moment on the steps, recalling an image from something I read years before, in a *Weekly Reader* when I was in elementary school. A mastodon, frozen in the instant when the ice came, a buttercup found fresh and fragile ages later in its huge mouth when archeologists unearthed the ancient creature from a thawing grave. Now, the mastodon has yielded a flower to my hand, and no one has seen that flower's delicate, uncertain petals for years.

My car is where I left it in the August heat, and there's no ticket on the window, despite the fact that the meter ran out hours ago. I make my way down the green slope that spills toward the street, remembering other August days, hot and humid and still, like this one. A day in my own mother's living room when I was yet certain that no living mother would have allowed Lee's story to happen. A day years before that, when, cold in my distance from her, I passed Lee going the opposite direction on the opposite side of the street.

I roll down all the windows before I start the car. It's been baking in its parking place all afternoon, and the accumulated heat inside has assumed substance. My glasses fog over and they slip down the sweat on my nose.

The radio comes on automatically when I turn the ignition. Thick heat comes back to me from the music, Mick Jagger's voice, bluesy and slow, on his way to an airport, on his way to a plane, living out his short, sweet life with no expectations at all.

That's right, I think. You have no expectations until you come face to face with what you're looking at, and then everything in you says, *I wasn't expecting this.* I didn't know what I was looking for when I set out to remember Lee at the beginning of the summer, but it hadn't been this: to witness a life I never saw.

I turn my car left from Court Street onto Prospect, heading to the south, for home. The route I'll take, the back way, stretches out in my mind.

In the first block, nearest the courthouse, two law offices, competing practices no doubt, Marsh, Marsh & Marsh, Harms & Harms, great names for lawyers, all that paperwork kept in the family, shuffled from father to son to son. Then, the corner of Wooster and Prospect, where the main street intersects with something like a promise. A gas station and a pizza joint on the right, the armory and the shabby awning and empty planters of the old Ross Hotel on the left. Beyond that, going east, a trail of fast-food restaurants, gas stations, drugstores, apartment complexes, motels point the way to the new side of town and the university.

Once it crosses Wooster Street, Prospect ambles through the old part of town, past large white houses, aluminum-sided now, with wide front porches and small front lawns shaded by maples and oaks that buckle the sidewalk. In the space of four blocks, three churches—four if you count the armory, where every August a revivalist camps out to save a few souls. The domed grandeur of the EUB Church. The stalwart gray stone of the Methodist Church. And the Baptist Church, a wood-frame house with a jerry-built steeple, the Baptists interlopers, never quite at home here.

Dog-legging through the center of town, I come to Pearl Street whose long stretch westward, not one stop sign along the way, articulates a history. First, nearest the town center, the Victorian *grandes dames* and painted ladies, a problem to heat now, the children gone, no servants, and the upstairs rooms closed off. After a block or two, they give way to smaller places, shingled upstarts wedged between narrow driveways. And then, past the railroad tracks the spaces widen again and the streets assume names like aliases: Hillcrest, Crestview, Donbar, Winfield, Parkwood, Knollwood, names with delusions of grandeur, names that pretend to an elegance or an elevation the streets do not have.

By Knollwood, I'm almost home. The way is as familiar as the creases in my palm.

In my mind, I've already made the trip, but in fact I've come only two blocks. The red light at the corner of Prospect and Wooster appears suddenly, unexpectedly. I brake without clutching, and the car lurches, then stalls.

I had started two months before with a puzzle I wanted to solve, a story I wanted to tell, vaguely uneasy that the pieces of my memory didn't fit into a coherent picture. That unease focused later on a grim question, to which I thought I could find an answer, the facts, at least, if not the truth. What had happened in Lee's life, that she could have been dead for over a year, and they found her body *by accident?* A conviction of my difference from her had prompted the question: *I* would have been found on purpose. Somebody would have been *looking* for me.

Somebody would have been looking for me. The words hum in my head over the growl of the engine, starting to life again.

Now, as I drive home from the courthouse, that old conviction of difference puts me on edge, like a lie I've told myself. The new thought, just taking form, seems hopelessly exaggerated. I try speaking it out loud: *You've just read your own life spelled out in a foreign alphabet.* And then immediately, the challenge: *Nobody's going to believe that. You don't believe that.* I haggle it out with myself while I wait in the heat of the afternoon for the light to change.

My father, a gentle, pious man. A minister, after all.

Lee's father, a handsome, educated man. A doctor, after all.

Pillars of the community, both of them. And no one dared think the structure unsound, the prop hollow, because pillars hold everything up.

Come on, you can't mean that. My father never tried to silence anyone.

He didn't have to. He was the silence himself.

I still hear his voice floating into my bedroom from behind the study door on Sunday mornings.

No, he spoke words for a living.

He spoke public words. What did he ever say at home?

The same words he said in the world. My father's no hypocrite.

Then why didn't he put all that "love thy neighbor" stuff to better use? You had a friend who was dying.

He probably didn't know.

Why didn't he know? Where was he looking instead?

But my father doesn't have a violent bone in his body.

Of course not. But if he did, who would believe it? And besides, how would you know?

The thought beats in me like a heart.

You invented your father, gave all that silence the shape you wanted it to have. The only true thing you can say is he's a mystery to you. You don't know him at all.

I had to admit I didn't.

In the folder on the seat beside me, the edges of the photocopies have curled up in the heat. They seem now a spooky mirror in which everything is spelled backwards, different languages for silence and noise. The father's silence makes the mother's noise possible, maybe even creates it. And the daughter dances around her father's silences and withers under her mother's noise, takes her mother's voice into her head because it's the only voice she ever heard.

But for Lee it must have been something like the opposite. The noise

Lee's father made, even if it was only a constant whisper in the daughter's ear, drove her mother into silence, where she evaporated like shallow water in the summer sun. And Lee danced around the empty place her mother made, imagined the comfort of her mother's dying, and her father's voice echoed in the hollow place inside: *Your mother never loved you. You are my ally. You, we, you, we have the power to undo her.* And then, did she carry her father's voice to her grave? Or did her mother's silence make the louder noise?

Now the light changes to green, and I move along Prospect Street, through a series of four-way stops I can almost glide past, slowing but not stopping. When I turn the corner onto Washington Street, I see ahead of me, at the next corner, another traffic light, and I shake my head and smile. The whole point of going the back way is to avoid the traffic lights.

A cluster of teenage girls, long and tanned, crosses the street in front of my car. One of them breaks away from the group, hurries a few paces ahead, then spins around to face the rest of them. She makes a scissors with her arms, up and down, up and down, and high-steps her knees almost to her chest, the perfect cheerleader in short shorts and a halter top. Then she doubles over with giggling. She reaches the curb, walking backwards, and doesn't miss a step.

Lee was braless, like this girl, when I met her that first summer at the fair. The loose freedom of her breasts had drawn my eye, and my imagination made us immediate allies. I'd been fighting with my mother about that bra all summer. At the time I imagined that Lee must have been fighting with her mother, too, but by then, of course, her mother was gone.

I fell in love with indirection when I turned eleven and sprouted breasts. For the last few minutes every afternoon that spring when I was in the sixth grade, I wandered off from wherever I was supposed to be, arithmetic problems or spelling tests or book reports, to dream a new way home. It challenged my imagination (lucky for me I have one), to figure out how I could get home without walking on any main streets. A straight shot down the length of Church Street would have brought me from the elementary school to my front yard, but the direct route seemed far too dangerous.

I imagined a route like this instead. Starting down the alley near the end of Kenwood Drive. Sneaking through what used to be the Warners' backyard. Climbing over a fence or two, never mind that I wore clumsy dresses every day to school. Ducking under a grape arbor in another yard. Stealing along another series of alleys, then slipping furtively around a detached garage, until I came to the gate in the fence around our backyard. Home free. And safe, I thought.

Along the main streets, grown men made lewd remarks about my breasts.

Bouncy, bouncy, bouncy, they called out to me from rooftops or porches or scaffolding where they were painting someone's house, a twisted version of the Ipana toothpaste song.

I tried to tell my mother that I needed the shield of a bra, but she wouldn't hear it. Maybe next year you'll need a bra, she said. Wait until you're older.

But I need one now, I said.

You have plenty of years ahead of you to wear a bra, she said.

Mom, men say things to me on the street.

You're not old enough to need a bra.

But look at me, Mother. Look at me.

She looked, I guess, but she didn't see me at all. Or she couldn't come to terms with what she saw.

I could have saved my money, bought my own bra, taken myself down to LaSalle's and asked the matronly woman in the lingerie department to help me. But the direct reproach to my mother's vision of me frightened me even more than the men on the streets. I felt abandoned to the world, dreamed that a bra offered the protection my mother couldn't give me, and I went the long way home.

I have worried that story all my life, like a rough bead in the fingers, rubbing it smooth and shiny, turning it into a pearl.

The last picture I have of Lee, taken a little over a year before her death, is a mug shot reproduced in the *Daily Sentinel Tribune.* I have that picture in the folder on the seat beside me, but I will never have to look at it again to see it. The picture cuts Lee off at the waist. Her hair is a long, dark tangle, falling well below her shoulders. Her dark eyes are clouded over with lid, swollen and heavy, the look of sleeplessness rather than tears. Her mouth is straightened along a grim line. A turtleneck in some pale color bunches up around her breasts. It doesn't quite fit. She isn't wearing a bra, and her nipples show through the thin cotton.

I hear the child's voice speaking from the picture.

My mother never liked me, she tells the social worker.

But it's my own voice I hear. *Look at me, Mother. Look at me.*

What does Lee say, without a mother to tell her yes or no? *I'll wear what I damn well please.*

My musings have brought me the length of Pearl Street. I make the turn onto Knollwood, almost home. I have arrived by the kind of route we in my family always travel, no matter where we're driving in town. We map out a series of side streets and four-way stops, to avoid the traffic lights, and the center of town. It's a long-standing habit, and like all habits, it no longer has any reason to it.

Now that I think about it, I'm not sure it ever did. The back way stops at two traffic lights. The front way, the direct route, has only one more, at the Four Corners in the center of town. Even if you hit all those traffic lights red, the long way, the direct route, would take you maybe three minutes more.

Not that anybody ever clocked it, probably. Because the motive has always been there, like a memory in the bones: *take the least direct route—it will save you time.*

It doesn't make much sense, but it's the way I know.

The peak of the roof of my parents' house comes into view. Suddenly, it returns to me, my misplaced anger at Eric, the messenger in my mother's living room a few days before. Now I begin to place it right.

Lee was my best friend and she didn't tell me.

No, that's not it. It's not a best friend's betrayal so long after the fact.

I was her best friend and I didn't know.

Guilt, then? Yes, some of that, probably.

She was Lee's mother and she left her, she let her go.

Yes, that's closer. But that's not all.

This was my mother and she didn't.

That sentence brings me home. Two mothers, two daughters. One mother, so damaged and frightened, she had to abandon her child, to give her up to the world unprotected. The other mother, daunted in her own way, too frightened to let her daughter go, to see her daughter's difference, to hear her daughter's separate voice. And strangely, that too was a giving up, a failure of protection.

To have a mother like mine was both my luck and my sorrow. My mother would have been looking for me if I'd been missing, as Lee had been, but she also couldn't see me when I was right there.

Had she seen me, had she heard my voice separate from her own, might I have trusted myself to look at Lee when she was right there? Might I have stopped that day when I passed Lee on the street, reached out for her pain, acknowledged her bruises, and taken her into my arms?

The garage door creaks open, folding back on its metal runners into the dark of the garage. The sunlight doesn't reach into the corners, and from the driveway where I wait, the garage looks cool and inviting. The car slips into the empty space, and I slide out. I know now where I'm going.

I have come home to witness lives I never saw, my own and Lee's, my parents' and hers. Lives that connect in a web of not knowing, a collusion of silence, a fragile structure that couldn't stand what threatened it. Lives that ran into danger—or caused it—because for different reasons and in different ways nobody was looking at them. Lives that called no witness when witnesses might have mattered.

Looking at them now, serving as a witness so long after the fact, won't change them, I know.

What's done is done. It's my mother's voice, practical, resigned. *You can't change the past.*

I don't want to change it. I want to see it.

You can't even know it, she says.

Then I can imagine it.

What you imagine will hurt a lot of people. It's my mother's voice still, fragile, endangered.

Let the dead bury the dead. It's my father's voice now, cadenced and biblical.

No, I say. *Let the living bury the dead and then go on.*

I make my way through the house, dustless and expectant, into the living room. I hesitate a moment when I come to the desk, and then I start opening the drawers.

I pass quickly over all the things I expect to find, the things I might find in anyone's desk. A few paperclips, blunt pencils whittled at the end with a paring knife, a broken key chain. I try a ballpoint pen or two, the advertisement from the bank or the insurance agency stamped along the barrel. All of them are dry. Here's a box of notepaper, half used, and another box, only the envelopes remaining. An old compact, the mirror cracked, the powder hardened around the edges, the puff thin and worn.

In the top right drawer, I find outmoded pieces of jewelry, circle pins, clip earrings my mother no longer wears since she had her ears pierced, golden flowers with pearly centers. They sleep there, uncovered, on beds of cotton, two to a box. In the top left drawer, a copy of the *Westminster Confession*, and a small New Testament, pocket-sized. An enamel picture frame, about the size of a fifty-cent piece, a gift, probably, too small to use. A copy of the *Beatrix Potter Birthday Book*. I scan its pages briefly. It's empty of names.

Beneath that drawer, in the file-sized drawer on the left, folders are arranged neatly, separated by wooden slats. Years of financial records, charts of stocks, tax accounts, kept in my mother's hand.

I've heard the story so many times. My mother tells it like a joke. How when they were first married, she entrusted my father with the bills. *I thought I was supposed to,* she says. *I thought the man took care of those things.* But my father had no mind for the bills. A second notice arrived in the mail, and a third, perhaps, with a threat to cut off the electricity or the phone. *I gave you that bill two weeks ago,* she would say to my father. *I forgot to mail it,* he said. She worried that she'd hurt his feelings, to claim for herself a duty he ought to have. But when she finally came to him, softly, gently, cautiously, to say, *Let me do it. I'm good at that,* he responded in relief. The world fell off his shoulders into my mother's lap.

I think of Lee's mother, more typical of her generation, or less gifted, perhaps, leaving all those blanks in the financial statements she had to complete in the process of her divorce, ignorant of or kept from the facts of her husband's salary. *Good for you, Mom.* I say it out loud. *It couldn't have happened to you.*

My mother's skill, the parable of the talents come to life, got her the house she wanted, the good furniture she prized. The investment extended to her children: she sent all four of us to college on my father's unworldly salary, never more than a third of what Lee's father made. I wonder, had Lee's mother been able to manage the world in her lap, might Lee's life have turned out more like mine?

The middle drawer, over the knee-hole opening, is caught shut, something stuck at the back. I jiggle it slightly, pull it open as far as I can, then reach my hand in to shift whatever has jammed the drawer. Now it pulls easily. I lift it off its runners, take the drawer out completely, and spread its contents around me on the floor.

Here are the snapshots that never made the albums, or that long since fell from the pages of the books in which they were kept. The yellow memory of tape crosses the corners on some of them. My own face squints up at me from behind plastic sunglasses, six-shooters pointing outward above the eyes. My brother poses stiffly for the camera in a fringed suede jacket, a Davy Crockett hat covering most of his dark curls. My little sister's bare bottom pokes up over the edge of a large pan in which my mother is trying to bathe her. All six of us smile back at me from a Christmas card photograph.

I open a blue leather folder, and find there photographs of my parents before they were married, studio portraits taken, perhaps, for some announcement of their engagement. Soft brown curls frame my mother's face, widened by a smile, naturally energetic. *You're a good kid and a peachy dancer,* my father used to say to the woman I never knew, the woman he married. Looking at this picture, I can see her jitterbugging.

On the other side of the folder, my father is sternly handsome, his dark hair thick and neat, his large ears less obvious in this pose, not quite a profile. His face is as thin as I have always known it. A smile barely plays on his lips above the definite chin and the clerical collar around his neck.

My mother's eyes look from the folder to the left, my father's to the right. If I took the pictures out and transposed them, my parents would be looking at each other. I pause for a moment to imagine the alternate life, whatever life they missed because they weren't looking in each other's direction. *I can do it for you,* I think. *What you can't do for yourselves.*

To imagine it for themselves would cast unbearable doubt on the choices they made.

I set the photographs aside, and start leafing through a stack of papers. I find my old school records, the year-end reports from the fourth grade, the fifth grade, the sixth. The feminine hand of every teacher I had looping the general sentences across the bottom of the page. *Ann is sensitive, attentive, gets along well with others.* In the formal grid at the top of the page, I locate the checkmarks in the best columns for everything but penmanship.

I remember my mother's determination to improve my handwriting. Nightly exercises at the kitchen table. *No, hold the pencil this way. For now, just make loops. Continuous loops. Fill up the page with loops. We'll practice letters later.*

She promised my brother and me a dog if, with constant practice, our handwriting showed measurable improvement. It wasn't until years later that I learned the truth. A dog, the miniature Schnauzer we named Misty, had been waiting all along, before I made that first loop, the pick of the litter offered to the family as a gift by one of my father's parishioners.

But my mother suffered life-long embarrassment about her own hand, and she wanted mine to be neat, at least, if it couldn't be graceful. Her teachers switched from one method of instruction to another in the midst of my mother's learning cursive script, and her handwriting never recovered. To this day, she forms one letter according to one system and another letter by the rules of the other.

My mother's hand is small, idiosyncratic, and perfectly legible. But it's one of those things she takes as a metaphor for her life, perhaps, and it needles her still. *They switched the rules on me. In the middle of my learning, they switched the rules.*

My own handwriting never learned much better. It grew smaller over the years, never prettier, or more consistent, despite my mother's nightly efforts at the kitchen table to instruct it. I am surprised to see it now, my own hand on a sheet of notebook paper in the stack of things before me. I look it over quickly, a note I had written my mother when I was thirteen, and the story, long forgotten, comes back to me all at once.

Why did she keep this all these years?

I had been at a dance at the junior high, an early-evening affair, and I'd promised to be home by eight-thirty. We had all walked home together, a bunch of kids from the neighborhood, five of us, three girls and two boys. I remember that clearly, because I used the mathematics of it to rationalize the way around my parents' rules: *no boys in the house when we're not at home.*

I made my way along Knollwood Drive, rehearsing the details in my head. *There are five of us. We're not going to do anything my parents wouldn't approve of. We're an uneven number. We're not even couples. We're two boys and three girls.*

By the time I got to the driveway, I'd made up my mind. I invited my friends in for hot chocolate.

My parents had taken my two little sisters to see *Lawrence of Arabia*.

They told me they'd be out late. It was a very long movie, they said. I figured we were safe.

I poured the milk into a saucepan, got the cocoa from the pantry shelf. We were all clustered in the kitchen, waiting for the milk to heat, when I heard my parents' car pull into the driveway.

We froze a moment in the kitchen, all of us having lived through this much adolescence under the same rule, then sprang into action.

Quick, I said. The front door.

The boys dived in that direction, but they weren't fast enough. My parents came in through the back door, each of them carrying a sleeping daughter, just as the boys had leapt off the front stoop. I hadn't yet closed the door, and my mother could smell my trick lingering in the air.

She hollered at me in front of my remaining friends, who hung their heads in stupefied embarrassment for me.

We weren't doing anything wrong, I hollered back.

If you weren't doing anything wrong, why did you shoo your friends out the front door as soon as you heard us coming?

Would you have yelled any less if I hadn't?

My parents sent my friends home, put my sisters to bed, and returned to the movie, where in a small town their ticket stubs got them in for the second half, after the intermission. We'll finish this later, my mother said, and she closed the back door behind her.

After she'd gone, still shaking with anger, I wrote my mother a note, the note that I am now looking at for the first time in twenty-five years. *You're mean*, I wrote. *My friends don't like to come here. None of their mothers are as mean as you.* I left the note on the kitchen counter, and went to bed.

My father woke me up when they came home, took me into the living room in my nightgown, and sat me down on the sofa.

I knew it was serious, because my father was scolding me, breaking his usual silence to let me know how deeply I'd hurt my mother. It was bad enough to have broken the rule. But to insult my mother on top of it, to hurt her feelings, that was completely inexcusable. He made me apologize, and grounded me for two weeks. I went through the motions of an apology, lived through the social restriction, and we never spoke of the incident again.

I had completely forgotten it until now.

My father might as well have said that night in the living room, *You have the power to undo her. Be wiser after this.* And here is the note, still in my mother's drawer, preserving all these years my childish hand, attesting to that power.

My hunger finally lets me know it won't be put off any longer. I leave the mess on the living room floor, and start for the kitchen to fix myself something to eat.

"What leftovers have I been torturing long enough?" I ask into the refrigerator. "What can I put out of its misery and have for dinner?"

Here I am, still talking to myself.

In my head I rewrite the note I left for my mother years ago. The words have hardly changed at all, but they say something different now. *You're mean, Mom. Small-spirited. Too small to let people be. You're closed up, locked in, you can't see, can't see anything that doesn't look like you. All these years, I haven't been able to look at myself. You made sure of that.*

I know you would have been hunting for me if I'd been missing. But I know I have the power to undo you and you have the power not to look. Yet here I am, Mom. This is who I am, Mom, angry and loving and smart and imperfect, with faults that are not your fault and virtues you can take joy in and I have a head full of things that matter and messy handwriting still and boys in the kitchen when you're not at home and friends you don't approve of and breasts and everything.

It's a childish impulse, and I know it, to write it all down again and leave it in a drawer for her to find who knows how many years later. *The indirect route,* I think. And then, *I am sick of the back way home.* And maybe it's a childish impulse again, but I reach for the telephone. When my mother answers, I ask if the old invitation, to make a trip to the lake once before the summer disappears, is still open.

"You have room for me up there?"

"I'd love to see you," my mother says.

"I want to talk to you," I say.

"I can use the conversation," she says. "You know your father, he isn't much company."

"I'll leave early," I say. "I should be there by mid-afternoon."

"Lock up the house before you leave," she says.

"There's a story I want you to hear," I tell her.

I've been asking questions and collecting information and proving my memory wrong about Lee and Eric since June. Now, with three weeks left before I have to return to my teaching job in New York, I have a head full of something that matters to me, and I want my mother to hear it.

"Don't forget to dump the milk so it won't spoil," she says.

Yeah, I think.

And then I think again. I am ready to move on. This is what it comes down to: I am here now, alive, and my mother, unsuspecting and loving, waits up north by the water to know me.

PART

THREE

1 9 6 9

*The next evening, my mother and I settle into our chairs, facing each
other in the bay window.*

"This story begins at Howard's." I start right in.

*Beyond the window, blueberry bushes and lush ferns stretch
through the birches to a point just above the water. The land drops
off there, and an embankment of rocks tumbles to the lake below.
Across the water, clouds gather into pinks and purples around the
sun, which won't set this time of year until much later, nine-thirty
maybe, or ten. We'll have another spectacular view of it, going down.*

*Despite my good intentions, I cannot keep the edge out of my voice.
Even now, years after it created a bone between my mother and me,
the mention of Howard's can set us off, and I know I am picking
a fight.*

"Howard's!" she says, refusing me already.

I went into Howard's once, when I was home from
college for Thanksgiving during my Freshman year. All
my friends were there, comparing notes on college life,
meeting up over pitchers of low beer, three-two beer we
called it, legal in Ohio for kids who were eighteen.

When I came soberly home that night, my father was
waiting up for me to let me know they knew. He paced
in the living room, his arms crossed over his chest. We'll
talk about this in the morning, he said.

Someone, nameless to me, but known to my father,
had been walking down the other side of Main Street,
had seen me step into Howard's that night, had gone
straight home to the telephone and called my parents.

"See," my mother told me the next day, what she had
been telling me for years. "People *do* notice your every
move."

My father's job made mine a special case, gave the line
a peculiarly restrictive twist. But fathers were a conve-

nient excuse. When I was growing up, my mother's argument repeated itself across kitchen counters, in family rooms, in bedrooms all over town, no matter who the fathers were. It had less to do with our fathers' places in the world than with our mothers' isolation in the home where they had too little life beyond the claims they made on ours. *Everything you do reflects on me.*

Our mothers took everything personally. There was no other way to take it. They didn't think they mattered otherwise.

There are real dangers and pretend dangers, and it's hard enough to know the difference. When someone who loves you so much tells you everything is dangerous, *everything you do endangers me,* you spin from danger to danger trying to figure it out for yourself.

I might have saved myself a lot of trouble if I'd been able to answer then what I can answer now. *Maybe those people on Main Street didn't have anything else to look at, except the mote in someone else's eye.*

Still I'm glad for it now, my knowledge of Howard's. It gives me a place to start.

"Howard's was the hub of the universe in 1969," I tell her, a grand verbal gesture I don't entirely mean.

She squints, as if to say, "Oh, nonsense."

All the universes of Bowling Green revolved around it. For the parents, who wanted to hang on to easier days, Howard's was the most obvious occasion of sleaze and disaster, a dirty old bar right on Main Street they wanted their children to avoid. The local kids who'd gone away to college returned to Howard's at least once a vacation, because they could be sure of finding their old friends there whenever the vacations coincided, or of finding the old friends who never left town. For the fraternity boys at the university, Howard's was the quaint local hangout, loud and amusing and full of chances to test a fake I.D. The politicos at the university found at Howard's another table to thump on when the Student Union was closed, and its South End, where the campus radicals usually convened, was off limits. For working-class men and women, Howard's was their own old neighborhood recently ruined, its value as property reduced considerably, now that the college kids and the creeps had discovered it. For the druggies, Howard's became the place where if you couldn't score, you were at least guaranteed of finding another paranoiac sitting in a corner or hiding under a table, listening

to the jukebox, watching the world go by, saying, wide-eyed and terrified, "Wow, man. What a bummer."

At Howard's you could dance, talk, drink, smoke. You could hit on
your own chick or crash somebody else's. You could make fun of
anybody or make fun out of anything. You could even kill yourself at
Howard's, like my friend Wesley did, sprawled out first on the floor of
his dingy apartment popping pills and listening to the Rolling Stones.
Then he wandered down to Howard's and started drinking.

"I could see the guy was in trouble," the bartender said later, "but it
was his life, you know?"

Howard's was the only game in town.

"You remember Wesley," I remind my mother.

*She nods wistfully. "His mother was so sweet," she says. "Whatever happened to her,
I wonder?"*

Eric and Lee met in Howard's that summer of 1969, about the time
another boy from Ohio was walking on the moon. Lee, just home from
Ohio State, was spinning dizzy circles on acid all over town. Eric, just
home from Vietnam, was running on empty. Lee took him home with
her that night, and one way or another, they belonged to each other for
the rest of her life.

*My mother winces slightly in the chair across from me. I can see the question on her
face.*

In Vietnam, whatever seemed the case wasn't. Just before Eric arrived,
in early November 1967, General Westmoreland had been encouraged
by an apparent shift in enemy tactics to something more like pitched
conventional battle, the kind of battle he thought his troops could win,
raging in and around Dakto for most of that month. Westmoreland
himself had come stateside in November to announce cheerfully that
"the enemy's hopes are bankrupt."

We eventually understood that this apparent shift in tactics at Dakto
and Khesanh was only a diversion on the part of the Vietcong, the initial
stages, in fact, of the Tet Offensive, which began in January 1968. It
demoralized everyone. It brought Lyndon Johnson before his fellow
Americans with a heavy heart. It spelled the beginning of an end which
was still not to come for years.

Why is she still so mad about the Vietnam War? my mother's face asks.

I hear the question in the third person because my mother isn't asking me. She's asking my sister. This is the way we talk to each other in my family about everything important.

It happened, she says to my sister. It was a long time ago.

"And it isn't over yet," I tell her now.

Uncertainty and false conviction and misapprehension belonged to the grand scale, to the strategies of the generals and the politicians. In his own way, the individual soldier knew better than his superior officers, knew with certainty and conviction, that some disaster was always about to happen. "After six-thirty," a friend of mine wrote me, "there are no innocent civilians. Everything that moves is either VC or NVA." A kid on a skateboard tosses a grenade. A grandmother peddling fruit or begging change disguises a gun in her basket. The boredom of hours stretched into days in the boonies, nothing to do but drugs, is relieved only by the sudden terror of incoming mortar. A meadow, a field in spring blooms with flowers and trip wires, and God help the point man.

Vietnam stories, in some ways, are all the same. Or the stories are vastly different, but the meanings are alike. The statistics are probably somewhat skewed by the fact that only the survivors can be polled. Some studies indicate that as many as 77 percent of American troops in Vietnam saw their buddies killed or wounded. Nearly 50 percent believe they killed or wounded somebody themselves. Twenty-three percent suffered war-related injuries.

"I suppose you're going to tell me this is some kind of Vietnam story," my mother interrupts.

"We know now about this war," I say. "An eighteen- or nineteen-year-old kid who could answer yes to any one of those questions might be troubled for life."

Eric, I tell her, could answer yes to all three.

"And this is what you're writing about?" my mother asks.

Eric's story happened quietly, in a little moment, devastation by a technicality. At least that's the way Eric remembers it now, perhaps because he cannot yet remember it any other way.

He had taken some shrapnel in the arm, in the leg, and enough morphine to dull the pain but not kill it. Waiting to be medevacked out, he was already out of it. His mind refused to connect with his body. He barely heard the words floating somewhere above him, the promise of a commendation, a medal, a tangible sign that all of this counted for something.

And a few days later, recuperating in a hospital, he was telling somebody about it, the fellow lying next to him, maybe, or somebody wandering through.

"He said I'd get a commendation."

"Don't hold your breath," the guy said.

"He promised," Eric said.

"That's what they all say. You got a name?"

"Back home they call me Coon."

"You're kidding? You're kidding! That's good. Keep it up, buddy."

Then Eric was back on the lines again, no more than an able body, and the promise was broken.

Everywhere he turned, someone was telling him he didn't matter. The people who counted told him he didn't count at all.

"But isn't it always like that?" my mother asks. "In war. For the ordinary soldiers?"

"Maybe," I say. "Or maybe this war was different. Eric got the message, that's all."

"So he couldn't stop fighting."

"He had to put the fury somewhere," I say.

"But he didn't have to turn it on the world."

"No. He could have turned it in, on himself."

"And what does that have to do with you?" my mother asks.

The fury and self-hatred that Eric learned in that war and brought home to Lee came home to me, too, in its own way. The man who wrote me letters from Vietnam, a man I almost married, wrote routinely about killing gooks, and casually about buddies suffering breakdowns or being blown to bits.

"He couldn't make love to me when he came home, Mom. He couldn't even touch me."

"You're not going to say that in the book, are you?" my mother wants to know.

Outside the window a distraction of children hurries by, beach towels around their skinny shoulders. At their age, I remember, they can stay in the water all day and not feel the cold. The boat from next door bangs against the hoist where a fisherman moors it for the night. The sun, still well above the tree line, makes a psychedelic mandala, a perfect Day-Glo circle against the pale sky.

"There's more," I say.

My mother stares out the window at the sun, and nods.

"There's Lee."

Lee Snavely considered Bowling Green home, and like most kids who grew up in a university town, assumed she'd go to college, and wanted to "go away." But like most of the kids from my high school, she didn't plan to go too far.

Her home address was the welfare office in Bowling Green, her official guardian Mr. Elliot M. Edwards, the signature scrawled on all the checks and forms. Her mother, who'd given up on being her mother, was still living in Cleveland. Any way one looked at it in 1968, Lee resided in Ohio and, using what was left of her father's money, paid minimal tuition at Ohio State University in Columbus.

She didn't last long there. After a year in Columbus, she came back to Bowling Green and took a job at Gray's Drug, the closest she'd ever come to medical school, stocking shelves with aspirin, first-aid cream, hair dye. She shared an apartment with Pam Robbins, a friend from high school who wound up years later as the weather girl on the Channel 11 News. They lived in a large Victorian house converted to apartments at the corner of Wooster and Maple.

The mention of a place she knows brings my mother back from the window.

"The big white house?" she asks.

"Two doors down from the Dunipace house," I say. "Across the street from where the Holdens used to live."

A lot of people passed through that big house on Wooster Street, or ended up there somehow, crashed there, or dropped in on Saturday nights. My mother wants to know who. People you knew, I tell her.

"Wesley lived in that house for a while," I say. "I used to go there to see him."

In that house he smoked this and he swallowed that, and he looked inside, and then he took to writing his return address on envelopes as "the Office of Internal Insecurity," before he moved to a basement apartment whose walls were painted black.

"Before he wandered off to Howard's, you mean, for his last drink," my mother says.

Eileen lived there, after Manny left her struggling with a baby and went off to deal drugs from Spain. Later Jimmy and Eileen lived there, before he put on velveteen bell bottoms and she put on a velveteen granny dress and they got married one February afternoon.

"It was one of two hippie houses in town," I say.

"I remember the other one," she says. "Down on Pearl Street. The Georges were just sick when those people moved in there, motorcycles and loud music and drugs."

"I felt safe in places like that," I say.

"It wasn't safe," my mother says. "You could have been arrested."

"Probably," I say.

"You hardly knew those people," my mother says.

"I felt safer with strangers than I did at home."

"What? But we loved you at home," my mother says.

Is this where I tell her she never looked at me? That the invisible don't feel loved? Do I have the love left myself to make her understand that?

But she understands it already.

"Strangers are easy," she says.

"Yes," I say. "And love is hard."

Pam and Lee tripped out of that big white house one night, and made their way down to Howard's, where they took a table in the back near the jukebox. From there, they kept an eye on the door, watched who was coming and going. Lee noticed Eric right away, taking command of the place from the moment he walked in. Even from the back of the bar she saw the luminous blond hair, the natural grace.

Eric Fletcher came to Howard's that night with Phil Donovan, one of his old friends from high school. The two of them wandered to the back of the room, bent over the jukebox, pointing at titles. Phil slipped a dime into the slot. "Ina Gadda da Vida," the short version. You still got a lot for your dime.

"Wait. Wait," my mother says. "What language is that?"

"It's English. Electric English for 'In the Garden of Eden,' " I say.

"I wouldn't have figured that out in a million years," she says.

"I wish we had headphones," I say. "I wish you could plug your headphones into my head, so we could hear the same music."

This is what I hear: the music, pulsing and extreme, almost overwhelms the flimsy words, but together they explode the myth of Eden into gibberish, prove it the lie that it is.

A small-town paradise in the fifties, unexercised and unbreathed, moved and changed slowly. It dreamed itself Eden, a clean and clarified world, free of evil, free of the serpent, whatever the serpent was. But that dream *was* the serpent's, squat like a toad at the ear.

We, parents and children both, followed the hiss of its promise, *it can't happen here, it won't happen here,* into the shelter of ignorance. We traded away knowing for safety, and ended up right where the devil could have us. The prince of darkness is a gentleman; we should have known him for a liar.

Whatever we gained in the devil's bargain, whatever we bought with not knowing, it wasn't our safety at all.

Ina gadda da vida. Pidgin English. The impossible grammar of the real.

I can't make my mother hear it; she hasn't let go of the myth herself, and still thinks what we don't know won't hurt us. In fact, everything we don't know will.

"The new words," I tell her, "are clearer to me than the biblical ones."

"Don't let your father hear you say that."

Then she studies me closely and can't stop herself.

"Whoever told you your life was going to be Eden?"

"Whoever told you?"

Lee watched Eric make his way back, tried to catch his eye on the way, but he didn't seem to notice much of anything. She figured she'd have to work a little harder for his attention.

He and Phil were picking out another title, and his back was to her. She imagined a dew of sweat in the crease of his elbow as she stretched her leg out under the table, pushed the chair toward Eric with her toe. She couldn't quite reach, and compensated by kicking at the chair a little wildly. It tilted, then knocked into the back of Eric's knees. And I imagine those knees crumpling a little and Eric whirling around, ready to fight somebody.

"What was that for?" he said.

"To sit in," Lee said. "Hi, Phil." They remembered each other from high school. Phil used to go out with Carrie Holden. The connection might help.

The men drew chairs up to the table, sat themselves down.

"What you girls up to?" Phil said.

"A little of this, a little of that," Pam said. "We've got an extra hit. You two want to split it?"

Lee brought a razor blade from her pocket and handed it over to Phil. He was studying business at the university, had an accountant's eye, divided the pill carefully, and pushed Eric's half across the table. He swallowed it with a gulp of beer.

"So what did I just take?" he asked.

"Chocolate mescaline," Pam said. "Pretty good stuff."

"What're you on?" Phil said.

"Windowpane acid," Lee said. "Cleans glass without streaking."

Lee had dropped the acid only a half hour before, and everything seemed perfectly clear. She looked directly at Eric, wanting to memorize his face before it melted in front of her, or turned into a cartoon. Rugged, almost gaunt, good cheekbones, eyelashes it wasn't fair a man should have. It had taken only a moment for her to know his eyes, wide and open as if lit from behind, ghostly in the dark of the bar.

A little more talk, and then Pam and Phil evaporated into smoky air. Eric and Lee took over a corner of the place, there where the music was blaring, the sounds from the jukebox dancing like neon. Before long the drug took hold, and Lee lost the distinction between the ends of her fingers and air.

She touched his arm, or thought it was his arm she touched, though it might have been sky or light. She dropped her hand to his thigh under the table, where her fingers sunk into denim or velvet or skin. They put their arms around each other and swayed in the middle of the dance floor when some sentimental drunk hit the numbers for the golden oldies on the jukebox, "Ramblin' Rose," or "Twelfth of Never." They bent their heads together over the pitcher of beer, watching the foam disappear slowly, or studied the sparks from Eric's Bic lighter, almost out of fluid and setting off a different configuration of light each time it tried to flame.

At closing time, they stumbled out together, took the back way home, played double dare on the fire escape at the back of the public library, draped themselves over the cast-iron deer standing in the Apples' front yard, dawdled on the steps of the junior high smoking a joint and laughing like children. Then they found themselves at Lee's apartment, led by a lodestar to the place where Lee felt at home.

Lee slid a record from its sleeve, set it on the turntable, and dropped the worn needle. Neil Young danced with his cinnamon girl. Lee watched the label spin until she felt a little dizzy. From behind her, Eric slipped his arm around her waist, and pulled her gently to the bedroom. They didn't speak a word, they said everything there was to say.

She, too, needed another chance, might even be happy the rest of her life.

"You don't have to show me what comes next," my mother protests.

"I want to see it for myself," I say.

"But why do you have to look at what's so private?"

"Because I can, Mom. Because I finally can."

It's taken me most of my adult life to be able to say that.

"Sex is so overrated," my mother says.

Speak for yourself, I want to tell her, except I already know she does. My mother excuses herself and gets out of her chair for a stretch. I've no need to compel her to listen, and take off on my own.

Circles of touch at Lee's temples, into her ears, around to the nape of her neck. Eric touched her breast and her toes twitched, as if pulled by a thread of light that connected them. He traced his tongue in secret circles around her nipples. She responded to nothing more than his hand resting on her inner thigh, his sweat sticking to her belly, to the surface of his body dancing along the surface of hers. He worked and reworked the length of her, his hands moving different directions, aimless and purposeful at once. Not hands at all, but shadows of hands, cool and dark, and not touching but dancing or dreaming along. She felt like a bubble, fragile and dappled with light, floating against a starless sky. Everything else she knew evaporated, lost hold, everything but this hand, this touch, this man. By the time he entered her, she was swollen and wet. She relaxed her neck backwards, sinking it into the pillow, and imagined water pulsing out of her with the contractions, eddying in little swirls between her legs.

"Besides," my mother objects when she returns to the window, "you cannot possibly know what went on in their bedroom."

"It's about seeing," I say.

"So you're making it up?"

"Eric told me about it. He says Lee had a gift for pleasure."

"It wasn't pleasure," she says. "They hardly knew each other. Real pleasure takes long acquaintance."

"You can imagine a world in a minute," I say.

"For your whole generation," she says, "it was something else. Not pleasure."

"Yes," I admit. "For most of us it wasn't that great."

Whether we moved away from our small towns, as I did, or stayed closer to home, for a whole generation of us, suddenly the bans were lifted and the possibilities changed. It was as if on January 1, 1969 (*"I can almost date it,"* I say), it was all right to be sexual, and we didn't know how.

"You learned fast," my mother says.

"And not always well," I add.

My mother nods, pleased by our agreement, but I don't let it go at that. The story isn't that simple, isn't that clear.

Nobody had ever told us our own pleasure counted for anything, so once the parietals crumbled, we found an empty structure on the other side of the wall. We didn't know what to do with the invitation.

"*It was scary,*" I say, "*and some of us retreated into celibacy or passionless marriage.*"

"*Where you might have ended up anyway,*" my mother finishes my sentence for me.

"*Yes, as if nothing had changed.*"

"*Since my day, you mean.*"

"*Since your day. But many of us just splurged on experience, without much thought to whether we wanted it.*"

"*See,*" my mother insists. "*It wasn't pleasure.*"

"*No, it wasn't always pleasure. But some of us got lucky.*"

"*Lucky?*"

"*Sure,*" I say. "*Some women found women on the other side of the wall. And whether that discovery was political or sexual, it moved us toward freedom and change.*"

My mother tilts her head, squints one eye, doubtful that I could be telling the truth, even for myself.

"*Come on, Mom,*" I say. "*It's probably the major thing we did right.*"

She doesn't get it—can't, or doesn't want to. She made her own connections over the years with women friends, and with each other they broke the silence that marriage to distant, emotionless men imposed on them. But to have turned that personal affection into political force might actually have altered their lives, exploded their boundaries, given them choices they longed for and feared.

"*It's a matter of where you draw the line,*" I say.

"*Or what lines you draw,*" she says.

For her the limit is real and certain and safe. She cannot see stepping over the Maginot Line, crossing the Rubicon that in her mind separates the affection of friends from the passion of lovers. ("I love my friends," she says, "but not like *that.*") She cannot understand a generation, her daughters and their friends, for whom no such line exists, or for whom passionate intimacy and public commitment reward the risk of crossing it.

"*And now we have all these horrible diseases, herpes and AIDS and people are dying,*" she says.

"*I know,*" I say. "*People are dying.*"

Many of us, children of the myth, inherited that old idea of Eden, and we bargained ourselves into a place where we could be innocently and openly sexual, as if we could touch a body without seeing the face. We renamed the great American pastoral, like a reaction, "free love." We thought that would get us back to the garden, but we were wrong: there was no garden to get back to, and love wasn't ever that free.

"We all would have been better off not knowing so much," my mother says.

"Don't you see, Mom? Ignorance doesn't keep us safe."

"But where did it get you, all that experience?"

"Here, Mom. Luckily, it got me here."

However we came out of the sixties and stumbled through the seventies, by 1980, the women of a generation were regretting the chances we'd taken, longing for chances we missed. We were buying how-to books, practicing our first orgasms, taking quizzes in *Cosmopolitan* ("How Sexy Are You?"), and receiving newspaper clippings from our mothers on the rise of venereal disease.

"Sometimes you're better off," my mother says, "sublimating your sexual energy. You have your work . . ."

She starts to say "instead."

"A simple trade is too risky, Mom."

"But does sex have to be so important?"

"It is, Mom," I say. "To me it is." This is who I am, Mom. This is who I am, a grown-up woman whose choices are different from yours. Who loves where she can. Who learned from its deprivation how much touching matters.

Perhaps for Lee, as early as 1970, sex was another cynicism, less pleasure than conviction, a power she craved as the only power she knew. I want to think otherwise, that here was a small chance she had, and here was the big chance she took.

"It was a big chance," my mother says. "Bringing a man home from a bar."

Another man Lee finds in a bar will take her home and kill her. I know that already, but it still seems true, what I speak next.

"Chance can also mean opportunity," I say.

The next morning, though they weren't sure how they got there, Lee and Eric worked out their lives together. Eric woke up edgy, but they both knew that any place else was nowhere.

"I'm not saying you have to understand it," Eric said over coffee.

"And I'm not saying I don't," Lee said.

"You just have to accept it, that's all."

"That's easy," Lee said.

"I won't take a job," Eric said. "I work, I make money, I pay taxes, I belong to the system. I spent enough time already being fucked over."

His fists tightened. He didn't look at her face.

"So, what I want to know is, how much underwear you got?" Lee asked.

"What do you mean, underwear?"

"I mean, I don't care if you have a job or not. But I hate doing laundry. If you have lots of pairs of underwear, like six weeks' worth, I won't have to do the laundry so often."

"I'll do the laundry," Eric said.

And that's the agreement they made. Lee kept on with her job at Gray's Drug on the east edge of town. And Eric stayed at home, did the cooking and the laundry, kept their place immaculate, a house husband ahead of his time.

"Some opportunity," my mother says.

Usually, they woke up together in the mornings, drank instant coffee and ate English muffins, then piled into the car, a yellow Volkswagen, and Eric took Lee to work. Days were long for her, running a dust rag over the shelves because the boss said nobody liked shopping in a dirty drugstore, or opening boxes of smaller boxes and bottles, stamping the price on the top before she lined them up on the shelves.

Most of all, she hated price change days. The boss said it didn't matter, just stick the higher price over the old one. Lee felt uncomfortable with that. Inflation. The new sticker barely covered the irrational jump. She broke her fingernails trying to get the old sticker off first. It killed her feet, standing up most of the day.

She preferred the days she got to run the cash register. If business was slow, she could take a paperback off the rack, sit on the high stool and catch up on her reading.

And the end of the day goes something like this: Eric meets her in the parking lot and they drive home, stopping off at the Dairy Queen halfway down Wooster Street for a Dilly Bar or a chocolate-covered cone. All the way home, they review their day for each other, so they can put it behind them and have the evenings scot free.

"I hope you had a better time than I did," Lee says.

"Big doings," Eric says. "Addie got run over by a truck."

"You're kidding? How did that happen?"

"Oh, she was out walking the baby, crossing the street, and she sees this truck coming. So she thinks real fast, pushes the carriage out of the way, but the truck runs smack into her."

"God," Lee says.

"See, Addie got cancer when she was pregnant, and she was supposed to die. But she didn't, so they named the kid Hope. Like, life is hope, get it? Then the next thing you know, this truck out of nowhere. Doug saw the whole thing."

"How's he doing?" Lee says.

"They'll have the funeral next Friday. They always have funerals on Friday."

"Gives him the whole weekend to mourn."

"Now things will start heating up again between Doug and Julie."

"Who's Julie? I forget."

"Addie's daughter from another marriage."

"If Doug marries Julie, then her husband will be her stepfather, and she'll be mother to her half sister, who's also her stepchild."

Eric stoops for a quarter he finds on the sidewalk.

"Here you go," he says.

"I don't know what I'd do if you got run over by a truck," Lee says.

So, the days are long, the nights brief as fire, and they manage just fine.

"And you approve of this, this life?" my mother asks. "Working at the drugstore, watching soap operas all day?"

"Approval's not the point. I want to understand it. I want to see it, that's all."

"Wouldn't you be bored to death by a life like that?"

"Probably. But they were who they were. What's so bad about that?"

"A mother wants more for her children."

"A mother wants more for herself. If I'd ended up in a drugstore, you would have loved me quite a bit less, I think."

"Oh, Ann," she says, exasperated.

"Think about it, Mom," I say. "I'm a reflection on you. It's your favorite idea."

In the fall their expenses increased dramatically. It became clear Eric would have to get a job. This was after the birthday party.

He turned twenty-one in October, and Lee decided to surprise him big. She worked out the plan for a party, and then gave Phil Donovan a call. He answered the phone about 1:00 P.M., sounding groggy.

Lee told him about the party she was planning, wanted him to come. He asked what he could bring, and she said the usual, chips, clam dip, Coke.

"You're talking serious horsing around," Phil said. "You want me to try and get Eric away from his soap operas?"

"The party's not a surprise. Only the presents are. I refer you to Columbus."

"Oh, I see. The OSU campus, overgrown with weed."

"Wait," my mother says. "I don't get it."

"It's a code, Mom. Coke for coke. Horsing around. Reefer. Weed. People worried about their phones being bugged."

"So anyway," Lee said. "I have Friday off, and I'm driving down there to do the shopping. You want to come?"

"You think they'll carry what you're looking for at Lazarus?" The major department store in Columbus bore the name of the resurrected dead.

"Sure," Lee said. "Sports and Recreation."

Lee and Phil Donovan drove down that Friday in the yellow Volkswagen, tooling down U.S. 23 at 70 mph, Janis Joplin wailing over Big Brother and the Holding Company, rattling on about Bobby McGee having nothing left to lose.

"What *are* those brothers holding," Phil laughed.

They passed signs for the Olentangy Caverns and the Indian Burial Mounds.

"I've always wanted to see those," Lee said.

It was a clear October day. They spun into the city a little after noon. Lee knew right where she was going, downtown, past the Capitol Building on Broad Street, turning right on High Street.

"Naturally," Phil said.

They headed toward the riverfront where they found what they were looking for easily enough. Lee had a way with the street kids, had kept in touch, after her fashion, since she'd left school.

They made it back to the apartment on Wooster Street in time to string the crepe paper and bake the cake.

It was the usual gang, Phil and Pam and Connie and Michael, some of them friends of Lee's or Eric's from high school, some of them new connections from the university, from wherever. All of them were smoking dope, some of them were dropping acid or mescaline, the purest they'd ever had, or cut with too much speed. The Grateful Dead grunted out the truth about Casey Jones, and Eileen sat in a corner, toying with a butcher knife. Pam sat under the kitchen table watching Randy and Barbara have a terrific argument.

"You should have seen their faces," she confided to Eileen later. "They didn't even look human anymore."

"You ever notice," Eileen said, staring at the lines across her palms, "how your hands don't really look like your own when you're on this stuff? I mean, they could do anything, and it'd be like somebody else was doing it."

"Wow," Pam said.

In the other room, Lee nestled into Eric's lap.

"Don't smoke that joint," she said. "I want you straight for later."

"What's later?" Eric said.

"I'm going to blow your mind," Lee said, close to his ear.

"When are we going to have cake?" Phil asked. "And how about the presents?"

"Hit the lights," Lee said, struggling her way into the kitchen. Randy and Barbara had made up nicely, staring now into the same empty air. And Lee came out, carrying the cake, all the candles lit. Everybody sang Happy Birthday, and Pam said, "Wow."

Lee placed the package on his lap, and leaning over the arm of the sofa, she kissed him.

Eric unwrapped it slowly, folding the ribbon, then the paper as he took it off. He brought out a bag, not a nickel bag, not a dime bag, but a real expensive bag, and he held up the clean, white powder for everyone to see.

"You really shouldn't have," Eric said. "Where'd you get it?"

"Phil and I went to Columbus for it," Lee said.

"So when are they going to start getting smack in Toledo?"

"You sure you know how to use that stuff?" Phil asked.

"Sure," Eric said. "I been to Vietnam."

Lee offered whoever wanted one a snort, but most of the rest of them were too out of it to pay much attention. Lee and Eric disappeared, hand in hand, into the bedroom, Lee singing the new version of the birthday song, composed especially for the occasion. *Happy birthday to you, this life makes me blue, you think like a junkie, oughta act like one too.*

Eventually, they needed works. Needles. Heat. A dish or the bowl of a spoon in which to reduce the powder to liquid. A place on the arm that hadn't been hit too many times already, a spot the size of a pinprick. Eventually they needed a lot of fancy stuff they'd have to plan for ahead of time. Eventually they'd be shooting themselves full of holes.

But they weren't ready for that violence yet. Now everything was within painless reach. A dusting of the white stuff over a lump of hashish in the pipe, like 10-X powdered sugar on a brownie. A fine white line stretched taut against a mirror or an album cover. A piece of paper rolled into a cylinder. A sudden taking of air.

This was as easy as flipping the silver lever on the pinball machine. Watching a cold steel sphere race to the top of a neon hill. Seeing it dance and spin and glitter under an electric sun. Smelling it go for its mark as if nothing stood in its way. Hearing it rattle past the destined place, over and back, back and over again.

This was like touching the lights. This was like tasting the score. This was as easy as breathing, as holding your breath, as easy as letting breath go.

Over the water the sun barely lingers, and the pine trees outside are shadows against that open light. Darkness has settled around my family's cottage. In the quiet that settles in on my mother and me, I can hear the water lap against the rocks, and occasionally an insect buzzes against the window.

My mother wonders if I'm sleepy after my long drive. You always sleep so well here, she reminds me.

It's true. I sleep more soundly in these woods, by this water, than anywhere else on earth. The words of a song she used to sing to me in childhood unexpectedly come into my head. You gotta give in, you said you would. You gotta give in so I'll be good. Tell me a story, and then I'll go to bed.

"There's only a little more," I say, "before bed."

Once he turned twenty-one, Eric took his responsibilities a little more seriously. By early in the new year, 1970, he had a job, driving the

Bookmobile for the public library, stopping at street corners all over town collecting and passing out books to children or old people who couldn't get downtown on their own. With both Eric and Lee working now, the dust collected in the corners of their house, the dishes didn't get done regularly, the laundry stacked up, and the days of Julie's and Doug's lives went on without them.

An employee of the county, Eric got his paycheck once a month, so they lived day to day on what Lee made at the drugstore. But the last Friday of every month, they spun off for Columbus where they blew Eric's monthly wad on High Street. Before long, though, the commute got a little easier: by late summer, Lee had found a heroin connection among the streetwalkers in Toledo, a mere twenty-five miles away.

Of course, they didn't need that connection for a while.

"Why not?" my mother interrupts, genuinely puzzled.

"Building a habit takes time," I say.

"But this was heroin, right?"

"We hear about first-fuck pregnancies and one-shot addictions . . ."

"And it happens like that."

"Often enough, I suppose, to keep us terrified. But for some people it's a way of life."

My mother wants to let it go at that. She will not ask the questions, make the accusations, because to do that she would have to confess to knowing all the things I never told her, to finding out what she could have known only by reading my mail.

"And this was happening," she asks instead, "here in town, just down the street, at the corner of Wooster and Maple?"

"Yes," I say, "just down the street."

For my mother, that's in the neighborhood, and close enough. It's not close enough for me.

"You know it could have been happening to me," I say.

By now the sun has dropped below the trees on the far side of the lake, a shadow of smoky red marking its passing. What light there is comes from under the door to the den, where my father has probably fallen silently asleep in front of the McNeil/Lehrer NewsHour. The bay window where I sit with my mother is dark and quiet, the only sound the squeak of the old wicker chair as my mother shifts her weight.

"I know all about it," she says.

"I know you do, Mom," I say.

I can't see her face in the dark, but I imagine it, startled by the fact, embarrassed. She sighs almost imperceptibly.

"*I was worried about you,*" she says.

"*I know, Mom. It's okay.*"

"*I'm not sorry for worrying,*" she says.

"*It was a long time ago,*" I say. "*And look. I'm here. I'm okay.*"

"*I'm still not sorry,*" she says.

"*I'm not sorry either,*" I respond.

I pause a moment, then, lest she misunderstand me, I tell her.

"*Yesterday I went through your drawers.*"

The light comes on at the cottage next door, and the neighbor comes out on the deck. He whistles low. His dog rustles through the ferns and the blueberry bushes, heading for home.

"*So,*" my mother comes right back. "*What are you telling me? That makes us even?*"

"*I didn't know we were keeping score,*" I say.

When I come downstairs the next morning, my mother is sitting in her wicker chair in the bay window, engaged in the morning ritual. The feature section of the Detroit paper, dropped in the mailbox before we are awake, is folded over on her lap, open to the crossword puzzle page. Her coffee steams on the window sill. She doesn't look up when I pass by on my way to the kitchen.

"The pot's on," she says.

I bring my own cup in with me, and take up my seat opposite her.

"Where's Daddy?" I ask.

"Out fishing," she says.

"Why does he bother? He never catches anything."

"Oh, he just likes to meditate out there," she says.

It's going to be awkward, starting again. I want to cajole my mother into listening.

"What happens next," I start, "is a point for your side."

"Who says we're not keeping score?" she asks.

"On April 9, 1970, Lee and Eric got married."

"Kind of a redundant exercise, don't you think?"

Her cynicism surprises me.

"They want the home-town stamp of approval," I say.

"Right," she says. "Make fun of us. It's easier."

She takes the crossword puzzle from her lap and starts working.

"And," I continue, "they both had jobs."

"And," my mother jumps right in, laughing already, "they both did heroin."

She has me, and I have to laugh, too. We run away with the list: They were a two-income family, I say. They saw each other through the flu, my mother says. They needed pots and pans, I say. They had credit cards, my mother says. Not yet, I say. They didn't have credit cards yet.

"She could use his G.I. benefits," my mother offers.

My mother has a good sense of humor, and a good share of her

own cynicism about marriage. Whatever the bargain two people strike, marriage makes
it for life.

   "What's a five-letter word for 'fence straddler'?" my mother asks.

   "Stile," I say.

   "I hate when you do that," my mother says.

Lee and Eric had a little trouble arranging the details, because Lee was
under-age and couldn't get married in Ohio without parental permission.
At first there was the question of where Lee would find a parent at all. Until
she came of age, the welfare office controlled her guardianship officially,
but the county couldn't very well give the bride away. And by this point,
Lee and Eric didn't have anything to do with her mother, didn't even want
to let her know, let alone ask her permission. In the end, they decided to
travel over the border into Michigan, Monroe County, almost next door,
where Lee was old enough and didn't need permission.

A girl runs off to get married if she can't do it at home, but that
doesn't mean she won't do it up right. Pam took Lee out shopping the
week before, bought her a new nightgown at the Powder Puff.

   "White," my mother says.

Connie threw Lee a shower, nothing fancy but a few little things to
get them started in their new life.

   "It's not like they went to the trouble of registering at Kleever's," my mother laughs.

Lee looked all over town for a new dress, and finally settled on a
simple cotton she'd found at LaSalle's.

   "That's the something new," my mother says. "What was borrowed?"

   "The flowers were borrowed," I say.

The night before they left for Michigan, Eric's buddies kept him out
late, but he was still up early the next morning, said he had some errands
to run before they could leave town. He came to pick her up early in
the afternoon. And when she opened the door to that little yellow
Volkswagen, she found the back seat swimming in forsythia, buckets,
pails, jars of yellow branches, the first blooms of the spring.

   "I been stealing them from bushes all over town," Eric explained.

Marriage didn't change much for them. They kept on with their lives,
kept to a few friends who understood or didn't ask too many questions.

On Friday nights sometimes they drove up to Westgate, wandered around the shopping center, ate at Grace Smith's cafeteria, took in a movie at the Cinema One and Two. In May during the week of Old Fashioned Bargain Days, when the local merchants in Bowling Green waged an extended sidewalk sale—the men grew beards and sideburns, the women dressed in calico skirts like pioneers—Lee and Eric strolled along the length of Main Street like anybody else, stole a couple of squirt guns from Woolworth's, and chased each other home, ducked into alleys and hid behind trees, and surprised each other with a well-aimed spray.

In August, they went to the Wood County Fair, kicked up a little dust on the midway, marveled at the size of the pigs in the livestock building, bought lemonades from the junior class booth where the high school kids were trying to raise money for the senior prom. By September, the flies were buzzing in the laundromat. Now that they were both working, Lee and Eric did laundry together.

"So basically," my mother says, "they were little kids playing house."

"They didn't know any better." I shrug.

"You mean nobody taught them better."

"I'm not saying fault, Mom. We imitate what we know, that's all."

My own marriage matched my mother's in so many ways. A good man, and loving in his fashion, with whom real intimacy wasn't possible, who moved away from me with every step I took toward him.

"We do the best we can," my mother says.

"I know that," I say.

The screen door bangs shut on the porch, and my father comes in, whistling.

"What you girls talking about?" he asks.

He doesn't wait for an answer. Talk makes him a little nervous. He heads on down the hall, and disappears behind the bathroom door.

My mother closes her eyes and shakes her head.

"Any other man in America," she sighs, "would pee over the side of the boat."

The sound of her voice says, what I've had to put up with, nobody can even guess. I think to myself, I can make a stab at it.

"There's a whole lot you can't tell by looking," I say.

To look at Lee and Eric, you couldn't know that doing laundry together was the major shift in the pattern of their lives. To look at them, you wouldn't know that they were making trips to Columbus more frequently, then making trips to Toledo twice, three times a month. To look at Eric, you wouldn't know that his old buddies shied away from him, or passed to the other side of the street when they saw him coming, mindful of the rumor about town, that he earned the extra cash he needed by turning over the names of drugged-out friends to the police. To look at Lee, you wouldn't know she'd found new friends among the streetwalkers who hung out in downtown Toledo, near the Scenic Bar, who thought this tough-talking white girl glittered hard and bright, so they got her whatever she wanted.

And like anybody else, Lee and Eric made love and had arguments, and if you passed them on the street you wouldn't know that somewhere along the line they had blurred the distinction between the two. You wouldn't know unless you looked close, or Lee was wearing short sleeves.

More than fifteen years later, long after Lee was dead, a neighbor living a couple of doors down remembered for me hearing the two of them at night. It was his only memory of his neighbors, the sounds that awakened him through his windows on summer evenings. At first he thought it was acid rock—not what you'd call music, exactly, but relentless and rhythmic and loud. Then he thought it was sex. Slowly he heard a noise more like animals, he said, a cat screeching in the dark and mistaken for a child, plaintive or angry or hungry, he couldn't tell which.

The cry of human pain, indistinguishable except for the sheer weight of it, from the cries of love.

And inside the apartment, the vision was just as clouded, just as uncertain. It always began with something simple, inconsequential, a casual complaint, a missing shoe, a late arrival. Even then, in the seed of it, Lee saw it coming, like an accident, a car hurtling at her in her own lane, lights staring her down in the dark. And then, the whole picture in front of her switched to slow motion and nothing looked real anymore. The car looked like a toy, the lights like flowers. She knew it was going to hit her, a toy, a flower, back and forth across her face, mechanical, steady, then a glove, something like a hand at her shoulder, then a flower at her face again.

"You don't have to make it look pretty," my mother says.

"It's the only way I can see it," I say.

"No," my mother says. "This is ugly, what you're seeing."

"Yes, and we do it all the time."

"Make it look like something else?" my mother asks.

"So we can outlive it," I say.

There was nothing Lee could do about it. So she told herself it wasn't real, it wasn't happening at all, and even her own voice sounded thick and slow, like a record winding down. She could see it, she didn't feel it, she took it, her arms at her sides like rags.

And later, when her face was enormous, she thought, how could it be otherwise? His weight against hers was both power and caring. His fist at her shoulder, his tender fingers at her breast were both the expression of the same hand.

"You cannot mean that," my mother says. *"That they felt the same."*

"I can, I do."

"There is a line," my mother says. *"We can draw a line between love and pain."*

"Yes, but how, when they feel the same?" I ask.

I really want to know the answer. And though I'm grown now, I still think my mother can tell me what I need to know. But perhaps my mother hasn't let herself ask the question yet.

"For most of us, the distinction is less clear than we'd like to believe," I say, *"and that's why we make it. That's why we draw the lines."*

But who can say, I wonder, where Woodstock slipped into Altamont? Who can say that they weren't next of kin in the first place?

"Woodstock, Altamont, I don't know what you're talking about," my mother says.

"You remember Woodstock," I say. *"All that peace and love."*

"All those dirty naked kids, and mud, and no bathrooms," my mother says.

"Yes, that," I say. *"And five hundred thousand people all getting along with each other. And then Altamont, the Rolling Stones and the Hell's Angels, and people getting killed and Gracie Slick screaming at them, saying, 'Keep your hands off each other unless you intend love.' "*

"Some Hell's Angel comes up to me, it's not going to feel like love."

"Yes, yes, but we can't always feel the intention in the touch. That's why touching is so scary."

"So it was a lie, then, all that peace and love at Woodstock? A cover for a violence underneath?"

"I don't know," I say. *"Maybe they're both true, Woodstock and Altamont, both at once, maybe. Like in a family."*

"Not our family," my mother says. *"I won't let you say that."*

"No family is immune," I tell her. *"We're not above them. It's a difference of degree, not kind. Eric loved Lee and . . . "*

"But," my mother says, *"you mean but."*

"No. I mean and."
Eric loved her and he abused her and Lee couldn't tell the difference.

By the time Eric turned twenty-two, in October 1970, he and Lee were ready to move on. The drugs had taken them over slowly, a trip to Toledo at a time. They became imperceptibly and, it seemed, irrevocably as much a part of the day as brushing their teeth, or going to work, or eating dinner. They found themselves in a way of life they couldn't maintain without considerable trouble.

BankAmerica knew where they were, and the Visa card people were out to get them.

It had all started with a letter, something that looked like junk mail. "Dear Honored Veteran," the letter read. "In acknowledgment of your recent service to your country, we believe you deserve credit."

Somebody had told Eric it would be a good idea to say yes, that a strong credit rating might come in handy as he settled into his life. He made this one concession to the workings of the system, but he didn't know when he'd applied for the little plastic card how well it would serve him.

When he first started needing the extra money, the card created access to a cash advance now and then. That was useful, but the bills came regularly, and the interest was high. So he and Lee put their heads together, and figured out a way to get the cash without paying the bills at all.

When you're a junkie, you need the drug, but when you're a smart junkie, the drug isn't enough by itself, because all it does for your mind is waste it.

"I thought that was the point," my mother says.

"Maybe that's what some junkies are after in the first place," I say, "and maybe all junkies get to wanting that eventually."

But at first at least that wasn't enough for Lee and Eric. They took a certain pleasure not only in the heroin itself, but in figuring out ways to get it, turning their minds on the process before they ever enjoyed the product.

"Like delayed gratification," I tell my mother.

"A twist on the Protestant work ethic," my mother volunteers.

"Sure," I say. "Work first, pleasure second."

They hit upon the plan naturally enough. They returned a wedding present without a receipt, without knowing even what store had sold it in the first place. They discovered that day that courtesy got them as far as they needed to go at the customer service desk.

They took to buying blenders in abundance, the perfect appliance for what they were after.

When an item cost under fifty bucks, K-Mart or Murphy Mart or Bargain City didn't bother to call in for a credit balance on the account when you charged it. A good blender went for about $49.95. So Eric waltzed into Bargain City, picked out an Osterizer, and charged it, no questions asked.

A few days later, the sales receipt slightly defaced so the clerk couldn't read the store's name or identification number, Lee walked into K-Mart, the Osterizer under her arm. She explained politely that her aunt, for whom the gift was intended, already had a blender; she was sorry to have to return it—she knew it was a good product—but K-Mart would surely understand.

K-Mart aimed to please and Lee walked away with a handful of cash.

And the next day, Eric charged a Proctor-Silex at K-Mart, and Lee got a refund from Bargain City.

Sometimes the clerk gave her a little trouble.

"We'd rather credit your account," the clerk said.

"Gee," Lee said. "I don't have my card with me."

"I don't suppose you know your account number?"

"I don't have much mind for numbers," Lee said. "Just this once, couldn't you make an exception and give me the cash?"

Well, she was so polite and sincere about it all. The customer service clerk couldn't help himself.

"So now they're petty crooks, and you want to make heroes out of them."

"Not heroes."

"But you think it's funny."

"It is sort of funny, like 'steal this book.' Ripping off corporate America."

"But who pays for that? We pay for that. Responsible citizens pay eighteen percent interest on those accounts."

"Well, that's what it means, I guess, to be a responsible citizen. Sometimes we have to pay for somebody else."

My mother reminds me that she didn't bring me up to think like that.

"Sure you did, Mom," I tell her.

Lee and Eric kept the scam going for a good while. It was surprising even in a small town how many different places a person could find to buy a blender. Eric kept BankAmerica at bay by paying a little now and then on his balance. But they couldn't keep it up forever. Before too long, they had stretched a $250 credit limit to $5,000, and they were running out of K-Marts.

So Lee and Eric decided they needed to disappear into the world for a while, without leaving a forwarding address. By that time, their habit was costing them fifteen blenders a week.

They had one conversation about it, and the choice was made.

They were at the laundromat on a Saturday afternoon, stuffing wet T-shirts and blue jeans and towels into the dryer, loading it a little too full.

"They'll never get dry that way," Eric said, the house husband.

"So, they'll get warm," Lee said.

Eric brushed a fly away from his face.

"Whatever you say, baby."

"Don't call me baby."

"Whatever you say."

Across the room, an exasperated mother was explaining to her little boy why he couldn't take a spin in the dryer.

"You'll get hotter and hotter and dizzier and dizzier."

"That sounds like fun, Mom."

"And then you'll explode," she said.

"But Mom," he whined.

Eric and Lee looked at each other over the sheet they folded between them, and in the air like a mirror, they caught a glimpse of themselves. Here they were, hopeless children, nothing but the future spinning around and around on the regular cycle. They were getting hotter and dizzier, waiting, maybe hoping, to explode.

"What do you want to be when you grow up?" Lee said.

"I want to be a junkie," Eric said.

"In this town? Not much room for advancement here."

"I guess not," Eric said.

"How about a transfer," Lee said, "to Junkie Land?"

"Walt Disney presents."

And that was that. They sold off a few record albums at a yard sale, the stereo, a few of their pots and pans, the one blender they kept; they borrowed money from their friends, took one last cash advance on their Visa card, made off with their final paychecks, and took themselves off to New York.

"It wasn't my New York they went to," I tell my mother.

I remember New York in 1970 from a trip I made there, buying grass in Washington Square Park, parts of the city not much different then than now. In the West Village, the only Village in those days, the Erotic Baker now on Christopher Street was then a head shop, the window full of exotic houkahs and hash pipes disguised as change purses. Somewhere along Hudson Street, I found a leather shop where I coveted my first pair of Frye Boots. I was a college student, on a budget, my imagination elevated to window shopping. But I picked up copies of *Narcissus and Goldmund* and *The Greening of America* at a little bookshop on Broadway. And on Bleecker Street, near Sheridan Square, I found a little hole in the wall that sold nothing but bumper stickers and buttons. I bought one for a souvenir and wore it on the brim of a floppy brown hat. "Seven with One Blow," it read.

"I remember that hat," my mother muses. "It was so, so East Coast."

She was glad for me to go away to school, hoped I'd have my horizons expanded. And then when I did, she didn't recognize me, and I scared her a little.

"My friends snickered at the slogan," I say. "I thought they all had dirty minds."

"A slogan like that," my mother says. "What else were they going to think?"

"William Kunstler," I say. "The Chicago Seven. Judge Hoffman. The outlaws against America."

"Oh, that," my mother says.

It wasn't the same city Lee and Eric found. They didn't take to window shopping or sightseeing, and most of my New York passed them by. But then, they were really just passing through anyway. They promised themselves they'd see the Empire State Building some other time.

It's a short trip across town to their New York. Tompkins Square Park was full of rats and drunks sleeping it off. Gangs of boys loitered on the street corners, passing joints, or ducking into doorways to buy and sell. At the shooting galleries near 4th Street and Avenue C, the lines stretched down the sidewalk and around the corner, men, mostly, waiting for their chance to get upstairs, where they'd find whatever they wanted, needles and junk and company, such as it was, a little shelter from the weather outside. Lee and Eric slept where they could, bought what they could, shared what they could, and didn't last long. By January, Eric's old Army jacket wasn't enough to keep her warm, and they decided to move on. Travel would be good for them, a life of itinerancy, no place to call home but each other.

They did odd work when they could get it, or had the energy, but mostly they didn't bother, didn't care. There was always some way to get money, a temporary job here, a scheme there. Sometimes, of course, their schemes didn't work, like the time they tried to lean on Lee's mother for a loan.

They needed the money in a hurry, and Lee thought maybe her mother would come through.

"It's not like she's ever done much for me," Lee said.

"That's the point," Eric said. "What makes you think she's going to start doing for you now?"

"She always liked Geoff," Lee said. "You could call her. You could be Geoff."

Eric didn't get it.

"He could be in some kind of trouble," Lee said. "He could be calling from anywhere."

"But she'll know it's not Geoff's voice," Eric said.

"I doubt it," Lee said.

"I played Mark Antony once," he said, warming to the idea.

"Piece of cake," Lee said.

So Eric called her, impersonating her son, told her he was in some kind of jam, needed bail money. Five hundred dollars would do it, he said.

She wasn't particularly cooperative, got off the phone as soon as she could, and didn't send the money order he'd asked for.

"That's the last time we try something like that," Eric said. "That was downright embarrassing."

My mother and I have gone through two pots of coffee already, and the bay window is getting warm.

"Let's move to the porch," she suggests.

"And I'll get something to eat when I pass through the kitchen," I say.

By the time I've cut my melon and buttered my toast, my mother is ready for me. She has trouble imagining any mother letting go, and she resents me for what she can't imagine.

"So a mother's supposed to take the abuse and the lies and the rejection," she says from her chair on the porch. "And she's still supposed to be there when the kid needs money? No matter what the money's for?"

"I'm not accusing Lee's mother of anything," I answer. "You don't have to defend her."

"Maybe she didn't have the money," my mother offers. "Maybe she saw through the lie."

"And maybe," I say, "she chose for her own good instead."

"This is the alternative?" my mother asks. "Saying yes to yourself means saying no to your child?"

"Maybe," I say. "Did it ever occur to you that motherhood is a great distraction? That women fill up their time with their children so they don't have to look at anything else?"

"Like what?" my mother says.

She looks away, searching out a better answer. Then she finds the last defense, the unassailable position.

"You can't understand. You've never had a baby."

It's true. I am not a mother, and I'm not likely to become one. Maybe I can't understand. Maybe I can only want to. Maybe I can only imagine. The need to protect when the need is there, the hand cradling the head, the hand sheltering the soft and dangerous place there. The need acted on or denied, and then transferred to the protector herself, who took to caring like a habit, whose hand cannot let go for fear it will wither away.

"The soft spot grows over, eventually," I say. "I have a pretty hard head."

"A child always has a soft spot," my mother says.

And she's right. I do.

Lee and Eric had other ways of getting money, and besides, money was less valuable anyway than the connections, which they came by easily enough. They tooled into some strange city, slept in the car, foraged in the seedier parts of town until they found somebody who needed a favor, another junkie happy to call the back seat of a Volkswagen home for a few nights, a cop, maybe, who paid good money for the information Lee and Eric came by easily enough. Occasionally, they looped back into Ohio, borrowed money from an old friend, from Eric's brother or his parents. And maybe somewhere along the line, they watched *Bonnie and Clyde*, became entranced with the spree, the last loving look, death in slow motion.

"*They probably didn't need the model for criminal behavior,*" my mother objects. "*They just needed the drugs.*"

"*You're right,*" I say. "*They didn't need the model. The rest of us needed that.*"

I'm just guessing, I tell her, trying to make sense not only of Lee and Eric, but of the way so many people—so many of their contemporaries, that is—remembered them.

"*It was amazing, Mom, when I started asking questions.*"

"*Who did you ask?*" she wants to know.

"*Anybody I could find who remembered,*" I say. "*The details shifted, nobody remembered it quite the same way. But the tone, the legend was always the same.*"

"*And you learned it from the movies?*"

"*Envy for the adventure of it,*" I say. "*Admiration for the style.*"

Eric Fletcher, a blond Warren Beatty, and Lee Snavely, a dark-haired Faye Dunaway, loving each other and off on a life of crime. Walking into places, pretty and polite as you please, making off with the cash, outlaws who charmed their victims, and managed for months on end not to get caught.

"*So you romanticize it,*" my mother says. "*You make a lie out of it.*"

"*A way of explaining,*" I say. "*Not exactly a lie.*"

"*Words, words, words,*" my mother says. "*Why can't you just see it for what it is? Common crime.*"

"*We do this in America,*" I shrug. "*In fact, Billy the Kid was probably a pathological killer, but we don't think of him like that. How many people did Jesse James kill? Yet the legend makes a 'dirty little coward' out of the man who shot him.*"

My mother doesn't buy that, and her questions keep me honest.

"*No,*" I say. "*That's true, too, but that's not it. That's not what I'm getting at here.*"

"*So what are you getting at?*"

"*I want a way in,*" I say.

A lot of us in those days thought of ourselves as living on the fringe, beyond the border, over the edge. We weren't really outlaws, I tell her, but we thought of ourselves that way.

"*And confronted with real outlaws?*" my mother suggests.

"*We turned them into an image of ourselves,*" I say. "*A picture of the outlaw we could tolerate in someone who looked like us.*"

It's as if we said, "If I were an outlaw, this is the outlaw I'd be, charming, winsome, not really dangerous." It takes practice—at first we can't imagine very far from ourselves.

"And what kind of truth is that?" my mother asks.

She's right, of course. It's a way we all have of not seeing. It's the way my mother has of not seeing me. To insist that we are the same under the skin. And I keep telling her we're not.

"But it's just the first step in," I say. "First you see yourself in the other, and then you have to . . . "

"See the other in yourself?" my mother asks.

"Something like that," I say. "Or see the other, period. As itself."

"But what are you going to do when the other is too real to look at? Too dangerous or too ugly to feel your way into?"

"That will happen soon enough," I say.

Beyond the screen, a jay swoops and chatters around the bird feeder, where two golden finches bob for the seed. Below them, a chipmunk races skillfully among the ferns and then around the corner onto the porch stoop. It sits up on its haunches, its white belly exposed, and sniffs at the air, curious and expectant. We used to name them, in pairs, after famous couples ("The Kissingers are long gone," my mother tells me), and we fed them peanuts out of the hand. The taming made them bold. One ventured once onto the porch, lost its bearings, and in a headless panic, ran wild all over the house.

I was surprised, when I finally got the story straight, how nearly the collective imagination approximated the truth. It happened for Lee and Eric, time and again, like this:

8:45 P.M., fifteen minutes to closing, safe time. Lee pulled up to the curb in the yellow Volkswagen, a few blocks from the drugstore, in whatever city they were in this time, suburban Atlanta, somewhere near Washington, or Richmond, or Philadelphia. They'd checked the place out earlier that afternoon, when it was still light, looking for the usual signs. A prosperous enough neighborhood. An isolated drugstore, away from the downtown area and the shopping center. A clothing store next door, maybe, that would close at five. They drove in concentric blocks around the drugstore for twenty minutes or so, planning Eric's route and finding Lee's parking space. They'd done this so many times before, she had the routine down pat, but still, now that it was 8:45 P.M. and they'd parked the car, Eric reminded her.

"I'm not back here by nine-fifteen," he said, "you just drive off."

Eric was leaning into the car, holding the door open with his right hand.

"And don't speed," he said.

"I know," she said.

She knew what she was supposed to do, and she reassured Eric every time that she would, in fact, leave him there if she had to. But she knew she wouldn't. She knew she'd wait until 9:30 or 9:45, or she'd speed off in the direction of the drugstore if she had to, one hand on the wheel and one on the door handle on the passenger's side, ready to whip it open as she drove past. A Volkswagen was small enough she could do that, and she and Eric were in this thing together.

Eric adjusted himself, slipped his left arm out of the sleeve of his Army jacket, hugged it to him inside the coat. Lee slid over the seat and zipped the jacket for him.

"How's it look?" Eric said.

"Just fine," Lee said. "The picture of the gimped-up vet."

Eric slammed the car door shut, and walked off in the direction of the drugstore, looking back over his shoulder once to wave at Lee, still sitting behind the driver's seat. He made it to the pharmacy in a few minutes, just in time.

"I was about to close up," the clerk said.

"Sorry," Eric said. "I'll just be a minute."

"Can I help you with something?"

"No, I just have to look. I won't be long, I promise."

The clerk turned the key in the lock after Eric was safely inside, and went back to the cash register. It was always like that, Eric had told me; arrive just at closing time and they lock you in. Makes the whole business safer, you're a lot less likely to kill somebody that way.

Eric wandered to the back of the store, to the shelves of shaving lotion and hair cream, looked quickly around to make sure there was nobody there but the clerk. Nothing but long empty aisles under dancing fluorescence. The clerk was just cutting the lights in the show-cases up front, leaving the watches and the cameras and the perfumes in the dark, when Eric stepped around the corner, carrying a sawed-off shotgun across his body, like long-stemmed roses.

"You want to open the drawer for me," he said, casual, polite, like they'd been friends for years.

"Sure, buddy, whatever you say."

"That little plastic bag'll be fine," Eric said, motioning with the end of the gun.

The clerk stuffed money into the bag, several hundred dollars, and fumbled with the change.

"I don't care about the silver," Eric said.

"Look, mister, I got kids, a wife."

"I'm not gonna hurt you," Eric said. "You'll be home maybe an hour late, that's all."

The clerk handed the bag of cash across the counter.

"How 'bout you come out from behind there," Eric said, "and come back here with me."

The clerk raised his arms above his head, and moved out from behind the counter.

"Where?" he said.

"Back here. At the pharmacy counter."

They walked to the back of the store together, the clerk leading the way, his arms in the air, carefully placing one foot in front of the other, a little unsteady.

"You gotta piss or something?" Eric said.

"Yeah."

"Well, don't worry about it. I'll be out of here in no time. You just be careful what you're doing. Unlock that case for me."

The clerk twisted the key in the lock on the narcotics case, and the glass door swung open.

"Now, almost finished," Eric said, pulling a wad of plastic from his pocket. "Just take this plastic bag here, and fill it up."

"With what?"

"What do you mean, 'with what'? With drugs."

"Yeah, but which drugs?"

"All of them," Eric said.

The clerk reached into the case, and in one motion pulled his arm and everything on the shelf forward. Bottles came spilling out, dropping onto the floor some of them, but most of them landed in the plastic bag. He started to hand it back to Eric.

"Next shelf," Eric said.

A few more repetitions, the next shelf and the next shelf and the next shelf, until he had raked out each one of them, and the plastic bag was full of every pharmaceutical you can name. Amphetamines. Morphine. Codeine. Methadrine. Librium. Thorazine. Ritalin. Darvon. Lithium. Quaaludes. Percodan. Uppers and downers, reds and bennies, even penicillin.

"Sort of extreme, isn't it?" my mother asks.

"I can understand the impulse," I say.

Less traveled myself, I used to carry both Thorazine and vitamin C in my pocketbook because somebody had told me that a hit of one was good for bad acid, a hit of the other for bad mescaline, home remedies, the old wives' tales of the drug days.

"*Back in those days,*" *I tell her,* "*you never knew what you might need.*"

"Thanks a lot," Eric said. "You want to let me out of this place?"

"Sure," the clerk said.

And Eric ran as fast as he could another block up, then cut down an alley to the next block over, and ran back in the direction of the car. He went a block past the car, in fact, just to be sure. Lee turned the key in the ignition the minute she heard his hand on the door.

"How'd it go?" she asked, pulling away from the curb.

"Watch the speed," Eric said.

"Right," Lee said.

She drove slowly, stopped at all the stop signs and red lights, remembered to use the blinker when she turned. They wanted to look like any couple, tourists, maybe, sightseeing a little.

"He was a real nice guy," Eric said. "Had a fine stock, too."

It was ten minutes after nine. They made it back to the motel in time for the second half of "The Mod Squad."

My mother rises from her wicker chair.

"*I don't know how much more of this I can take,*" *she sighs.* "*And pretty soon I'll have to worry about your father's lunch.*"

"*There's not much more for now,*" *I say.* "*Sit just a minute more.*"

She has been patient, and I want to let her go. She sits back down again, and prompts me on.

"*How did they manage not to get arrested?*" *she asks.*

"*They kept moving around,*" *I say.* "*It happened like that sixty, maybe seventy times, before they finally got caught, and then it was only Eric, and they were back in Bowling Green again.*"

"*Well,*" *my mother says.* "*Most serious accidents occur in and around the home.*"

"*Within twenty-five miles of your own driveway,*" *I say.*

Lee and Eric had returned to Bowling Green, for Christmas, were staying with Eric's parents. Lee had something else to do that night, an old friend to catch up with, a book to read, a cover to keep so the

Fletchers wouldn't know what they were up to. Eric went out that night on his own, one of the few times in their history together that he'd operated by himself, without Lee behind the wheel. On December 6, 1971, starting about eight-thirty or so, Eric made his way into Shaeffer's Pharmacy on Central Avenue in Toledo. He left a few minutes later in the yellow Volkswagen with his gun, a bag full of drugs and $250 in cash. And he might have made it home safely, except that a cop stopped him on Route 475 on account of a broken taillight.

"That was just as well," my mother says.

"By then," I say, "it was either get caught or kill somebody."

Eric was tried that winter in Toledo, convicted of armed robbery in March 1972, and sentenced to fifteen years in prison at Mansfield. Lee moved in with a friend, Connie Humphrey, out by the university for a while, then rented her own place, an apartment in a house on Main Street, wrote Eric letters regularly and visited him every Saturday.

The visitors' room was stark and white, a guard or two at the doors, small white tables on pedestals scattered about the room, little families seated at them, eating picnic lunches, fathers bouncing babies on their knees. Lee and Eric took a table in the farthest corner, held hands across it, spoke low.

"You have to promise me something," Eric said.

"What's that, baby?"

"You'll write me, tell me what you're doing, no matter what."

"No matter what," Lee said.

"I know it's going to be hard," he said, "on your own, I mean. But I need to know what's going on, whatever it is."

"It doesn't matter what," Lee said.

"It'll be easier to know," Eric said. "I got nothing but time to imagine. And I can imagine worse than you can do."

"Sure, baby, whatever you want," Lee said.

"Promise," he said.

"I promise," she said.

"Shall we shake on it?" he said.

"I got a better idea," Lee said.

She looked in the direction of the nearest guard, who was chucking a fat-faced baby under the chin, not paying much attention to anything else. Pulling her chair closer to Eric, she reached her arms around him, dropping a needle in his lap.

"I have one, too," she said.

And as far as anyone in the room could tell, visiting hours would be over in a few minutes, and Lee and Eric, like anyone else under the circumstances, embraced their last goodbye. She pulled as close to him as she could get, as close as she needed to be. He dropped his blond head to her shoulder. Her black hair, long now and thick, spilled down her back, fell across her face buried in Eric's neck. Folded carefully in each other's arms, she found his vein and he found hers.

"You know what they say," she said.

"To live together's human," Eric said.

"To come together is divine."

In the kitchen, my mother busies herself with lunch. From the porch I hear the drawers open, the silverware clatter, her feet shuffle across the pine planks as she moves from stove to sink. This is the sound track accompanying whatever drama of irritation or relief she has spinning in her head now that she's in the other room and away from me.

Beyond the screen of the porch window another little drama engages my attention. A small squirrel climbs a few feet up the trunk of a birch tree, then hurls itself into the air, aiming for the cylindrical bird feeder my parents have strung on clothesline five feet above ground and a good distance in all directions from the trees. It's their latest innovation.

On the third try, the squirrel manages to grasp the bird's perch at the bottom of the feeder. From one claw, the creature dangles in the air, then drops to the ground. Sudden chatter fills the space among the ferns and blueberry bushes there.

When it comes around to the tree again, the squirrel climbs past its usual launch, up to the place where the clothesline attaches to the trunk. It hesitates a moment there, measuring the treacherous distance out to the feeder, then takes a few steps along the rope. It pauses, then backs up, then starts out again, this time in a hurry.

Halfway to the feeder, it slips and spins a half circle to the underside of the clothesline. Its tail twitches to balance itself, and the squirrel stretches its neck down and back to eye the prize hanging in the air a few feet away. Slowly it pulls itself, upside down, along the rope. When it's within a body's length of the bird feeder, it stops again and the noisy chatter starts up like encouragement. Then, in a moment of perilous conviction, its front feet release the rope and stretch across air.

Its grip at last secure, it inches itself head first down the feeder, finds the opening at the bottom, and stuffs its cheeks with birdseed.

I turn away from the window, and see my mother standing in the doorway. She heard the noise.

"Darn that squirrel," she mutters on her way back to the kitchen.

I drop my head to my hands, and hold it, as if trying to keep in a headache. My files are full of newspaper articles and records of interviews, and I know more or less what happened, how Lee managed on her own without Eric, who she hooked up with, what kind of trouble she got herself into. But I heard the news long distance, and I can't quite put it together now, long after the fact.

I have been playing Quentin to my mother's Shreve, the questioner, the adversary, the resident of a distant, cold climate. But in the early seventies, Bowling Green was my mother's town, her home. If not a Compson or a Caulfield, at least she was a witness. She read the papers, she talked to other women waiting in line at the grocery store, she had a daughter at home still, and still probably tapped into the network of mothers. By the time the news reached me, off in graduate school, caught up in another life, it had already distorted into an echo.

But my mother was there. My mother heard the noise.

She brings lunch out to the porch, balances her sandwich and cup of soup on a paper plate at her knees. I pull up to the table. Tomato soup stains.

"Why didn't they ever tear down the old Ross Hotel?" I ask.

Once stately and impressive, a dark red carpet in the lobby filled with Victorian furniture, a mahogany desk from behind which the clerk received guests, the Ross Hotel stands at the corner of Wooster and Prospect, a block from the Four Corners crossing that marks the very center of my home town. It's miles away from where we are now, but my mother doesn't notice right off that my question comes clumsily out of nowhere.

"Oh," she muses. "Somebody was always coming up with a plan to do something with it."

"Like what?"

"The welfare office housed migrant workers there for a while," she says. "And then somebody made it into apartments for senior citizens."

I don't know who stayed at the Ross when it was just a hotel. Bowling Green didn't have any businesses to speak of to attract out-of-towners. Parents coming to collect their children at the university rarely spent a night in town, since most of them came from other little towns within an easy day's drive of Bowling Green. Pure passers-by, having no connection with us, might stop over for a night now and then, en route to somewhere else, but that didn't happen often until they finished the highway, I-75, stretching north and south from Michigan to Florida. By then, the university had expanded and motels had sprung up on three out of four edges of town, motels with big parking lots, conveniently located near the Dutch Pantry or the L and K. Strangers could pull in, eat a meal, spend a night, and be back on the highway the next morning, five minutes after breakfast.

"Whatever made you think of the Ross Hotel?" my mother asks.

"I heard, you know, when I was nosing around, that in the early seventies somebody tried to run a brothel out of the Ross."

"Local gossip," my mother says, and dismisses it with a wave of her hand. "Surely you don't believe that."

"There's always a life below the surface," I shrug. "Even at the Ross Hotel."

"You think that's how Lee got started in all that," my mother pauses, and her face wrinkles into a word she doesn't want to say. "That, business."

She doesn't mean "profession." She means a particular act, a deed, a messy scheme that landed Lee in prison in 1973. I'm not ready to ask about that yet.

"Nah," I say. "I think Lee was in business for herself."

It started casually. When Eric was arrested in December 1971 and sent to prison later the next spring, Lee went on with her life alone. She'd never been the sentimental type anyway, and she had a habit to support. She worked part time as a sales clerk at Uhlmans, and took night jobs waiting tables at Petti's Alpine Village and Kaufman's, the two decent restaurants in town. A spaghetti house and a steak house, basically, frequented mostly by families and students. But the habitual loner stopped in now and then, or the occasional husband whose wife had taken the kids to her mother's for a couple of weeks. Lee picked them up, took them home, and made a little extra on top of her tips.

"I don't think that's right," my mother objects. "We heard she was working in Toledo."

"It happens every place, Mother," I say.

"She couldn't have had many clients here. There."

Summers create distance between my mother and the place where she lives the rest of the year. She's spent her life in small towns. Together, we have often rolled our eyes at the small towns we come from, pipsqueaks, unresourceful and ordinary, not even given to particularly interesting vices. But it's easier for me to condescend. I don't have to return there in September.

I can tell already that it's going to be hard getting the information I want from my mother. She is herself a local girl, caught up in whatever the home town is.

"You remember that breather who used to call you on the phone?" I ask.

"Huh?" my mother says.

"You know, the one who was enamored of your feet?"

My mother releases air in something like a laugh. "Do I," she says.

"He used to tell you how sexy your little feet looked coming out from under your choir robe in the alto section. That means . . . "

"He was probably the tenor across the aisle," my mother says. "But I still think Lee would have had better luck working in Toledo."

I can let her have the distance she wants, a kind of job placement service that gets the local hooker out of town.

"She worked Toledo, too," I say.

It was the easiest way Lee knew to make money, once she lost her day job at the department store for sleeping late one too many mornings. She worked a restaurant out on the Airport Highway, close enough to the airport to attract salesmen stopping over for a night or two, staying at a nearby motel. Or some nights she hit the Scenic Bar, downtown, a neon martini glass tilting out over the sidewalk. It had a reputation for seediness, a good place to pick up men.

Occasionally she took some trouble there from the other girls' pimp, who didn't care much for a white girl horning in on his business. When gentle persuasion didn't work, he escorted her out the door and roughed her up in the alley behind the building. But the next night, or the next, she was back on the job again, joshing it up with the rest of the girls. White girl like you, they told her, ought to do pretty well for herself in a place like this.

The other girls took to her, were curious, admired the way she stood up to the boss, saw her the way she wanted to be seen, slick and hard, treated her like a sister.

"What's your story, honey?"

"Same as yours, I guess," Lee said.

"What name you go by?"

"Lelah."

It was the name she used when she was working, right up to the very end.

"I'm Othelia Jones," the other woman said. "That's with a *-th.*"

"Nice name," Lee said.

A man pulled a stool up next to Lee, draped his arm around her neck, fiddled a little with her breast.

"So, sweetheart, where you been all my life?" he said.

"Looking for somebody better dressed than you," she said, and turned back to her drink.

"I got my pockets full," he said.

"Small change," she said.

"Pardon me for interrupting," Othelia said. "But we have to make a little trip to the ladies' room."

When Othelia suggested that Lee watch out for this guy, a mean one, a weirdo, a man with a reputation, Lee insisted she could take care of herself.

"You in this for the pain?"

"I'm in it for the drugs."

"It's your pretty white ass, sister," Othelia said.

If he pushes her around a little, or wants something weird, she outlasts it. She looks ahead to something down the track a ways, to avoid what's putting itself in her face. At the end of a long line, she'll find a quarter for the pinball machine, a little spare change, not much of a price to pay for all that light and noise. The horse she'll bet on runs, shows, places, wins. The snow, when it falls, tumbles thicker and thicker, each flake gorgeous, sparkling with light, each flake its very own self. Pretty soon now, she'll be poking around the junk shop, feasting on smack and macaroons.

Sex with a stranger, and she hardly has to be there at all. A body going through familiar motions. A hand here, a mouth there, a part, a thing, a nameless power.

And if sometimes they show a little interest, ask personal questions, wonder if she isn't about the same age as a daughter they have at home; if some of them rent fancy rooms in the Commodore Perry Hotel downtown and let her order from room service whatever she wants; if sometimes when she wraps up with him, she catches herself twirling her fingers through curly dark hair, tracing her tongue along the crease of sweat at an elbow, or buries her face in a crotch where she catches the memory by a smell like yeast and talcum powder; if sometimes the memory makes it almost like love, come morning, she can forget about all that. She's out on the street again, tired, and ready for the drive home.

My father comes in from the patio, carrying an empty paper plate and his coffee cup. The screen door bangs behind him.

He doesn't participate much. Most of my childhood he spent looking the other way, not paying attention. But there's a sweetness to him it's hard to be angry at. Sometimes I think he arranges it that way, simply by bowing out, making himself unavailable, floating like a comfort at the edges of my life, so my mother takes the heat unfairly. Maybe we all should be more angry at our fathers.

"I see you girls made it out to the porch," he says.

"We'll come outside in a little bit, maybe," my mother says.

The breeze through the shade of the porch keeps us comfortable, makes us lazy. Even walking outside sounds like an effort. My father exchanges his paper plate for a paperback, a potboiler, summer fare, and returns to the patio.

"When you first read about it in the papers," I start.

"Read about what?"

My mind has skipped on ahead to the troublesome part. I forget that I left my mother behind.

"You know," I say. "Lee's escapade." I'm careful with my choice of words.

My mother nods.

"What did you think? I mean, what did people say about it?"

"I don't remember it all that well," my mother says.

"What did people talk about? The money? The sex?"

"Well, it wasn't like the president of the bank or the high school principal got caught with his pants down."

"Right," I say. "The local clientele probably drop their pants in Findlay."

"We didn't know the people involved," my mother insists. "Except for Lee. And we'd already heard enough about the way she was living, you know, her lifestyle—she sort of advertised it. It didn't come as a great surprise."

"It surprised some people," I say.

When I first started digging around for the story myself, I began at the police station. It had recently been remodeled, and didn't look anything like the place I remembered from my having appeared there once a year as a kid for my bicycle license and official police-issue reflectors for the back fender. Now it was a maze of shiny floors and arches leading into dark corridors. I waited patiently at a window cut into a wall. The sign beside it said INFORMATION, and that was what I was after.

A policewoman, about my own age, dressed in a navy blue skirt and crisp white blouse, asked how she could help me. I explained that I wanted to know something about this case that involved the police some years before.

"It must have been about fifteen years ago," I said.

She explained that police records were closed to the public. I could find out what I needed to know at the courthouse, or maybe from the newspaper.

"Yes," I said. "But I don't know the date. I need the date."

"I see," she said.

She turned from the window, and called out into the large open space in the office behind her where a number of people were working busily at desks.

"Somebody here wants to know about the Fletcher case. Can we tell her when it happened?"

Another woman's voice came from a nearby desk.

"I remember the night we brought her in. It was February 1973." I didn't wonder that she remembered so precisely.

That same voice then called back into the office.

"And what was the name of the man?"

I had imagined the incident living this way in local memory. One voice calling to another voice, that voice calling to another still, the details coming clear as they echoed in an empty room.

A man's voice responded.

"Hang on a minute," he said.

I heard a rustle of papers, a chair scraping the floor, and heavy footsteps coming my way. A tall man with sandy brown hair approached the window. He wore a gun in a holster.

"Woodman," he said. "A Findlay man named Carl Woodman."

"Who was he?" I asked.

"He was the man they shot," the officer told me.

"See," my mother says. "He didn't come from Bowling Green."

I try to prompt my mother's memory. You must remember something else, I tell her. The man was shot.

"Lee had an accomplice, didn't she? Some woman from out of town?"

I'd been hearing that kind of remark about Connie Humphrey all summer, a vague suspicion of the out-of-towner in the whole affair.

She was cute, somebody told me, the cheerleader kind of cute, perky and energetic. You'd never guess she was up to no good. She wasn't strung out, I heard, but she'd try any drug that came her way, just for the fun of it. She'd turn state's evidence on her own grandmother, someone else told me; the woman had no scruples. A clerk from one of the little shops downtown told me they all knew her for a shoplifter. She'd come in, say she was just browsing, and she'd move slowly from rack to rack, running her hands over everything, pulling something out now and then to check the color in the mirror. They never actually saw her take anything, but then at the end of the day, a blouse or a sweater would turn up missing.

"Did you know anything about that?" I ask my mother.

A friend of my mother's ran a little dress shop out by the university. I thought maybe my mother had heard the rumor from her.

"No," my mother says. "That's news to me."

Connie was an import, a college student who came from somewhere else. She hadn't grown up in Bowling Green. For all the extremity of Lee's experience, an uglier picture in so many ways than Connie's experimental life, the collective memory might have been kinder to her. Lee was, after all, a local girl.

"So maybe you thought Connie was behind it all?" I ask.

"No," my mother says. "I don't think that was it."

My mother isn't being much help.

Connie had been in on it from the beginning, I tell her. She was the first to know about the man Lee'd met.

"Aren't you dolled up," Connie said when Lee came home that morning from work.

"Been to the Top of the Tower."

"Moving uptown, huh?"

"I get tired of the lowlifes," Lee said. "It does the heart good sometimes to put on the dog for a high-class bar."

"Well, you look real pretty."

"I spent the night with a man."

"I figured you weren't having a sleepover with Othelia."

"No, I mean, this is different," Lee said. "I made another date with him."

"You're not . . . "

"Of course I'm not. I'm a married woman."

"I was going to say," Connie said. "I mean, just because Eric's in prison doesn't mean you should give up on him. It's so romantic, having somebody to visit in prison."

"This guy could be useful to me," Lee said.

"You want a cup of coffee?"

"Sure. He owns a business south of here. Weighs grain, I think, for the elevators."

"Probably tips the scales," Connie said.

"He makes plenty. Great big house, wife and kids, the whole bit."

"The devoted family man," Connie said.

"Oh, you know. He's losing his hair," Lee said. "Besides, he prefers his sex uncomplicated."

"And money keeps it simple?"

"You bet."

"I have to go to class," Connie said. "Hot dogs okay for dinner?"

"I won't be here for dinner," Lee said.

"So Lee met the man when she was working, right?" my mother asks.

"That's what Eric told me."

"So it couldn't have been an accident. I mean, he didn't just walk into her house, land in the wrong place at the wrong time?"

"No. It was all planned."

After Lee met Carl Woodman in a bar in Toledo, she went out with him a couple of times. He was decent enough, paid her well, talked a lot. It didn't take long before she had all the information she thought she needed. Then she tried the idea out on Eric on visitors' day. Since he'd been away, she'd written regularly, visited him when she could, faithful after her fashion. And she never flinched from telling him who she was seeing, what she was up to, just like she promised, no matter what.

"It's made to order," she told him. "A prominent citizen in a small town. Churchgoer. His wife thinks he's a saint, and he wants to keep it that way. But here he is, seeing me once a week for money. I don't see why it won't work."

"How much you think he's good for?" Eric asked.

"First time, about five thousand. And we might be able to hit him up again."

Eric pulled at the edges of his Styrofoam coffee cup, then took a drag on his cigarette, watched the smoke drift off over Lee's dark hair. He offered her a drag and Lee shook her head.

"I'm trying to quit," she said. "Filthy habit."

"Yeah," Eric said. "Expensive, too."

"You don't like the idea?"

"There are other ways," Eric said. "You could live with my parents, get straightened out."

"I have to learn to take care of myself," Lee said.

"But do you have to do it this way?"

"He's not going to miss the money," Lee said. "And I need it."

"That's not my point," Eric said.

"So what is your point?" Lee was getting irritated. "I've been honest with you. I've never covered up what I've been doing."

"I feel like I've let you down."

"Don't be silly," Lee said, softening, reaching across the table to stop his fingers from demolishing the Styrofoam cup. "And don't worry. I'll be careful."

"It sounds a little too easy to me," Eric said.

"How can I lose? The state's taking pretty good care of you in here, isn't it?"

"You ought to have some kind of back-up," Eric said, "in case this guy doesn't want to cooperate."

"I ran into Tommy Matson the other day on the street. You remember him from high school?"

"That willow?" Eric said. "I wouldn't count on him if I were you."

But Lee didn't take Eric's advice. The man moved in with her a few days before the scam went down. Lee wanted him there. Tommy was a freckle-faced boy, but he owned a gun.

My mother stretches out of her chair.

"We've been sitting here all day," she says. "And it's so pretty out."

"You want to go for a walk?" I suggest.

"I'll go get my shoes," she says.

The road we take wanders through the pines and birches, passes mailboxes that mark the few cottages hidden from us beyond the trees. It's about a half mile out to the main road, the standard journey we take on our walks, down the woods road, out to the main road and back. In the late afternoon, the sun slants through the leaves and dapples our path with shade and light. My mother wants to walk for the exercise, but as usual, I stroll, slowing the pace.

We haven't passed the first mailbox before my mother returns us to the story I'm reluctant to tell.

"You know more about it than I could ever remember," she coaxes.

It has to be my story in the end. My mother can't help me tell it. I've imagined it already, many times over, and now I have to claim it, that's all.

Lee turned twenty-three on February 5, 1973, and she used her birthday to get Woodman to her place, where she'd feel more in control. She'd learned, after all, a thing or two about control from the B movie of her childhood. The man was practically old enough to be her father, but he was small town, didn't have her father's finesse. She could use his weakness, his reputation, his secret connection to her to get from him whatever she wanted.

She was going to throw herself a little party, she told him, just the two of them. She'd cook for him, something yummy. When he put her off at first, had some family business to attend to, they made plans for the week after that.

Twenty minutes before the man was to arrive, Lee sliced up some apples, sprinkled them with cinnamon, and stuck them in a slow oven. It was a little trick she'd learned from her stepmother, who sold real estate. Have something with cinnamon baking in your oven, her stepmother always told clients, when people come to look at your house. It smells like childhood, makes people feel at home, they're a lot more likely to pay the price you're asking.

"This is going to be fun," Connie said, when Lee positioned her in the bedroom closet.

"Make sure you get him in the act," Lee told her. "And get his face."

"Got it," Connie said.

Lee stationed Tommy in the kitchen pantry, told him to wait there. Be patient, she said. She left the light on for him because the dark made him nervous, and he might be there a while. If everything went well, in fact, he wouldn't have to come out at all.

"How will I know?" he asked.

"I'll signal if I need you," Lee said.

"Mmmm. What smells so good?" Woodman said when he arrived, right on time, about 3:30 P.M.

"That's for later," Lee said. "No dessert for you until you've licked your plate clean."

She fixed him a little scotch, the way he liked it, neat, let him swallow some of the warmth, get cozy on her sofa, before she went into the routine she'd been through so many times already in her mind. She slipped her hands under his jacket lapels at the shoulder, eased their way back toward his shoulder blades so the coat pulled away from his arms as she leaned forward to kiss him. He struggled a little, his arms caught behind him.

"No," she said. "I want to do it myself."

She circled the button with her tongue, breathed wet air against his white shirt, and bit the top button right off.

"What was that?" he said, sitting upright on the sofa.

Lee heard it too: the sound of Tommy's nervous elbow colliding with a can of cling peaches.

"The oven, coming back up to temperature," she said.

She managed herself up off the sofa and went into the kitchen, pulling the oven door open, and shutting it again noisily. Then she moved quickly to the pantry, put on a stern face and pressed her finger to her lips, the schoolteacher shushing small children.

"Sorry," Tommy mouthed, waving his hands in front of his face, to say he'd keep the noise down.

"The perfect little homemaker," Lee said, holding up a needle and thread when she came back into the living room.

"I don't think I need the button," he said.

When she got him into the bedroom, she slid herself into the rumpled bed. He fell heavily on top of her, his chin knocking against her collarbone as he kicked his pants free from his feet. He pressed the palms of his hands into her shoulders and raised himself above her, ready to enter her.

"Now," she said.

Woodman thought he knew what she meant.

Instead, Connie threw open the closet door, the light of the flash fracturing into tiny stars in the air around the bed. Lee put a little spin on the shove as she pushed him off her, and he fell to her side.

"Right there in the open, in front of God and everybody," Connie said, snapping pictures as she walked around the bed.

"And worth something to your wife," Lee said.

She was already rummaging through his wallet. She pulled out $300, and waved it in the air. Woodman didn't notice. He lunged at the camera, ramming his shin against the bedpost. Connie turned quickly and left the room, going straight to the kitchen and knocking on the pantry door.

"Get your pants on," Lee said once Connie was out of the room. "We've got some talking to do."

So she talked. She explained her offer reasonably and calmly. Five thousand now, she said, and later they'd negotiate a price for the negatives. Or she'd have them developed and mailed to his wife. It was his choice, she said. She might even make extra copies and send some to his kid.

"No more sneaking peeks at *Playboy* for the Little League team."

Woodman hadn't looked at her once while she worked out the arrangements. He studied the buttons on his shirt, took care with his zipper, hooked his belt in the comfortable hole where the leather was creased and supple. Then he walked around the bed to where Lee stood, faced her squarely, pulled his arm back, and let go with the back of his hand against her jaw. She stepped back with the blow, caught herself from falling as she reached her arm to the wall behind her.

"You whore," he said.

"That was never in question," Lee said.

"Take the three hundred," he said. "But you're not getting another cent out of me."

"Tommy," Lee said.

"Go ahead and send your dirty pictures to my wife. I can straighten this out with her, no sweat."

"I wouldn't be so sure of that," Tommy said.

Tommy had pushed open the bedroom door, was standing there clutching the gun with both hands, its barrel pointed directly at the man's head.

"Who's this punk?" Woodman said.

Tommy looked over at Lee, the question on his face. Suddenly he couldn't remember his own name.

"Meet my friend Tommy Matson," Lee said.

"What the hell are you doing?" Tommy said, turning to Lee.

"I'm going to walk out of here, right now," Woodman said.

He hesitated a moment, then moved toward the door, expecting to breeze past Tommy and out into the world again.

Tommy gestured toward Woodman with the gun, and the man took a few steps back.

"Come on, kid," he said.

Things had gotten out of hand, and Lee moved in quickly to set it right again.

"It's okay, Tommy," she said. "We can keep the three hundred."

"But you told him my name."

Woodman took advantage of their little squabble, and started moving again toward the door.

"Where do you think you're going?" Tommy said, waving the gun wildly in his direction.

Lee moved toward Tommy, reaching out her hand to take the gun, but she was too late. His finger twitched nervously. The gun exploded in front of him. Woodman clutched at his chest, staggered back, and fell against the side of the bed, pulling at the sheets as he dropped to his knees, then crumpled into a pile on the carpet. A dark red stain seeped into the sheet.

"Look what you've done," Lee said.

"Oh my God," Tommy said, staring blankly at the mess in front of him.

Connie came shrieking into the room.

"What happened?" she said, took one look around the room and burst into tears. "Oh my God, what are we going to do?"

"God's not going to give us much help with this one, honey," Lee said.

"I didn't have anything to do with this," Connie said.

"Like hell you didn't," Lee said. She wasn't thinking very far ahead yet, but she was the only one thinking at all.

"Look," she said. "Here's what we do. First, we separate. Matson, you get rid of that gun, and these messy things."

"Blood," Connie said.

"Of course there's blood," Tommy said. "I shot the guy."

"Burn the sheets," Lee said. "I'll take Connie with me, we'll try to lose the cops, and the three of us will meet up later somehow."

"We gotta get out of here," Tommy said.

They gathered up the things as quickly as they could, made some sketchy plans, and headed out of the apartment. And on her way out the door, Lee remembered something else.

"Jesus," she said. "The apples."

Before she left, she turned off the oven. The cinnamon was charred black, and had long since lost the fragrance of childhood and home.

I pause a minute and wait, listening.

"A car's coming," I say.

My mother and I move to the side of the road to let the car pass. The road is narrow through the trees, but cars drive slowly, make noise, and their approach never surprises.

"You mean they went off and left the man for dead?" my mother says.

"Yes," I say.

My mother shakes her head.

"She was desperate," I offer.

"She was tired," my mother says. "What a life."

"She was betting on the power of a secret," I say.

And given what she came from, where she lived all her life, it was an odds-on bet. My mother laughs a little, has her own way of seeing it.

"She runs into somebody too sleazy to give a damn about secrets. Even his own."

That's it right there, homespun respectability.

My mother wants to know what comes next.

"The newspapers said Lee and Connie went to Fremont, to Connie's parents' house. They left Lee's car and borrowed the Humphreys'."

"But surely her parents didn't cooperate with that, not knowingly?"

"They must have worked out a lie on the road," I say.

All the way to Fremont, Lee watched her speedometer and tried to calm Connie down. After extortion, armed robbery, probable murder, that would be just what you'd expect, found out on account of a hysterical blonde and a speeding ticket.

When they finally got there, after a few detours along the way designed to lose the police, who were probably following by now, Connie took one look at her mother and went to pieces all over again.

"Oh, Mama, it was awful," she said. Tears spilled into her mother's bathrobe.

"What, baby? What happened?"

Lee stepped in right there, wedged herself between Connie and her parents. They'd have an interest in protecting Connie maybe, but Lee would be out on the streets again in no time. And she wasn't going to go through this alone.

"It's nothing, really, Mrs. Humphrey." Lee knew how to handle parents, never having had them herself. "We hit a dog out on Route Six. Couldn't help it, it ran right out in front of the car."

"Sure, baby," Mrs. Humphrey said, patting Connie gently. "You couldn't help it, it wasn't your fault."

Lee saw it right away. It was all too easy for Connie. With a mother like that, nothing would stick.

"Most people have mothers like that," my mother interrupts.

"So Lee was probably jealous," I say.

Connie's father was a little suspicious, wondered what they were doing out on the highway at this time of night, anyway. Lee said they'd just up and decided to drive to the lake.

"Kind of cold this time of year, isn't it?" Connie's father asked.

"A lot less crowded, too," Lee laughed.

She paused a minute, waiting for Connie to take the cue, but she was all wrapped up in her mother's bathrobe.

"We were wondering if we might borrow your car?" Lee said, without enthusiasm.

"That's right," Connie said, finally collected. "Lee's car's really old, isn't very safe."

"You might have called first," Mr. Humphrey said, getting the keys.

"Sure, baby," Mrs. Humphrey said.

In no time, they were back on the road again.

"Boy, are you confused," Connie said, when Lee headed the car west out of town. "The lake's the other way. You know, Exit Seven off the turnpike."

"We're not going to the lake," Lee said. "We're going home."

"But aren't we wanted for a crime at home?"

"They won't be expecting us to show up there," Lee said. "Besides, we ought to find out what happened to Tommy."

"Gee," Connie said. "I was looking forward to the beach."

"Connie," Lee said. "It's February."

"What difference does that make?" Connie said.

"That's right," Lee said. "What difference does it make?"

Nothing, not a different car, not a state line, not another country, Canada, just a few hours away, could do her much good anymore. They might as well go home. Lee headed down Route 6 again, retracing the road they'd come.

"What's that?" my mother asks.

"They went back the way they came," I say. "Back home."

"No," my mother says. She reaches out for my elbow to stop my walking. I'm trying to think of one more explanation, but I don't need it.

"Shh," my mother says. "Look there."

A deer stands in the middle of the path, a doe, long-legged and puzzled by the human intrusion. She stares at us, absorbed, then darts off into the woods. When we look through the trees after her, there's no sign of her passing. She disappears as if we had imagined her.

We take up our walking again. My mother wants to know what the police were doing all this time.

"The Keystone Cop routine," I say.

The local police weren't used to this kind of thing, outright crime against persons.

Their part in it started when Woodman staggered into the parking lot of Al Smith's Chrysler-Plymouth across Dill Street, bleeding from a gunshot wound in the chest, a .38 caliber Smith and Wesson. For somebody in his condition, he certainly had his wits about him. He provided exact names and exact addresses, like he'd been keeping it all in a book, before he collapsed and was carted off almost dead in an ambulance.

So the police had all the necessary information at their fingertips. In no time, they surrounded the house at 937 North Main, not a block from the car lot. Every squad car and every patrolman in town swarmed the place, sirens blaring, revolvers at the ready.

"It must have looked like a circus," I say.

"They were doing their jobs," my mother says.

When the chief got on the bullhorn and ordered everybody out, nobody came. So the chief sent his best men up the stairs. Two flanked the door, and one of them busted it open, all of them waving their guns and shouting at once that they were the police.

After all that trouble, the apartment was dead empty.

"You can't blame them," my mother insists. "They didn't have much experience."

"They had the beer riots," I say.

In the late fifties, when one of the bars in town had refused to serve under-age college kids, they took to the streets, first ten, then fifty, then hundreds of them, breaking windows all along Main Street, and demanding beer on campus. The local police took off after them. They bellowed into megaphones, and when they couldn't establish order that way, they swung their night sticks into as many heads as they could.

"How old was I then?" I ask. "Eight or nine?"

"I suppose you're still mad at your father and me for that," my mother says.

I raised my own little ruckus at home, angry that my parents wouldn't let me go watch.

"I got over that a long time ago," I laugh.

Once the university added the Cardinal Room Bar to the Student Union on campus, the students stayed happily drunk, but they kept their noise on campus. It threatened to break its intended boundaries once since then, during the political troubles in the early seventies.

In 1971, the South Enders and druggies activated the campus in response to Kent State. They planned to disrupt an ROTC awards program. The university officials feared they might have another Kent State on their hands, eighty miles west of the original. President Moore called in the local police, asked them to stand by.

"He also called off that parade," my mother reminds me. "Things didn't get out of hand."

"Yeah," I say. "And the local boys figured they missed their chance to beat up hippies."

My mother shakes her head. It's that Vietnam thing again.

"And then, a few months later, half the police force got itself arrested," I remind her.

"Well," my mother says. "That was more a public embarrassment than a crime."

This is the kind of town it was then: when people went off on vacations, they didn't need automatic lights to make you think they were home. They just called the local police station. They'd say, "We're going to be away for the month of June. Would you mind sending an officer by the house a couple of times a week, to make sure everything's okay?"

They were glad to do it. There wasn't much else to occupy their time, especially in the summer, except occasionally root a bunch of kids out of a condemned house they thought was haunted, or drive through the park to make sure everybody was out by dusk, or pick up a few drunk and disorderlies who got out of hand now and then.

It all turned out too good to be true, so many people out of town, and the police knowing all about it. Five or six of them, more than half the force at the time, including the lieutenant himself, cooked up this scheme, keeping track of who was away when. Then they rented trucks, backed them empty into people's driveways, and unloaded all those houses of their furniture, stereos, TVs, blenders, all over town.

"*The policeman is our friend,*" I say.

My mother's response takes me by surprise.

"*You cannot write that in your book,*" she says.

"*It was in the papers, right on the front page. I'm not giving up anybody's secret.*"

"*It was a long time ago,*" my mother says. "*Think of their lives now, their families.*"

"*It's the truth,*" I tell her.

We have been to the end of our path through the woods, turned around, and come all the way home again, back where we started out with each other.

"*You can say what you want to about Lee,*" my mother tries another tack. "*She's dead.*"

"*So what is this?*" I ask. "*We take a girl out once a year and stone her so . . .* "

"*And I'm still alive.*"

"*Corruption is everywhere,*" I say. "*Learn to live with it.*"

I think of it as liberating knowledge, a protective recognition that opens whatever precarious margins we find. But my mother needs the center.

"*I still have to live in that town,*" she says.

"*We dump all the judgment on one head, and protect the rest of them, even if they don't deserve it?*"

"*Let's talk about deserving,*" my mother says. "*She was a prostitute, she committed this crime, and you want to excuse her.*"

"*I'm not excusing her,*" I say.

We're not listening to each other anymore. We're screaming now, out by the patio.

"*What does it mean, all the things that happened to her, all the things she did? That we don't have to think anymore about the way we live?*"

"*And why do you care more about some dead girl you hardly knew than you do about me?*"

"*I don't, Mom. I don't.*"

I don't, I don't, I don't, my head throbs with the sound of it. That isn't it at all. My father looks up from his book.

"*Hey,*" he says, friendly, soothing. "*What's going on here?*"

"*Oh, go jump in a lake,*" my mother says.

"*That's a good idea,*" my father says. "*Let's go swimming.*"

My mother and I look at each other. I reach up to my mouth, try to pull the corners back down to a serious look. And then we can't help it, we both start to laugh.

"*Yes, let's,*" my mother says.

She takes my arm and turns me toward the cottage.

"Your father lives on another planet," she says.

"And I wouldn't have him any place else," I say.

Later that evening, I'm upstairs, packing my bags. It's time to go back, and I plan to leave in the morning. I have work to do. I stand at the window, taking a little break, looking out at the evening sky.

"I brought you a cup of tea." It's my mother at the door.

"Thanks," I say.

"Can I help?"

"I'm just about done," I say.

"I'm sorry," she says. "About earlier."

"I'm sorry, too," I say.

"If you roll your blouses," my mother says, "they won't muss so much."

"Mother," I say.

She holds her hand up in a little salute.

"I really want to hear the end of the story," she says.

"There's not much else to tell," I say. "Just the facts."

When the police found Lee's apartment empty, they investigated. A neighbor said that two women left in a Volkswagen bug, but they didn't know what happened to the man who had been there. The police got the license plate easily enough, since they knew who was driving, and shortly afterwards, the car was spotted by the highway patrol, heading east on Route 6, making for the turnpike maybe, and they set off in pursuit. They followed leads through Findlay, Fostoria, all the way to Fremont, where they found the car sitting in a driveway. The Humphreys said they didn't know a thing about it. The girls just showed up and wanted to borrow the family car, so they'd traded.

Ten hours later, 2:30 in the morning, after numerous phone calls and radio signals, and ten-fours and over-and-outs, they picked up the two women in a room at Baker's Motel on the south side of Bowling Green, right where Route 6 dumps into Route 25, the beginning point of the circle they'd raced around. They were just sitting there, waiting.

The police found Tommy Matson in his own apartment on North Enterprise Street three hours after they apprehended the women at Baker's Motel. He had tossed the gun and the bloody sheets into a ditch along Tontogany Road, and he led the police to the evidence.

The story hit the front page of the *Daily Sentinel Tribune* on February

13, a simple story pulsing with journalistic control. According to the local press, Carl Woodman made his way into the garage at Al Smith's Chrysler-Plymouth about 4:30 that afternoon. "Help me," he said. "I've been shot." He was taken by ambulance to Wood County Hospital, where he was listed in critical condition with a gunshot wound in the chest.

The new wing of the hospital, only recently constructed, where he was treated, and from which he was released three weeks later, to return to his wife and family, had been named in memory of Lee Snavely's father.

The three of them, Lee, Connie, and Tommy, were arraigned before Judge Dunipace, and later indicted on three counts: extortion, armed robbery, and attempted murder, crimes decidedly against "the peace and dignity of the State of Ohio." Connie got out on bail almost immediately. Tommy's case and Connie's were continued until late summer of 1973. Tommy pleaded guilty to the charge against him, the shooting itself. By the time Connie's case came to trial in August, continued that long through the agency of a fancy out-of-town lawyer, she pleaded no contest to a reduced charge, aiding and abetting in an attempt at extortion. She never served any time.

Lee didn't have the money herself, and nobody to round it up for her. She was declared legally indigent and given her choice among public defenders. She asked for David Holden, the oldest son in the family she had lived with in high school.

She pleaded innocent at first, when she appeared in court without her lawyer, but David convinced her to trade in her jury trial for a reduced charge, to plead guilty to aiding and abetting in an attempt to kill. It didn't really take any convincing, David told me later; she knew just what she was doing, and didn't have to be talked into anything. She always was smart, he said, and knew the score.

Nobody out there worked the angles for her, nobody got the case continued like Connie's had been, and Lee didn't have to wait long for her trial. She used the time well. Once they brought her back to the jail on Prospect Street, remodeled since her last stint there, she amused herself by cutting clippings of her crime from the *Daily Sentinel Tribune* and the *Toledo Blade*, correcting the typographical errors, underlining the "Miss" in Miss Fletcher as if to say "what fools they are," and sending the articles off to Eric, still in prison himself. When the sheriff supplied her with the list of news items published by the local radio station, she took pleasure in noting that her story was the headliner. "Top billing, no less," she printed neatly across the top.

"You must be making that up," my mother says.

"No," I say. "A few weeks ago, Eric turned all the clippings over to me."

"It's unbelievable, isn't it?"

I can hear her tongue clucking.

Lee was arrested in February, tried and convicted in March, sentenced on April 23, 1973, to confinement in the Ohio State Reformatory for Women, in Marysville, for a period of not less than one (1) nor more than twenty (20) years. In May, following the usual procedure in these cases, David Holden appeared before Judge Adams, requesting that his client's sentence be commuted to probation. The judge refused.

She had had prior convictions for prostitution, and he saw no reason to trust in her own recognizance. The court did agree, however, to subtract the time she spent in the Wood County jail, about two months, from the length of her full sentence.

But before they shipped her off to Marysville, Lee was ordered to pay the costs of her own prosecution. In an official writ, Sheriff Rife's office was entrusted with the responsibility of collecting that sum from Lee, whose name the forms consistently mistake for a man's.

"If she'd been a man," my mother starts.

"Things probably would have turned out a whole lot different," I say.

According to the statement of the sheriff's deputy, the attempt to collect those funds was duly made, but "for lack of goods or chattels, lands or tenements whereon to levy, I now return this writ wholly unsatisfied."

"In the end," I say, "the county picked up her tab."

"So that's what it comes down to, huh?" my mother asks.

"An unpaid bill of $135.65," I say.

"That's sad," she says.

"There isn't much else to say," I tell her.

I run the zipper around my suitcase to close it up tight.

"All packed," I say. "Let's go build a fire."

"There is one more thing," my mother says.

"What's that?"

"You're alive, too."

It's dark outside now, and no-see-ums, small enough to slip through the screens, have begun to gather at the bedroom light. I nod at my mother.

"Yes," I say. "I'm alive, too."

My mother takes my arm and pulls me to her. I drop my head to her shoulder.

"And I would have paid your bill," she says.

I pull away a little, so I can look in her face.

"I wasn't ever that expensive," I say. "Besides, you're not responsible for me."

"I know," my mother says. "That's not the point."

"I love you, too," I say.

We find our way down the darkened stairwell to the living room. Things are still messy with my mother, no neater now than when I first came, and maybe they'll never be clean, until one of us stops fighting or dies. But there's a knowing between us, and we can live with that.

I have come to know myself better by looking at Lee, by telling the story I made myself see. Yes, we came from the same time, the same place. We listened to the same music, we kissed the same boys, and on compatibilities as sure and as fleeting as that we seemed briefly identical twins in shorty pajamas, one dark-haired, one blond. We fell into our adult lives, for different reasons and in different ways, unprepared and unprotected. We turned some of the same corners, made some of the same mistakes. Yes, I see myself in her, through her, and feel myself alive in the reverberations of her story with mine. And I come to my mother as the woman I am now for having looked at Lee, angry and loving and guilty and knowing. But I also come to my mother because I can, and because Lee cannot come to hers. I do not always feel safe in my mother's arms, nor she in mine, but in that embrace we know the beating of the other's heart.

When my mother and I get downstairs, my father has already started the fire.

I leave the lake early the next morning. Despite the thermos of coffee and the good lunch my mother has packed for me, I'm not prepared for the trip.

For the time being, I am done with Lee, happy, in fact, to leave her in prison, where I know she's safer than she will be when she gets out.

Now the road is taking me somewhere else. It stretches out ahead of me, a weird confusion of geography and time. I reorder it as I drive. The story these signs and places mark is what's left for me to imagine, what's left for me to know.

I've driven this way countless times, from Ohio to Michigan, from Michigan to Ohio, but it's a strange landscape now. By the time I'm halfway home, the reality of the route has changed completely. All the landmarks have shifted, and the road looks new.

PART

FOUR

I drive along I-75, reordering time and space as I go. Here is the town where Lee was graduated from high school in 1968. Here is the county line she crossed in order to get married in 1970. Here is Tecumseh, Michigan, where the car she was driving was found, abandoned in the parking lot from which she disappeared in 1974. And a little farther south is Toledo, where she lived out her last days, after prison. Where, according to information in the papers, she made her curiously elaborate plans to meet up with a man she encountered in a bar there, where she arranged to drive herself into his Irish Hills.

As I move south I pass exits for Detroit and its suburbs, to the east, Pontiac, Royal Oak, Bloomfield. Nearer by, Ann Arbor, Lansing, Ypsilanti. All of them landmarks, scenes from his story, places he knew, places he traveled, during the course of Lee's life. I cross the same rivers he crossed, riding in the back seat of police cars, transported from hospital to jail and back again, rivers that bear the names of their own past, the Tittabawassee, the Cass, the Rifle, the Bad.

I'm in his territory now, Gary Taylor's, the man who killed Lee. He killed other women, too, who shared nothing with Lee except her sex, who may have shared nothing with me but mine. And where is the shelter from that?

Speaking out of their own fears, from generations of instruction whose purpose is not women's safety, our mothers warn us. "Do not be sexual," they say, "and you will be safe, from the catcalls of construction workers on the street, from the misogynist's bullet." The warning echoes in myriad ways, in a chorus of frightened voices. Do not wear skirts on the stairwells. Do not let your knees drift apart. Do not be friends with that dangerous girl. Do not step into the pool hall. Do not experiment with your life. Do not acquaint yourself with the world. Do not hold another woman's hand in a public place. Do not write this book.

The wheels spin along under me. The landscape blurs by. I fiddle with the radio dial to find the Detroit stations, KISS 99, CLASSIC 101. My mother has arranged my lunch on the seat beside me so I can reach into the cooler, retrieve half a sandwich, fresh vegetables, sweet cherries, without stopping. She says I should make myself a picnic at a roadside rest, stretch my legs a *bit ("Don't go into the restroom," she says, "unless you see plenty of people around"). It's good advice, but I prefer to keep driving. The trip seems shorter that way.*

Near Ypsilanti, where Gary Taylor was incarcerated, the road sign bears a warning: CORRECTIONAL FACILITY IN THE AREA. DO NOT PICK UP HITCHHIKERS. *Now there's a rule a woman can live with, a rule she can follow, and be.*

The road I'm on converges with I-75, the length of interstate that links everything together on the map in my mind. It unravels before me like a sleave, a thin filament of gray silk drawn out from a skein of threads. One road, sleepless and undreaming, extends past Detroit, past Toledo, past Bowling Green, through Ohio's flatlands into its hills, through the mountains of West Virginia and Tennessee, into Georgia where the land goes flat again. If I keep driving, if I stay awake, I'll make it all the way to Florida, and back again.

1 9 5 4 – 1 9 7 5

The national weather map in the paper shows snow for Detroit, but here in St. Petersburg the front yard is growing oranges. Puny and hard, more like golf balls than anything you'd eat, but oranges, for sure. Gary Taylor looks from the map to the window, the map to the window, the map to the window, reducing the motion slowly to a shake of his head. Florida, he thinks, might as well be another planet.

His mother insisted on having Christmas anyway, though there is no season for it here. The man at the nursery suggested a citrus sapling instead of the usual pine. In the old days, he said, in Williamsburg where he'd been once, they decorated for Christmas with lemons. They made the house smell clean, he said. Besides, for their first Florida Christmas, 1954, a lemon tree or an orange tree in a pot would be just right. They could plant it in the yard afterwards, keep track of their stay year by year, by watching it grow.

But no, she said, she wanted it more like home. They bought a pine tree after all, puny like the oranges, hardly worth the trouble of decorating.

Gary loosens his tie, and flips the newspaper page away from the weather map. All dressed up and somewhere to go on Christmas Eve. He isn't much interested in the party, but it will get him out of the house for the night.

He folds the newspaper over on itself, and rises from the sofa.

"I'm off," he says.

"Take your coat," his mother says.

"Hnh," he says, something like a laugh.

"This is Florida, not Africa. They have frosts down here, plenty, and the price of oranges goes up all over the country."

"I'll be out late," he says, and brushes quickly past his mother.
He is eighteen years old.

When he arrives at the boss's house, nobody meets him at the door.
He is clearly expected to make his own way among the people milling
about, many of whom have spilled out through sliding glass doors into
the yard, the patio. He ladles for himself a cup of eggnog, and talks for
a while to some guy he recognizes from the loading dock. Then he
wanders out to the patio, fenced on one side, lined by small orange trees
along the other. He reaches absently for an orange drooping off a
branch, thinks he just might pick it, though it is puny and patched with
green.

"Found yourself a souvenir?" she says.

He knows the voice right away.

He remembers her from the day he went into the office to fill out the
application for the job. He is used to it, that tone, knows just what it
means. You can sit here, she said, by me. Just fill out the top part, she
said, and I'll do the rest. Spinning sugar in and out of the words the way
women do when they want something they aren't asking for. Don't you
walk off with my pen, she said, the flirtatious accusation, when she was
the one who'd just been caught looking out from under her eyelashes.

This voice is the boss's wife.

He pulls his hand away from the orange.

"I'm sorry," she says. "Have we met?"

"I'm Taylor," he says. "Gary."

"Well, Gary, how about another drink?" she says.

That voice again, the sugar in and out of the words, an assault of
sugar and intention. She rests her hand briefly on his elbow, guiding him,
directing him, turning him toward the bar. He draws his arm in quickly.

"I'm not quite ready yet," he says.

"I'll check back later," she says. "We want you happy here."

Once she's gone, he takes in air in short, quick breaths, almost a pant.
He can't quite place the constriction, inside, around his lungs, or
outside, like a weight on his chest. He pulls at his tie, flexes the muscles
in his neck as he turns his head, pushes his chin up slightly. It sure got
warm in here all of a sudden, he thinks, and then remembers he is still
out on the patio.

He wipes his palms on his pants, feels the car keys bunched in his pocket. He has things under control after all. He can always get out of here.

He parked his car a few doors down, on the street, knowing that at a party he might get boxed in. On his second try, the engine jumps to life, and he pulls out, squealing the tires on the pavement. He speeds off down the Boulevard, then turns from the main drag onto streets named for states and numbers, losing himself in the maze once he is far enough away from the house. Third Street, Fifth Street, Eighth Street at the corner of Ohio. California, Michigan, Maine. The place has no geography. Every yard with a house just like every other house, slung low to the ground, tile, cement blocks, terra cotta, and a yellow porch light, shimmering through frosted glass covered with a net of dying bugs.

When he sees the woman on the street, he finds himself again and reaches for the wrench under the dash.

He meets up with her just beyond the back of his car.

"I'll give you a ride home," he says.

"I don't want a ride," she says, struggling to free her arm from his grip.

"Shut up," he says.

He brings the wrench down against the side of her head.

Another blow, and then another, but he can't get her squarely because she won't stop making all that noise, and it distracts him. He brings the wrench down again, hard this time, compensating with force for the failure of aim. The woman crumples, quiet finally, on the grass, and a light comes on in a house a few doors down. Then another light across the street.

Gary throws the wrench into the car, slams the door, and hurries around to the street side. All this time the engine has been running. He slides into the seat, pulls at the brake, and speeds off before he closes his door. Once he is out of the neighborhood, well on his way home, he glances at his watch. 11:00 P.M. Not Christmas yet.

In his own mind, Gary Taylor has a reputation already, long before his wrench meets up with this woman on the street. Years later, he speaks with a certain pride about it, about how much he managed to get away with, and for how long.

The Phantom of the Bus Stop, he says they called him in the local papers, the *Tampa Morning Tribune*, the *St. Petersburg Times*. He haunted the bus station, he says, watching for women getting off buses alone, coming into town late at night from who knows where.

He took pleasure in it, satisfaction, he calls it later, seeing the look on their faces when he loomed up in front of them from around a bus, a corner, a cigarette machine, the terror once it became clear what he had in mind. The police arrested him for it once, but they hadn't been able to make the charges stick. He enjoyed that too, he says, giving the cops the runaround.

They talk it up at work, the rest of the guys, who are impressed with the spookiness of it, some creep fading in and out of the bus station. I find out my wife's been hanging around that part of town, one says, I'll whup her for sure. My girl's terrified, another says. She won't go to the Piggly Wiggly by herself. And get this, she has me folding clean socks with her at the laundromat. They better catch this phantom quick, he says. I need help with those socks.

One of these days he'll kill somebody, another offers.

Gary joins in like a regular fellow.

The guy must be nuts, he says.

The wrench would have been enough that Christmas Eve to keep the woman quiet, but Taylor doesn't count on the lights coming on down the street. He doesn't stay around to finish the job.

And apparently, incredibly, Pearl Washburn, his victim, manages to get his license number, or part of it. The neighbors, alerted by her cries, call an ambulance, and she describes her assailant or his car after she comes to in the hospital. On January 24, 1955, exactly a month after the assault occurred, a warrant is issued for Taylor's arrest.

He is arraigned in March, the trial date set for June, but his lawyer manages to postpone it until the following November. The lawyer also recommends trial by jury. Six women who had been assaulted in the bus station identify Taylor in a line up, but by Florida law, the jury will be instructed to ignore that. (*"Such evidence with respect to this Defendant and said other women, if you believe such evidence to be true, must be considered by you only on the question of the Defendant's identity, and his plan or design if you find that he had a plan or design."*) A jury can consider only the evidence directly connected with the Washburn case. And her testimony will be easy to discredit—it was dark that night now nearly a year ago.

Besides, they can come up with at least the appearance of an alibi. An alibi, the lawyer explains to Gary and his father Milo, doesn't have to be airtight; they won't have to prove the alibi beyond a reasonable doubt. All they have to do is raise sufficient question in the jurors' minds that the defendant could have been present at the time the crime occurred. They have the testimony of the boss's wife, who can't remember exactly when he left the party. They have the word of his father, that he had been home early that night. By Florida law, the jury will be obligated to acquit.

The jury acts precisely as the lawyer predicts. Ordered by the judge to discount as irrelevant the testimony of Rhonda Olson, Pauline Leggett, Imogen Crosby, Beth Ann Drake, Mona Hopkins, and Myra Fosdick, all of whom came into St. Petersburg on a bus, the jurors silence Pearl Washburn, too. On November 16, 1955, on the third day of the trial, they acquit Gary Addison Taylor of charges of assault against Pearl Washburn on the basis of an alibi defense, provided by the defendant's father.

Two days later, Milo Taylor reclaims State's Exhibit #1, a ten-inch stilson wrench he carries in his car.

Years later, Gary Taylor is still laughing about the runaround he gave the cops, the lawyers, the jury. And about all the other things he managed to get away with. He joins the Navy briefly, and the Navy moves him to other cities: Baltimore, Newport, Boston. Join the Navy, they say, and see the world. In each new city, he finds whores he can beat up, and nobody ever catches him at it. Otherwise, he doesn't like the Navy much, and is released after less than a year on Corporal Klinger's dream, a Section 8. They try to keep him in a uniform, but he finally tells them he'll wear what he damn well pleases.

By the time he is twenty and his family has returned to Detroit, Taylor has quite a reputation in the city, and around nearby Toledo, Ohio. Cab drivers get so they won't take him where he wants to go. They know what he's after, and don't want to dump him off at a bar if all he's going to do is beat up girls. That doesn't matter much, Taylor says. There are plenty of bars he can walk to.

I pass Toledo myself in the late afternoon, and I drive into town, home again, when the shops are closing up along Main Street. Changes in the face of things along here have occurred over the years, but they don't add up to much. The public library stands now where Howard's once drew in the crowds of college students and locals home for vacation.

Howard's itself moved across the street, where it boasts a fancy orange sign and a paneled facade. It's still a hangout for the students, though it hasn't much atmosphere now, and three-two beer is a thing of the past. An ice cream parlor replaced a drugstore, restaurants moved into vacant spaces here and there with names that belong in other climates. The Blue Peacock. Sun Dance. South of the Border.

Across Main Street from Keeter's, long since disappeared, they're shooting pool at the movie theater, where the marquee announces The Color of Money. *The one theater of my childhood still stands, keeping up with the times, converted to two screens now: the Cla-zel Theater. When he built the place, the man who owned it couldn't decide who best to honor with its name, his mother Clara, or his wife Hazel.*

The theater has occupied the center of the block near the center of town for as long as I can remember. As a fifth grader, I won an essay contest sponsored by the management—"Why I Want to See Gulliver's Travels" *in twenty-five words or less—and free tickets to the movie, inspired by voyages to monstrous places even then. The same year, they offered \$25 to the first comer who could sit in the theater alone through a special midnight showing of* Psycho. *At ten, I had my limits, and I didn't try for that. Now I can sit, open-eyed, through almost any movie. I have a high tolerance for violence in the movies. It worries me sometimes.*

At the Cla-zel Theater, the distinction between mother and wife marked by a neon hyphen between their truncated names, Paul Newman teaches Tom Cruise the flash of the con, the deft trick of the trade; the young man learns from the old man, then outstrips his mentor, takes to his lessons a little too well. There's a woman involved somewhere, a woman between them somehow.

I pass the theater, stop for the red light in the center of town, and glance into the rearview mirror where I can read the back side of the marquee, the second feature at the Cla-zel. Back to the Future, *it reads. A blockbuster movie, I hear, a cherished fantasy, like trading places with your kid. There's been a spate of those movies recently, too. I wonder, if we could go back to the past and change it, what lessons would old men be teaching young men now?*

They line up in my mind, as I drive down Main Street, past the landmarks of my childhood. Men who confuse their mothers with their wives, take out their anger at one on the other. Men like Lee's father, who, angry perhaps at his own mother for leaving him orphaned, insists upon control, as if he could assert his will over death itself, as if death came in the shape of a woman. Men who are taught by their own fathers and in turn teach the lessons to their sons, who then rap their knuckles on bar stools to have some fun with a girl. They line up in my mind, men at the bar, psychiatrists and lawyers this time, not in a pool hall but a courtroom, not in T-shirts but business suits, mustached or bearded but not likely tattooed. Men who speak for Gary Taylor (he's learned his lessons too well: death comes in the shape of a woman). Men who want to excuse him because he looks a little like them, or like their sons. And here and there a police officer or a judge, the persons behind or beside The Court, who don't seem to have so much stake in things, who cannot count the women or name their names, who cannot see them, perhaps, as women at all, because they see them as equal under the protection of the law.

I step into this world, a bizarre and distorted film, a nightmare buddy movie, when I track Gary Taylor's history down through the next transcript, or the next. It's something like walking into Keeter's pool hall, a dangerous place for a girl, but a place that a girl needs to know.

At home again in my mother's house, I spend the evening sorting through my files, scattered over the dining room table, on the shelves of the study upstairs, labeling them, arranging them neatly in boxes. Each transcript bears the seal of the circuit court of this county or that county in Michigan, certifying officially to the accuracy of the record contained there. Under the seal, a woman's signature, the county clerk who prepared the material for me, a woman with an ordinary name, working an ordinary job, her paycheck coming once a month from the state.

It was hard going for me at first, finding the information I wanted, a process full of false starts and misapprehensions of the way a world in which I haven't lived is organized. I sent the record keeper a trial date, and she asked for the defendant's birthday. I sent someone else his birthday, and she asked for his aliases or his Social Security number. But slowly, one piece of paper led to another, and then another, until the trail was clear.

It seemed odd to me when I first read it in the transcript of Case # L41657, the record of Taylor's sanity hearing before the Circuit Court of Oakland County, Michigan. After years of watching cop shows on television, I expected the familiar rehearsal: "You have the right to remain silent. Anything you say can and will be used against you in a court of law." But this is 1957, more like Dragnet *than* Cagney and Lacy. Miranda v. The State of Arizona *won't alter TV shows for good until 1966.*

On the evening of February 7, 1957, shortly after 8:00 P.M., Gary Addison Taylor was apprehended by the local police, just west of Garden Road, on Albert Street in the city of Royal Oak. Detective George Tedder responded to a call over the police radio, and assisted in the arrest of the suspect. He had been working for several months on similar cases, and he was sure now they had the shooter.

Since December 1956, the police in Royal Oak, Southfield, Bloomfield Hills, Birmingham, Michigan, all of them suburbs of Detroit, some of them little more than a string of fancy shops and grand houses for GM executives, had been receiving reports of a phantom sniper taking potshots with a rifle at women and adolescent girls. They were walking down the streets on their way home from work, waiting at bus stops, or padding barefoot across their own living room carpets, passing by a plate glass window on their way from the sofa to the fireplace to stir up the embers on a winter's night. From a distance, through that glass, they might have looked like women on TV.

"You have got a lot of trouble," Tedder said, when he climbed into the back seat of the police car with the suspect. "Do you want to talk about it?"

"I know I've got trouble," Taylor said. "I don't know if I want to tell you or not."

"That's entirely up to you," Tedder said. "But a man who did the things we suspect you of doing, that man would need a lot of help. If you want help, you should talk to me."

Taylor sat silently in the back seat for a few minutes, as the police car pulled away from Albert Street and headed down 13 Mile Road toward the station.

"I am," he said finally. "All right. I'm the man you're looking for. I'm your sniper."

That February evening, in the back seat of the police car on their way to the station, Taylor began with that sentence, then recreated for Tedder the shape of the past few months, searching back compulsively over the past several years of his life.

"I have this dream," he volunteered, almost right away. "It isn't quite a dream, I might be awake, but it's like I'm dreaming. I've had this dream for years."

"What dream is that, Gary?"

"She's coming fast down the slope, all bundled up. I can hardly tell she's a woman."

"Where are you in this dream?" Tedder asked.

"I'm hiding behind some trees."

"Who are you hiding from?" Tedder asked.

"There's a jump at the end of the slope, and suddenly she's in the air. That's when I shoot."

"Huh?"

"I've got her in the scope," Taylor said. "And right then, when she's suspended in the air, when she doesn't have the ground under her anymore, I blow her out of the sky. *Kabloom.*"

"Isn't there a movie about that?" Tedder said.

"Yeah? Maybe. It happens like that a lot on television."

"What happens?" Tedder asked.

"Sometimes," Taylor said, "I see women on television, and I can't help myself. I almost can't stop. I want to shoot at the screen."

"So what do you want to do," Tedder said, "after you have this, uh, dream about the skier?"

"Last December," Taylor said, "I went down to Hudson's and bought a gun."

"What kind of gun?"

"A .22 caliber rifle. I was going to fix it up with a four-power scope, so I could see well enough. So I wouldn't make a mistake."

"And did you use that gun?"

"I took a pair of binoculars out to Telegraph Road. There's a ski slope out there, you know. I walked through all this snow, about a quarter of a mile of it. I was looking for a place to hide. A place to shoot from."

"But what if you made a mistake?" Tedder said. "What if that was a man coming down the slope and not a woman at all?"

"I'd feel bad about that," Taylor said. "I wouldn't want to shoot a man."

"But you didn't shoot anybody then, did you?"

Taylor shrugged. "I didn't have my gun," he said.

Later, from the witness stand, Taylor made another black joke like that to his defense attorney, Gilbert Davis. After his arrest for the snipings, he said, being in jail, he didn't have the chance to hurt anybody. So sometimes circumstances prevented Taylor from having his way. But other times, through the strenuous exercise of his own will, Taylor could keep himself temporarily under control. He reported to a court-appointed psychiatrist sent to examine him that when he saw a young woman walking down the street, he wanted to hurt her or kill her or rape her. To control himself, he wrapped his mouth around the steering wheel and bit down hard. He often left marks in the metal or the heavy vinyl with his teeth.

On the evening of December 21, 1956, both Taylor's active will and the circumstances cooperated with his impulses. He told the police detective about it, about shooting Cathy Estabar in the back as she walked along Catalpa Drive. Cathy was fourteen years old.

"What happened after you shot her?" Tedder asked.

"She just kept walking," Taylor said. "She didn't fall down, or anything. But I guess I got her."

Tedder remembered the incident well. He had been called in to investigate the shooting. A bullet had, in fact, penetrated Cathy's back, coming out of nowhere as she walked east on Catalpa Drive.

Within fifteen minutes of that shooting, Taylor was at it again, taking several shots at a woman seated at a bus stop near Memorial Park, at 13 Mile Road and Woodward. He then proceeded into Southfield, to a deserted driveway near the local dump. A car was parked there, its windows all steamed up.

"You know what that means," Taylor said. "A car, parked at the dump late at night. The windows all steamed up."

Taylor locked the young man in the trunk of the car, and, at rifle point, pushed the young woman into the well under the dash on the passenger's side, and crammed her mouth against his exposed penis.

"What can you expect?" Taylor told the police officer. "A girl like that."

"What kind of girl is that?" Tedder said.

"You know," Taylor said. "The flirty kind. If they only knew what I was thinking, they'd be scared to death."

That set Taylor off on the waitress.

"I go into a restaurant," he said, "and there's a particular kind of waitress there. You know, she wiggles her ass at you when she walks you to your table. Or she complains about the heat, and fans herself, where her uniform is cut down in a V. It happens, you know. Women notice me."

"Sure," Tedder said. "You're a good-looking guy." Taylor's brown hair swept back from his broad forehead. He affected a slight curl in the lip, the Elvis Presley look, Tedder thought.

"So if this girl, this waitress, walks by and smiles or something," Taylor continued, "I smile back, and they think I'm flirting with them.

But if she knew what I was thinking. I'm probably thinking something like, 'Boy, I'd like to shoot you.' "

Later, at his sanity hearing, Taylor described in detail the events of the night he had been apprehended. He'd been drinking at the Fox and Hounds, a bar in Bloomfield Hills. A painting of the chase hung over the bar, and it may have given Taylor ideas, the fox running like crazy, helpless against all those dogs. This peculiar quality to his fantasy life, one of the psychiatrists testified, is what makes Taylor dangerous. The murderous fantasy is not all that unusual in itself. But this man doesn't distinguish clearly between the fantasy in his head and the reality outside it. He imagines a picture, and then he walks straight into it, as if he were moving from one room to another. And here was a picture—he didn't even have to invent this one—of a fox tormented by a pack of hounds.

"So you were drinking at the Fox and Hounds," the prosecutor, Fred Ziem, said. "What did you have to drink?"

"A shot and a beer."

"And when you left the Fox and Hounds on that date, what did you do?"

"I went to Pontiac and bought a rifle."

"Then what did you do?"

"I started riding around. I was going down Woodward Avenue towards Pontiac, going back down to Birmingham, and I saw this woman."

"Where did you see this woman?"

"I don't know the exact street. It was somewhere in Bloomfield Village, north of the Fox and Hounds, on the same side of the street. I was heading toward Pontiac."

"Then what?"

"Well, I drove down the road she was walking on. It was a dirt road. I went down about a quarter of a mile, I should say."

"Did you drive past her?"

"Yes, and I got out of the car with the rifle."

"Then what did you do?"

"I jumped over a couple of fences."

"Then what did you do?"

"I rested my rifle on the fence."

"Then what did you do?"

"I shot her."

After shooting at Sheila Evers as she walked into her home, Taylor went to the Town and Country on Telegraph Road. At the bar, he had another shot and a beer. Fred Ziem wanted to know what he did after that.

"Well, I went out for more people, looking for more people to shoot. At that moment I was trying to decide what I wanted to do. I knew what I wanted to do, and I knew what I should do. I should have gone home."

But he didn't go home. Once he got started, he said, he couldn't stop. He knew it was wrong, he knew the maximum sentence was life in prison if he got caught, but all that was too much to think about. He went out again, riding around past the place where the earlier shooting had occurred. Then he rode around Birmingham, Southfield.

"Well, what happened after that?" Ziem asked.

"That was already covered by the officer," Taylor responded. "Everything the officer told is the truth."

Officer George Tedder had testified that after the Evers shooting, Taylor shot at two women at a bus stop on 14 Mile and Woodward roads. One bullet went into the woman's back; another passed through the lapel of her coat, and zipped under her chin. He then shot several times at another woman waiting at another bus stop before driving home to change his clothes. He then took a shot at a young girl walking along a street in Birmingham. Then he parked his car near Greenfield and 13 Mile roads, and shot through plate glass windows, he couldn't remember how many, whenever a woman appeared there, like a woman on the television screen. All told, on the evening of February 7, in a few short hours between his beer at the Fox and Hounds and his apprehension at 8:35 P.M., Taylor had aimed his rifle and pulled the trigger upwards of twenty times.

But the shooting itself seemed a little erratic, the bullets often missing their apparent targets. Tedder had located a lot of bullets, so he knew Taylor hadn't invented the shootings, imagined them. One bullet missed the woman entirely, and embedded in the bench where she was sitting. Another hit a nearby parked car.

"Did you intend to kill these women?" the prosecutor wanted to know.

"No, sir, I didn't. I just, I'm not sure."

"Didn't you tell the doctors that you intended to kill?"

"I never had any intention of killing anybody," Taylor said from the witness stand. "I would like to bring out that I used the .22 rifle instead of a high-power rifle, which I had."

Everyone in the courtroom remembered the rifle Taylor had bought to equip with a scope so he could shoot the woman plummeting down the mountain, or suspended in midair.

"I used .22 short hollow points," Taylor said.

"What is the purpose of hollow points?"

"They flatten out, won't hurt anything through a coat."

"They also don't provide clear ballistics evidence, right?"

"Yes, that's true. That's part of the reason."

"So you couldn't be traced."

Gilbert Davis, the defense attorney, had been seated silently behind his desk for most of the testimony. Taylor had been doing fine, going on about "irresistible impulses" and "urges he couldn't control." In the State of Michigan, "irresistible impulse" provided one acceptable test of legal insanity. Taylor's testimony fed naturally into the defense case, convincing everybody he was crazy by that definition. But at this line of questioning, which exposed Taylor's rational intent, a malice afore-thought, Davis objected.

"I don't like to object facetiously," he said. "But it seems to me the groundwork is being laid here for a criminal trial, not an insanity hearing."

The Honorable Frank L. Doty agreed.

"I don't think it's necessary to go any further," he said. "It is all right as far as you have gone. I don't think we need any further testimony."

The case was concluded in the Circuit Court of Oakland County on March 22, 1957. Judge Doty ruled that Gary Addison Taylor was an insane person, incompetent to stand trial, and that he be forthwith removed to the Ionia State Hospital for the Criminally Insane, there to be safely kept until his sanity was restored, at which time he should be returned to the same court for trial.

Everybody got what he wanted. Fred Ziem got Taylor off the streets. Gilbert Davis had on record the basis for an insanity plea, should the case ever come to trial. And Gary Taylor didn't have to go to prison after all.

After he spent almost three years in the Ionia Hospital, and under some pressure from Milo Taylor to have his son transferred closer to home, the authorities agreed to move Taylor to the Lafayette Clinic in Detroit in November 1959. The Lafayette Clinic operated under more open conditions; it provided expanded freedoms for the patients, and thus a better test for the quality of their treatment. A year later, in November 1960, while a patient there, Taylor severely misused the privilege, failed the test.

He had read about a woman who had received some favorable publicity in the papers, and he took careful note of her name and address. When he was released from the hospital to attend a welding class, he made straight for a phone booth. He called the woman, gave himself a new name, promoted himself to FBI agent. He needed a reference, he said, for one of her co-workers who was applying for government work. A routine matter that required her signature, so he couldn't take her recommendation over the phone. He won her confidence, set up an appointment, and easily gained access to her apartment. Then he sexually assaulted her, and robbed her of $13.62 she had in her purse.

Taylor returned to the clinic that evening, no questions asked, and the local authorities did not connect him with the crime. A few months later, however, another of his escapades came to legal attention. On April 12, 1961, Taylor watched the space launch with the rest of the patients in the day room, and later that day, went off on a rocket of his own.

He had received permission again from the hospital to go into town to register at the local trade school for an electrical wiring class. His first stop on the way was a sporting goods store, where he made his purchase without arousing the clerk's suspicions. Once back out on the street, he accosted two women, a mother and daughter, and threatened them with the machete he had just bought.

The two women reported the incident, identified Taylor as their assailant, and he was arrested on charges of assault with a deadly weapon. The worst the court could do to him, though, was to send him back to the Ionia State Hospital for the Criminally Insane, and that's what they did.

Taylor was actually tried for the sniping incidents in 1967, nearly ten years after they occurred, when the courts decided he was sane enough to understand the proceedings against him, to participate reasonably in his own defense. Lawyers and doctors lined up on both sides, one set providing witness for the petitioner who sought release through a writ of habeas corpus on the grounds that if found innocent by reason of insanity for those long-ago crimes, he had already served an appropriate sentence, and no longer posed a threat to society. The doctors rehearsed statistics (Taylor presented a "40 percent threat," and a "risk worth taking"). They analyzed deductive patterns of sociopathic behavior ("it isn't necessary to study the details of any particular case"). They recognized in the patient "some hostility toward women," yes, but the consequences of his actions had not been serious. Besides, he behaved so badly only when he'd been drinking.

The other side pointed to repeated incidents of rape and assault, consistently paranoid interpretations of reality, a complete failure of moral sympathy for his victims, abuses of the little freedoms he'd been given over the years, an insufficient system of internal controls on his behavior to warrant his release into an ambiguous world. In the middle, the judge, at the fulcrum of the seesaw, weighed the case in the balance, the potential freedom of one man against the lives of countless women, and decided on the interests of the state. The judge ordered Taylor to be remanded once again to the Ionia State Hospital for the Criminally Insane.

Back at the hospital in March of 1967, Taylor continued participating in his therapies. He followed politics in the newspapers, anti-war demonstrations, assertions of student power. He got himself a copy of *The Portable Nietzsche* and set about contemplating supermen. He memorized passages from *Mein Kampf.* He read the journals of another prisoner, Rudolph Hess, imagined him pacing the length, the width of a little room in Spandau, keeping himself moving in confinement.

And he complained about the restrictions on him—to his parents, to his lawyers, to the psychiatrists they sent to see him occasionally, to anyone who would listen. Finally, on March 4, 1970, almost three years exactly since his trial, they transferred Gary Taylor to the Center for Forensic Psychiatry in Ypsilanti, Michigan. This prison operated on a different principle. It was the express purpose of the Forensic Center to introduce patients found not guilty by reason of insanity back into the community.

I didn't count on the extra trip to Michigan at the end of the summer to see my mother, and now I'm on a tight schedule, only a few days left before I have to take up my duties at the college in New York. So I can leave early in the morning, so I can make the twelve-hour drive in a day, I pack up my car that night, backing it half into the garage, leaving the trunk open and the garage light on. I carry one box after another out from the dining room, page after page of his story, palpable evidence that I haven't made Gary Taylor up. Each case is neatly numbered and labeled, as if I can contain his story, control him somehow, in file folders.

I travel today on an even-numbered interstate, stretching east and west. I suffer some from confusing them, east and west, and have to think in broad terms when I see the huge green signs along the highway. Interstate 80, East—toward the Atlantic Ocean, Europe, the rising sun. West is the Pacific, where the sun sets. North and south, up and down, the oddly numbered interstates, give me no trouble at all.

Even after I am on the road the next day, grateful to leave the Ohio heat behind, my thoughts drift back the other direction, west and a little north, into the Irish Hills of Michigan, the world into which Gary Taylor walked disguised as an ordinary citizen in 1973, about the same time Lee was released from prison.

Once he was settled at the Ypsilanti Forensic Center in 1970, Gary Taylor set about convincing the people in charge that thirteen years in a mental hospital had made a painful impression on him. When they asked him the psychoanalytic questions, he knew how to answer. When they asked him about his violent responses to women in the past, he looked down, rubbed his forehead, squeezed his eyes shut, as if he were trying to force out the ugly pictures, erase the bitter memories.

But they didn't ask too many questions like that. Dr. Ames Robey, the Center's chief administrator, wanted to guarantee his patient's future by designing programs for him that would "verify the controls" he was already beginning to establish for himself. He wasn't going to pull all that Freud on him; the doctor was talking behavior mod.

It was a constant test. How about a weekend pass? Taylor asked. How about a visit home? He always wanted something a little too soon, and they always told him no the first time, maybe even the second time he asked. They wanted to test the level of his frustration, the response of his patience. The world, after all, was a very frustrating place. It wasn't going to fall over and play dead just because he asked it to.

Slowly Taylor earned privileges that permitted him to move around more. A grounds pass, and eventually a work assignment digging shrubs, or replanting tulips, or scoring the newly laid sidewalk to prevent the concrete from buckling under pressure. And slowly he traveled beyond the hospital grounds as well, day trips into Ann Arbor to shop, a visit home for the weekend, the responsibility of accompanying another patient to the dentist's office in Ypsilanti. By the time the case came to court again, to be reviewed as Michigan law required, he had won the support of many of the hospital staff.

Dr. Robey had to be a little less enthusiastic, because he was in charge and had a professional responsibility to be cautious. But even Dr. Robey suggested to the court that a behavior modification program could be instituted outside the hospital; a series of checks on Taylor's behavior could be developed. Robey had worked out a convincing description of the rules: gradual release over a six-month to one-year period; continued Antabuse treatments for ten years or so to control his drinking; no marriage without medical approval; limited contact with his parents; the necessary security and control exerted by Taylor's successfully finding and sticking with a job.

Robey had to admit when the lawyer asked him that Taylor had been and still was a sociopath who had not confronted the underlying causes of his problems. He had to admit that the recidivism rate among sociopaths was relatively high; even so, it fell off considerably after the patient turned thirty. And Gary Taylor was thirty-four already.

By the simplest legal tests, the right-and-wrong test, or the uncontrollable-impulse test, his lawyers could present a convincing case that Taylor was not "insane." But the law was more detailed than those simple tests might suggest. According to Michigan Act 151 of 1923: "The terms 'mentally ill' or 'mentally ill person' . . . include every species of insanity and extend to every mentally deranged person, and to all of unsound mind . . . and may include persons whose sexual behavior is characterized by repetitive or compulsive acts which indicate a disregard of consequences or the recognized rights of others or by the use of force upon another person in attempting sexual relations of either a heterosexual or homosexual nature."

With regard either to Taylor's past history or his current status, that wording remained subject to interpretation by the judge, who was not likely to accept as definitive the word of those hospital personnel who had been watching over Taylor all these years. The Court recognized from the outset a wide range here for discrepant opinion, and sought accordingly a wide range of expert testimony.

On the highway, a truck driver in a flatbed rig has been having fun with me for the last fifty miles. Passing me and slowing down, passing and slowing, laying on the horn, waving to me, calling out obscene greetings. He's in front of me again now, the mud guards flapping against his back wheels, the outline of a leggy, big-breasted woman etched in white against the heavy rubber flap. He slows to about forty, so I'm forced to brake or pass. When I pull into the left lane and come even with the cab, he speeds up again so I can't get around him, then raises his cupped fingers toward his mouth and tilts his head back, as if chugging a beer from a can. He points to the exit sign, and raises his eyebrows in an eager question. How about a drink, sister? I shake my head, then drop my speed, and slip back into the right lane behind him. Once he's too far past the exit ahead to make the turn himself, I put on my blinker and slide off the highway, figure I can lose him for a while at least.

To best protect the interests of his client, before the case came up for review, Taylor's lawyer arranged for examination of his client by Dr. Behan, a civilian, a psychiatrist in private practice. Called before the bench of Judge Ross W. Campbell as a witness for the petitioner, Dr. Behan reviewed what he saw as the central features of this case.

Behan explained that Taylor had divided women into two large classes, those with whom he developed some kind of emotional attachment, and those against whom he committed violence. It was as if he said, "That one upsets me because I am attached to her," and, "This one is going to pay for it." In Taylor's mind, virtually no overlap existed between the two groups. He experienced involvement with a particular woman as a kind of stress that stimulated ambivalent feelings and an urge to violence. Having made, however, such a clear distinction in his own mind between two kinds of women, Taylor never acted out against the woman by whom he actually felt threatened. Only strangers, on whom he artificially imposed his negative responses and from whom, as a result, he felt no threat, provided appropriate targets. He had no feelings for them whatsoever, and precisely that failure of affect gave him "permission," so to speak, to commit violence against them.

Behan suggested that this pattern of behavior could continue until Taylor came to terms with his underlying feelings about women. Nevertheless, Behan insisted that Taylor had come a long way toward recognizing his responsibilities and limitations. While he didn't fully understand the cause of his problems, Taylor realized his inability to relate to women, and intended to avoid situations in which his ambivalence might be aroused. If he could avoid complicating relationships, he could live in society without menacing it.

Mr. Arthur D'Hondt, Assistant Attorney General, cross-examined Dr. Behan carefully.

"You testified under direct examination that Mr. Taylor, and I quote, has 'integrated thought processes,' and 'no gross inability to test reality.' Could you explain to the court as simply as possible what that means?"

"Of course. Taylor's past history shows a repeated pattern of elaborate projection. If he wished something to occur, and it did, he assumed that he caused it to occur. He has also been unable to distinguish his own experience from the intentions of others. If he feels threatened, he assumes that someone is actively threatening him. It is typical of the psychotic to assume that the world is a play put on just for him, that reality is driven or created by his own mind, and it has no validity independent of his perceptions of it."

"And it is your opinion that the petitioner's relationship to reality has changed, that he is no longer insane, is that correct?"

"It is."

"Can you demonstrate for us his improved relationship to reality?"

"Here is one simple example. There was a time when Taylor's paranoia would assume that anything he read in the paper had something to do with him, was evidence that someone out there was 'after him,' or persecuting him. He continues to read the newspapers regularly. But now his mind is engaged, even exercised by politics, for instance, by issues about which he can form opinions separate from his own experience."

"For example?"

"He has described to me the current 'political kick' as 'infantile.' "

"This is in reference to agitation over American involvement in Southeast Asia?"

"I believe so, yes."

Dr. Behan went on to explain that it was not his position to assess the quality of Taylor's political judgment. The point was, Taylor was better able now to form opinions about what he read, to make connections that carried a certain logical force. He was fascinated, for example, by Nietzsche's concept of the superman. Nietzsche's thought has frequently been applied, however erroneously, by sane persons to political situations, to justify, for example, political intervention on the part of a superpower. The doctor did not mean to suggest that Taylor's fascination with Nazis was evidence of normalcy, but neither was it in itself a sign of insanity.

After all, we do not lock a person up simply because he is a right-wing fanatic.

The attorney for the State of Michigan, however, wanted some assurances that Taylor would comply with whatever restrictions would be imposed on him on the outside.

"Mr. Taylor is a unique individual," Dr. Behan said. "I cannot predict with absolute conviction how he will respond to his freedom. But certainly, he fully understands his own limitations."

"On what do you base that conclusion?"

"The patient has said as much, that he knows his sobriety acts to inhibit his responses. He has stopped drinking altogether, even when he is away from the Forensic Center on passes."

"Is it not likely that the patient will naturally encounter situations, opportunities for entering, say, into a sexual relationship with a woman, even if he is on convalescent status?"

"It would indeed be hard for him to avoid such situations completely, given the control his sexual urges exert over him."

"Such situations, sexually charged situations, induce stress in him?"

"Primarily when he's been drinking. But I feel certain that he would cooperate with our efforts to control that. And I have considerable experience working with alcoholics."

"If you had the authority, then, you would recommend restricted release?"

"Yes. But if convalescent status were not available to him, I would discharge him outright."

"Have most of the alcoholics with whom you've worked as a consultant exhibited the degree of criminal behavior evidenced in Mr. Taylor's past history?"

"I have acted as a consultant in the treatment of a rather unique population," the doctor said.

"And what population is that?"

"Alcoholic clergymen, actually."

Halfway across Pennsylvania, I pull off for gas at my favorite truck stop. Clean restrooms, a good cup of coffee, and a shop full of trinkets, key chains that look like license plates, mug holders, pocket maps, caps bearing the Harley-Davidson insignia, a reflecting plate that shows a woman winking back at you, puckering up her bright red lips, when you turn it in the light. I wander up and down the aisles, pause at a compact tool kit for the glove compartment, wonder over the fancy devices they sell these days to truckers—computerized maps, fuzz busters, special calculators to mount on the dashboard. I pass it all up, pay for my coffee and a box of Archway cookies, and head out to the car again. I have another five or six hours to drive.

The next witness before the court had considerable experience with cases like Taylor's, having examined several hundred criminal sexual psychopaths in the course of his career, having been personally responsible for releasing into society over two hundred who had been inmates in the Ionia State Hospital alone. He allowed that Taylor had made progress toward becoming a real human being, but that he still had a long way to go. His basic conflicts remained unresolved. He still had dangerous impulses he did not understand sufficiently to control.

"In the hospital setting," the doctor testified, "his ability to control his impulses is very good. But these abilities will not necessarily carry over to his life in society."

"And why is that?" Mr. D'Hondt asked.

"It's very difficult to control, in fact, I would say, it's virtually impossible to control all the circumstances in which a person might find himself in the course of ordinary life. He will meet women regularly, and there's nothing to prevent his becoming involved with a woman."

"Even if he enjoyed convalescent status?"

"Taylor's main motivation for control is fear of punishment. He has not internalized the moral values that might otherwise restrict his behavior. Unless he were convinced that he would be locked up within twelve hours of committing an action, he will in every likelihood act out dangerously, shoot someone, or be otherwise lethally dangerous."

"Would you recommend his release under any circumstances?"

"At the present time, I would say the chances of his acting out dangerously are about fifty-fifty. If he could, through extensive therapy, work through his problems with his parents, if he could stay away from his parents on the outside, and avoid any meaningful relationship with a woman, those chances might improve."

"And how likely is it that those conditions could be affected if he were released?"

"About as likely as a moth's not flying at a flame."

The next testimony set Taylor's case back even further. This doctor had appeared as an expert witness in approximately one thousand court matters of this kind, had personally examined nearly two hundred murderers and four to five hundred criminal sexual psychopaths. He spoke with great authority and conviction on the matter. Sociopaths, he said, are notorious liars; you can't safely believe anything they tell you. Despite his expressions of remorse, in fact, the evidence in this case suggests that Taylor has no conscience whatsoever, has undergone only superficial improvement in the hospital, continues to fear his own impulses, and would most likely repeat his past behavior if he were released.

"Can you categorically state," Taylor's attorney asked, "that after thirteen years in a mental hospital, the petitioner has no conscience whatsoever?"

"More accurately," the doctor said, "he has some conscience, and he lacks some conscience. But he believes fundamentally that the world was created for his benefit and pleasure. One cannot assume that such a person will act consistently in accordance with 'conscience.' "

"How does this interpretation of his character, Doctor, square with the fact that he has conducted himself so successfully on day release from the hospital?"

"You will recall, sir, that he assaulted at least three women while on day passes from the Lafayette Clinic. Besides, the key word here is 'consistently.' "

These impulses, the doctor explained, are not constant. Perhaps Taylor had not had violent impulses when he'd been away from the hospital on passes. Or perhaps he exerted limited control over himself on occasion because he wanted to be released. After all, his capacity to "con" people in authority had been amply demonstrated. But the psychiatrist concluded that Taylor could successfully maintain the appearance of sanity for only so long.

"Are there any circumstances under which you would agree to Mr. Taylor's release? Any restraints you would find acceptable?"

"Sure," the doctor said. "Handcuff a policeman to each wrist."

Looked at one way, Gary Taylor had an airtight case. No psychiatrist was going to say outright that Taylor was insane. Psychiatrists didn't even use that word much any more. Instead, Taylor had a character disorder. That's not a disease of the mind, so he was not insane, so he should have been released from the custody of the Department of Mental Health.

The law, however, is full of ambiguity in this area, and the judge had plenty of room for interpretation. The judge allowed that "the petitioner was not psychotic," but concluded that Taylor's "character disorder" was sufficiently dangerous to warrant his return to the hospital.

Admittedly, character disorders could not be "cured," as some "mental illnesses" could be. But according to the judge, a dangerous condition does not become less dangerous because it is not susceptible to treatment. The judge recognized degrees of "character disorder," some less dangerous than others. But whatever ambiguity existed in the complicated area between legal and medical definitions of "insanity," the statutes were clearly intended to protect society from potentially dangerous persons rather than to provide medical attention and care for the committed person. And it was not as if Gary Taylor had some minor neurotic quirk. In what amounted to a litany of Taylor's problems and abuses—extreme selfishness and narcissism, impulsiveness, lack of conscience, an inability to learn from experience—the judge had expressed clearly the danger Taylor posed.

By the end of his hearing in 1971, Gary Taylor was on his way back to the Forensic Center. But despite all the ambiguity his lawyers talked about, the law seemed quite clear on one score: the judge's decision was not irreversible. Michigan law gave the medical superintendent the statutory power to "discharge any patient whose discharge in the judgment of the superintendent shall not be detrimental to the public nor the patient because of mental disease." Dr. Ames Robey didn't think Taylor was insane in 1971; he didn't think Taylor had ever been insane.

Taylor was dangerous, Robey argued all along, only when he was drinking.

Robey was convinced that under controlled conditions, Taylor would get along fine in the world. So he worked out a plan by which Taylor would report back to the hospital on a regular basis, so they could make sure the drinking problem was regulated properly. And in July 1972, Robey sent Gary Taylor out into the world.

Almost immediately, Taylor entered into a "complicating relationship" with a woman. That same month he married his defense attorney's secretary, Helen Mueller.

He took a job with General Motors. For a time, he kept up with his regular visits to the hospital, where he received his medication and some continuing therapy. Sometime in the fall of 1973, before November, when he was first listed as missing, Taylor walked away from the responsibility, stopped taking his medication, stopped checking in at the hospital. Around that time, he bought a $40,000 brick home on a wooded lot in Loch Erin, an all-but-empty and secluded subdivision near Onsted, in Michigan's Irish Hills, the house where Taylor lived with his complicating wife, the house where Lee died.

I know that part of Michigan, where Gary Taylor settled, by heart. For several years when I was a child, I vacationed with my family at a little lake in the Irish Hills of Michigan, just north of Onsted, a lake with a mucky bottom. It was full of catfish, ugly as sin. We caught them with the ease of Eden, leaving our bamboo poles fixed to the dock overnight, the lines baited with fat crawlers and jammed with fish by morning. A few doors down from the cottage we rented, a natural spring emptied into a cement pool. People kept watermelons, too big for their refrigerators, cold there.

It has become my business, I've made it my business, to know what I can about Gary Taylor's life. I have heard his voice speaking from page after page of trial transcripts, not invented, but recreated in my mind. I have learned his Social Security number, his driver's license number, his birthday, his aliases, any distinguishing features or marks by which he might be recognized, anything I need to know to put myself in touch with the record he left behind him.

Despite everything I now know—perhaps because of it—one picture still threatens to overwhelm another. It must be like that for Jerry Smeenge and his wife Dee, their hopes superseded, their memories distorted, replaced, owned by this man they never knew, who still reaches into their dreams. They bought his house in the spring of 1975, came upon it by accident after they had already settled on another one, in Tecumseh. They were ready to close the deal, in fact, but arrived early for their appointment, decided to drive around the countryside for a while, killing time. One turn in the road led to another, and they found themselves pulling up at the house of their dreams.

They knew the minute they saw it. Loch Erin, the development was called. The Smeenges had never been to Ireland, but they imagined it must look just like this. The woods out back. A great yard all around where Jerry could play ball with the boys. A sparkling blue lake down the road. Fishing in the early summer, swimming when the dog days arrived, snowmobiling in the winter. It was a house for all seasons, Eden at a perfect price, the kind of place they might have imagined retiring to, and here they were owning it when Jerry was only thirty-six.

Naturally, they had some work to do on the place, but you had to expect that. The house hadn't been occupied for about a year, the realtor said, and the previous owner had left in something of a hurry. That probably reduced the price. The basement windows were all boarded up, and Jerry thought that a little odd. Maybe the guy had been into photography, or swinging parties. That could explain the strange little room in the basement, padded with extra insulation, like it had been soundproofed.

Whoever the last owner was, he didn't seem to know much about housekeeping or fixing things. Dee had noticed a strange odor in the basement, for which they couldn't determine a source, and the walls had all been painted over. And then there was that bizarre paneling in the bedroom, just kind of stuck up here and there, every which way, as if the owner didn't know what he was doing, or gave up before he'd barely begun.

When the weather turned warm in May, about a week after they'd moved in, Jerry and his wife began to think they'd bought somebody else's problems, a sewer backing up, or a bad septic tank, a drainage problem of some kind. Dee was home all day. She traced the smell to a spot outside their bedroom window.

"We had no idea it would be something like this," her husband told the reporter, whose story I read in the papers.

Now, driving east along Route 80 again, I imagine Jerry Smeenge standing at the picture window, looking out over the front yard, his fingers hooked through his belt loops. He sighs. He loves the neighborhood so much, and he knows now he'll have plenty of trouble convincing his wife to stay when it's all over. But it will never be over. It's not like he's having nightmares, but things like this go through your mind forever.

It is Thursday, May 22, 1975. Men from the Lenawee County Sheriff's Office and the state police have come into his yard with a backhoe. They had information from a lawyer in California that a bunch of bodies were buried in the yard. Later that afternoon, they unearth a shallow grave right under Jerry's bedroom window, pull out a garbage bag from a hole about two feet deep into the sandy soil. It contains the nude *bodies, severely decomposed, of two women, one bound in rope, the other in an electrical cord. One woman had been shot twice—a bullet destroyed her chin, and another found its mark between the eyes; the other woman had been shot once in the head, the bullet entering behind the ear. They send the bodies over to Bixby Hospital in Adrian to be identified. About that time, Dee packs up the kids and takes them to nearby Holland, where she will stay with her sister. She isn't going to sit around and let the children watch this horror show, she says. She wants them to sleep at night.*

Another bag, buried in a second hole, contains a couple of burnt and blood-stained sheets, home insulation material, locks and handcuffs, some women's clothes, a pair of cheap earrings, a slip of paper with the name Lelah Fletcher *written on it, and a library card issued to someone whose name is smudged and illegible. All that, and they are still digging. The sheriff says his information has it that at least two more bodies are buried somewhere on the property.*

The sheriff's men have been studying the basement pretty thoroughly, too. They find traces of blood and human flesh on the walls, under all that paint. The sheriff says it looks like there was some kind of torture chamber set up down there in a soundproof room.

Just west of Wilkes-Barre, where Route 80 meets up with Route 81, the even-numbered interstate with the odd, the traffic slows and finally stops. Several lanes are blocked off for construction, just where the merge is supposed to occur. Ahead of me and behind, as far as I can see in either direction, the cars line up. Tempers no doubt flare in the heat. Husbands scowl at their wives, mothers scold their children, acting boisterous in the back seat. No matter what day of the week I drive, the highways are jammed with cars.

Given the way we move around in this country, Taylor's house has probably had several occupants since the Smeenges decided they couldn't live with the memory of events they never witnessed, and left that house ten years ago. I have pictures from newspapers and a magazine to go by when I make my trip to Loch Erin in the summer of 1986. I try to find the house from the picture. A brick ranch with dark shutters. A big yard. A rail fence. The woods stopping short at the backyard. A stream beyond that. But over ten years have passed since the pictures were taken, pictures crowded with men bearing shovels, wearing bandana handkerchiefs over their mouths and noses. The neighborhood has changed with time. Then it was only a few houses scattered about, seven, to be exact, much of the land uncleared, the woods separating one neighbor from the next.

Now Loch Erin looks like any other subdivision. Brick ranches. Raised ranches. Aluminum-sided colonials. Wood and brick split levels. Many yards with rail fences. Yards big enough for barbecues in the summer, for snow angels in the winter. I cannot tell in 1986 which house would have cost $40,000 in 1973, which house would have been one of the originals.

I drive aimlessly up one street and down another, distinguished one from the next by their Irish names: Cork Road, Kerry Road, Killarney Lane. Dingle Drive. For a moment I think of the developers, laying out streets with a map of Ireland in front of them, reinventing a world they may never have seen, spinning a suburban landscape from a slim idea of its looking like someplace else. One of them has leprechauns, pots of gold, rainbows in his head.

And then I pass a house that might be the one, a brick ranch on a rise, back from the street whose name I've forgotten to notice. I imagine my way into the lives of strangers, an invasion of the privacy the suburbs were designed to protect, imagine my way into the lives of people who live in the house I'm not sure I've found.

With the first prospective buyers, the real estate agent likely took the man aside. "I feel it's my obligation to tell you," she said, "that two women were murdered in this house." And the information scared them away. But the next couple, or the next, or the next, conferred about it quietly, began to imagine how they could remake the house to rid it of its memories. They decided they wouldn't tell the children, but they could live with the house, make it their own.

The basement is now a rec room, a rumpus room, a den with highly polished pine paneling and wall-to-wall carpet. A bar stands at one end next to a pool table. A swag lamp, modeled vaguely after the set for The Sting, hovers above the table, sheds its light on the dark green felt. In a little room off to the back, a washer and dryer rumble through their cycles. The delicates, rescued from the heat, hang on a wooden drying rack nearby.

It's Saturday night, perhaps, and the basement fills up with the noise of teen-aged girls. They sculpt their hair with mousse and gel, arrange it into spikes and waves. They laugh raucously at dirty jokes they do not understand. In a corner, several of them practice the moon walk, the androgynous artifice of their dreams. Others work on their splits, or try to build a human pyramid. I wonder, though: perhaps it's not splits anymore, but contortions more complicated, elaborate aerobic routines in perfect synchrony. Perhaps they do not long for bulky wool sweaters and pleated skirts, but imagine competing for French-cut leotards and spandex leggings, showgirls sidelined by the game.

Sleeping bags are strewn around the floor, next to each one a backpack stuffed full of the necessities. Three of them have forgotten their toothbrushes. One girl has carried with her a pink vinyl case shaped like a hatbox. The picture of Barbie on the top, peeling off now, reminds her too much of childhood, and it embarrasses her.

It is getting close to midnight, and the mother brings down one last tub of popcorn. When you've finished with this, she says, I want you to put the lights out and go to sleep. The girls eye each other knowingly, and nod politely. Yes, Mother, they all say at once.

When the lights go out, the chatter subsides to a whisper. One girl falls asleep right away. She'll miss all the fun.

It starts, casually at first, rising out of the conversation, a story they've all heard before and never tire of hearing again. The one about the couple parked on lovers' lane, making out in the front seat, listening to the radio, hearing about some maniac who has escaped from the mental hospital. He has a hook for a hand.

The whispered tales end with shrieks and giggles, and once or twice the mother calls to them from upstairs to tell them to keep the noise down.

And then one takes up the story that will beat them all. "Did you know," she starts, "that a woman was murdered in this house?"

She bets all her friends a quarter that no one will be able to stay all night in the basement after she tells this story.

"It happened on a night just like this," she says.

One of her companions pulls the sleeping bag over her head.

"It happened in this very room," she says.

Another girl reaches across the circle to take her friend's hand.

Maybe the teller knows. Maybe when she first moved to town, the distinction gave her a kind of cachet on the playground ("See that girl? She lives in the murder house"). It's more likely she's never heard the truth, and she can tell the story anyway, because this is the kind of story they tell late at night when the lights are out, when they're spread out in their sleeping bags, like spokes in a wheel, their heads making a smaller circle in the center.

The story itself is short and grim, swift in its action, body separated violently from soul, a hand severed from an arm to get at a bracelet that wouldn't come off. She works hard to make it real, because to win her bet, the ghost story has to have the ring of truth, because the purpose of the telling is the haunting that comes afterwards, when the deed is done.

"And sometimes, late at night, her ghost wanders all over the house, looking for the missing part, calling out 'where's my hand?' " At first her voice is deep and low. And then she repeats the refrain, the pitch slightly higher, more plaintive this time. "Where's my hand?"

The teller reaches over to the girl lying beside her, and plays her fingers lightly on her friend's arm.

"Where's my hand?" she intones. The music now has the edge of desperation.

"Cut that out," the other girl says.

And then she reaches for the nape of another girl's neck, barely touching along the ruffle of her nightgown.

The girl shivers involuntarily. "I'm going upstairs," she says, and wraps her sleeping *bag around her shoulders. She gets halfway across the basement, halfway to the steps, and turns back to the group. "Somebody come with me."*

"Where's my hand?" the girl calls one more time.

"What was that?" another girl asks.

A noise outside the back door, a rustle in the bushes, a scuffling sound on the patio, a wheeze in the air, a creak in the steps, a footfall, a shudder in the window. Everyone goes quiet, even the teller of the tale, and they all listen attentively, waiting in dead silence for a confirmation of the sound.

"You've got it!" the teller shrieks suddenly, and her hand clutches at the nearest body she can find.

They all scream, and then they laugh, but by morning, the mother finds them all sharing sleeping bags, draped over furniture, pillowed in each others' arms in the living room upstairs, breathing evenly in their sleep. And over breakfast, the teller of the tale collects a quarter from every one of her friends.

From every one of them but me.

PART

FIVE

I pull into Poughkeepsie late in the day, my nerves on edge. From a distance down the road, through trees that are a little too green, a little too real this time of year, I see the thick stone chimneys that rise from the roof of my building. They take me by surprise and my breath catches. Every time I return to town after a long absence and a long drive, those chimneys trick me into pleasure at coming home. It's probably only relief I feel that the wheels of my car no longer spin underneath me. After twelve hours on the road, I can park it in the lot and shake the hum from my ears.

By the time I've lugged a few boxes to my second-floor apartment, I remember the chore of it. This is my life, I think, on my own.

But it is a privilege, too, this faculty apartment building, hard won by single women of another generation who taught at the college from its founding. They resented living in the dormitories with the students, serving as substitute mothers, when their male colleagues, who had wives and children of their own, lived in large, opulent houses across the road from the school. The separate space of this building, constructed at their demand on the leeward side of the street, told them that they mattered, as themselves.

Once I am settled into my apartment, the boxes stacked in corners, under the bed, behind the desk, my feet curled up under me on the sofa, I try to recover for myself the comfort and excitement of a place to call one's own. Here is the furniture, grown-up furniture, purchased slowly over the years according to my mother's sound advice ("Buy one good piece at a time," she said). A few antiques. A rug brought to me from Turkey. A china cupboard, inherited from my grandmother, filled with the compensations of my divorce. A collection of hand-blown paperweights, like those in my mother's house. An arrangement of silk flowers, not to my taste, but a gift from a lover I no longer see and want to remember fondly. Books and records my students examine furtively when I invite them to my home, as if they could know me from what I read, what I listen to. And they could be right. Perhaps they can know me by those visible signs as well as I now know myself.

I am not at home here, any more than I was in my mother's house. It isn't the memory of the wheels spinning under me, or the hum still in my ears, that displaces me. I have given over my life to ghosts in the closet, ghosts under the bed, ghosts in the basement, ghosts in the boxes I have carried with me all summer. I am a transient now in my own life, stopping over wherever I am, living only in the story I have to tell.

Maybe when the weather turns cold, here among my things, I'll feel at home in my own life. Perhaps this winter, I'll get firewood in again.

The next morning, early, I sneak over to the campus to collect several months worth of junk mail that has accumulated in my absence. The first-year students have started arriving. I will have to meet them eventually, mother them, perhaps, without meaning to, but for now I enjoy the anonymity, slipping among them on my way to the mail, unrecognized, unknown.

I have seen them all before. Fathers, short-sleeved and breathing hard, who rest for a moment on the tailgates, sigh, then load one more carton on the dolly. Mothers who begin to imagine rugs, curtains in their children's rooms, to make them look more like the homes they've left. Sons and daughters, who want to stay up late and drink too much and use their time unwisely; who want to make their own mistakes, look out their own windows, and want their parents to head back to Great Neck or Rochester, to Connecticut or Ohio or Tennessee, so they can start.

Later that afternoon, a daughter stands in the driveway, waving the station wagon off, squinting to see her mother's figure grow smaller and smaller. The hand flutters out the window and the familiar voice calls out last-minute advice and reassurance. She's only a baby, and so much can still go wrong.

Putting my things away that night, I struggle myself against the impulse to relax into the comfort of the sheltered space that endangers as it protects. In the odd floor plan of my apartment—a triangular bathroom, alcoves that were once closets, so many fireplaces, two main entrances, a kitchen long and narrow and clearly added on—I try to read the history of the place I call home.

My apartment was once three single rooms for single ladies, taken care of here and watched over, who trooped downstairs together at the sound of a dinner bell, ate meals in a common dining room cooked by someone else in a common kitchen, who shared baths at the end of the hall. They had to sign out in advance if they were to be absent for a meal. Someone would know if they were missing, and there must have been a comfort in that. But I suspect they also chafed against the discipline of their common life. They broke the rules when they had to, they lied for each other after lights out, they slipped out of their rooms in pairs on cool spring nights to look at the stars reflected in the lake behind the building, they scurried down the darkened halls late on winter evenings into someone else's room for tea and gossip and love.

This is what I'm doing now, imagining history from the distortions of a present floor plan, seeing my way into lives of women, like me and not like me, all of them one way or another on their own, Lee and the others who followed different paths to the same terrifying end.

Lee Snavely served a scant nine months of the one- to twenty-year sentence she'd received in March 1973, then popped out like a baby after her term in the womb, born again but not innocent, and ready to take on the world. The problem was where to go.

She exchanged letters with her brother Geoff about it, and he suggested that she share his place in Cleveland where they could make something like a home together. The idea appealed to Lee, but the parole board wouldn't hear of it, the two of them, hardly more than kids, looking out for each other.

Eric urged her to accept the more promising arrangement. His parents, still living in Bowling Green, had agreed to take responsibility for her. Knowledge of his parents' concern for him had helped Eric turn himself around, even in prison. He hoped they could provide the same solid ground for Lee.

She must have dreaded the prospect, being cooped up in yet another prison with a couple of fun-loving Baptists. But she went along with the plan, made for her by official people and willing hearts, because she didn't have much choice. On December 18, 1973, in time for the holidays, Lee was paroled, and the Fletchers waited in the visitors' room to take her home.

They turned northeast out of Marysville on Route 4, toward Marion, Ohio. Eric was in prison not fifty miles away, and he'd been looking forward to this particular visiting day.

Further north and west, where they headed eventually, Ohio was flat, like a headache, but this was the pretty part of the state. Millions of years ago, the glaciers made their way south, dredging out the Great Lakes, leveling everything in their advance, pushing the resisting land ahead of them, like a carpet nudged into folds. When the earth shifted again and the big thaw came, the ice melted back, leaving a line across the middle of what was now Ohio, the flatlands, rich brown soil that grew just about anything, to the north, and gently rolling hills, mining towns and auto plants, rivers, to the south. Now those hills were covered with a fine dust of early December snow.

Mr. Fletcher moved cautiously into the left lane to pass the Amish farmer in his buggy, loping along at the shoulder, and Mrs. Fletcher chatted on from the front seat of the car.

"We'll come back this way in a few days with Christmas presents," she said. "We thought you'd want to get him something yourself."

What do you get the man who has nothing? If she'd been on the ball, Lee might have made him an ashtray in the prison shop.

When they reached the visitors' room, the Fletchers insisted that Lee go in alone first. She was his wife. The two of them would have private things to share.

The guard looked over her pass casually, and disappeared behind a locked door. At the sight of Eric returning with him a few minutes later, her first look at him in nearly a year, Lee softened. She'd written him regularly, but it wasn't the same. He put his arms around her waist, and lifted her off the floor in his arms.

"You've put on weight," she said, when they'd taken seats at a small table in the corner.

"Good home cooking," he laughed. "I've been working out some."

"You look great," she said.

"You look tired," Eric said.

"I stopped plucking," she said.

Her eyebrows had thickened, a smear of dark paint closing in over her eyes.

"I know it's been a strain," Eric said. "But things are looking up, right?"

"Sure," Lee said.

"You got plans?" he asked.

"I'll be with your parents," she said, "until I'm on my feet again. I've got a parole officer in Toledo who's supposed to help me find a job."

"Doing what?"

Eric turned her wedding band around on her finger.

"I'll be out as early as next spring," he said. "We can do it right next time."

"Sure," Lee said. "I can hang on that long."

She reached across the table, brought his hands together between hers. She wanted to touch him some other way. She wanted to drop her head to the table and weep, but a stiffness between them, a fence she wasn't sure she could get over, startled her. And she resented it a little, that even now this stranger had such a claim on her soul.

"How did you manage to quit smoking," she said. "In here?"

By the time the Fletchers pulled into Bowling Green, the day was well into darkness. Red and silver tinsel wreaths circled the street lights downtown, and a garland of bright green spanned the intersection at the Four Corners.

"I'll take the long way home," Mr. Fletcher said, "so's you can see the way folks jazz up their houses at Christmas time."

"Some doctor out on Conneaut Road is competing with himself," Mrs. Fletcher said, "to see how many lights he can string up on his property. It's a sight."

The car wound through the northeast section of town, where the Fletchers lived, a block out of the way here, two blocks there. A sleigh and eight reindeer paraded through one front yard. Santa Claus waving mechanically from the seat. A crèche, life-size, showed in a spotlight on the courthouse lawn. In another yard, tiny white lights hung from the branches of spindly, leafless trees.

"It looks like God hung those lights on air," Mrs. Fletcher said.

For a time, the lights put Lee in the Christmas spirit. She tried to help around the house, to be patient and cheerful, to say please and thank you like no mother had taught her, to appreciate the Fletchers' efforts, to feel that she'd actually come home for the holidays. But it wasn't going to work. Soon, she bickered with her mother-in-law, looked for excuses to leave the house, paced about, restive, anxious, bored. When she stayed in, she sulked, resented having someone looking over her shoulder all the time, and made everybody nervous. She managed to hang on through one more visit to Eric, through Christmas Eve, then Christmas Day, then New Year's Day.

Just after the first of the year, the Fletchers notified Lee's parole officer, and told Eric, that Lee had made off with a little cash from the cookie jar. They didn't have any idea where she'd gone.

She went off in search of her future, which was taking its sweet time getting there.

On Friday, August 18, 1972, exactly a month after Gary Taylor was released to outpatient status from the Ypsilanti Forensic Center, Irene Waters pulled into her driveway, tired. When she reached the bottom of the stairs leading up to her second-floor apartment, she pulled the newspaper out of the box. It weighed a ton.

Mr. Nixon grinned up at her from the front page. REASON TO SMILE, the headline read. The Republican Party had agreed to the President's platform, and they were all gathering in Florida to confirm his nomination.

Irene resented all the attention the big politicians got. Just last week that poor woman had been murdered, dragged from the Thrifty Mart parking lot, strangled and stabbed and dumped in a ditch out near Hastings. Already that story was lost on the back pages of the *Journal.* She preferred reading local news herself. She'd lived in Lansing all her life, had gone to high school here, knew the town pretty well by now, and she'd gotten her information partly by keeping up with the local news. Lansing still seemed like a small town to her, even if it was the state capital.

Now this convention, nothing more than a chance for otherwise respectable grown-ups to act like kids on national television, whooping and hollering and carrying on, talking about the great state of this or that, carrying signs, throwing confetti. That, and a chance for advertisers to sell their products. And all that foolishness was going to preempt her favorite programs on TV.

Irene lived with her eighty-four-year-old mother in a quiet little apartment on Seymour Street. There wasn't much else to do at night except watch TV.

Irene dropped her purse inside the front door, and went in to check on her mother, her own pulse picking up speed as she walked. One of these days she'd come home and find her mother dead.

Now, she was napping in the back bedroom. Irene stood in the doorway a moment, watched her mother's thin chest move slightly with her breathing; then, calmed, she turned toward the kitchen to find something for their dinner. It was too hot to cook anything. But she could boil up that chicken for salad, serve it with a little fresh fruit and a green vegetable. Or there was the meatloaf left over from Wednesday. They could eat that cold.

She went back into the living room, kicked off her white nurses' shoes, and pulled her feet under her on the sofa. When she reached for the paper, her elbow bumped over the picture frame on the end table. She set it right, then looked for a moment into her own eyes looking back at her. That picture was almost forty years old, and her mother probably still thought of her that way, the smiling, eager high school graduate.

Irene had watched her brothers grow up, get married, move away to New York or California, where they raised families, had good jobs, homes of their own. With each year, until she reached middle age, she watched her own possibilities diminish a little. She'd done nothing in particular to reverse that trend, and now, she'd stopped watching altogether. This was her life, the dutiful daughter, fifty-eight years old, mothering her own mother in the little apartment they shared.

They passed the meal together that evening in the usual conversation, something like silence. How was work today? her mother asked. Fine, Irene said, same as every day. I like that Dr. Bassett, her mother said. Yes, he's very nice. You getting along any better with the nurse? her mother asked. We get along just fine, Irene said. I tell you, her mother said, you have to stand up for your rights down there. An office can't run without a good receptionist. You're the first person the patients see. Yes, Mother, Irene said.

After supper, Irene suggested they head to the Dairy Queen for dessert.

"There won't be anything on TV, anyway," Irene said.

"That Nixon," her mother said. "Don't you just know he's a crook?"

As I dress for bed myself, I feel my way even into her dreams. I see into Irene's life easily in that narrow apartment, simple, tasteful, a knickknack shelf in a corner somewhere, a coleus on the coffee table, pictures of her nieces and nephews scattered about, reminders of the life she never had for herself. She spends quiet evenings with her mother, watching television, reviewing the day, their conversations filled with the little resentments that rarely bubble over into anger anymore, the accommodations each of them makes to the other. From a newspaper article, simple and spare, the whole life emerges, and none of it on Irene's word. The newspaper took the story from her mother.

Irene went to bed early that night, well before eleven. She fell into a deep sleep, and dreamed she got mixed up in a noisy parade, confetti like snow, in the Thrifty Mart parking lot, and couldn't find her own car.

At 5:00 A.M., the telephone beside her bed rang. Irene jumped awake. Something had happened to her mother. By the second ring, her mother was standing in the doorway, and Irene realized foolishly that if something had happened to her mother, she'd be *making* a call, not getting one. She picked up the receiver.

"You the woman who works for the doctor?" a man's voice asked.

"Dr. Bassett. Yes." Irene was not quite awake yet, though her heart was racing with the fear of telephone calls in the dark.

"There's been a fire at the office," the man said.

"Oh, my goodness," Irene said. Had she remembered to turn off the coffeepot, she wondered.

"Nobody was hurt," the man said. "The fire department contained the damage."

"Well," Irene said.

"But the office is in pretty bad shape," the man said. "The doctor would like you to come down and help him sort through the papers."

"I'll be right there," Irene said.

She replaced the receiver. Her hand flew to the open neck of her nightgown and fluttered there.

"Oh, Mother, the most terrible thing," Irene said, and told her mother the story.

"Yes, but who was that?"

"Why, I didn't even ask him," Irene said.

"I didn't hear any sirens," Irene's mother said.

"The office is across town," Irene said. "You were sound asleep."

"I don't like it," her mother said. "You going out by yourself at this hour."

"Mother," Irene said. "I have to go. It's my job."

"That doctor better pay you for your time," her mother said.

Irene pulled on clothes that were convenient, brushed her teeth, grabbed her purse by the door, and hurried down the stairs. She crossed the alley to the garage, fumbling for her keys as she walked. When she reached the car, she managed to get the door unlocked, and threw her purse across the front seat. Just as she was about to climb in herself, someone with a knife grabbed her from behind and pulled her, screaming, back into the alley.

Her mother heard the screams from the apartment above. She threw on a housecoat and hurried down the stairs, still spry for her eighty-four years. When she reached the ground floor, she looked out, saw nothing but the earliest light of day. By the time she found her way to the backyard, her daughter was dead.

All the neighbors heard Irene's screams, too, and as soon as the commotion started, lights came on in most of the houses on the block. Right away, telephone calls lit up the police switchboard. Somebody's trying to kill a woman out here, the neighbors said.

By the time the police arrived a few minutes later, people had gathered in the driveway. A few of the older women tried to comfort Mrs. Waters. Others were eager to talk to the police, to tell them what they saw. One witness saw a man disappear down the alley. Several others had gotten a good look at him.

"He was wearing a trench coat," one said. "Gray, I think."

"No, it was green," another said.

But surprisingly, for the hour and the rudeness of the awakening, the witnesses agreed on most of the details. The man they saw was white, in his mid-thirties. He was well built, fairly tall, about six feet. He had dark brown hair receding from a broad forehead. And he wore heavy, dark-framed glasses. Police Lieutenant Robert Brown made a composite drawing of the man from the witnesses' description.

The killing of Irene Waters appeared completely motiveless. No suspect could ever be identified, except the man in the composite drawing, who didn't look like anyone Irene knew.

Irene's mother was certain of that. "No, no," she said. "I can't think of anyone who would want to hurt my Irene."

I sit up late in my bed, a beautiful four-poster canopy my mother made for me, and compare the pictures once again, the composite drawing with a photograph of Taylor taken about two years later. I see the same oval face. The same dark eyes. The same set of the mouth, slightly off center, like a pout. The Adam's apple shows distinctly in both necks. Both men have dark hair, broad foreheads, a receding hairline. Both men wear heavy, dark-framed glasses, the only difference between them the style, which might well have changed in two years. In the summer of 1972, when Irene Waters was killed, Gary

Taylor, six feet tall, was thirty-six years old. He lived somewhere near Ypsilanti, less than an hour's drive from Lansing.

If he did not actually know her from a visit to Dr. Bassett's office, from a casual conversation on the bus, or from a more complicated acquaintance, Irene Waters's killer must have planned the murder, at least learned his victim's name, watched her go to and from work, found a telephone booth in advance near her apartment. Admittedly, Taylor usually encountered his victims by chance, walking along a street, the first woman he came to once his rage or sense of insult took hold. At the same time, Taylor's history reveals his capacity for obsessive fascination with victims he imagined, his playing over the possibilities in his mind like a broken record, a futile effort to control himself during the lag between the conception and the act. The same kind of obsession might have attached itself to a real woman, probably about his mother's age. And at least once before, he acted with considerable premeditation, inventing a story over the telephone in order to gain access to one of his victims, the woman he assaulted in 1961, on day release from the Lafayette Clinic in Detroit.

He had never committed murder before, but that history had to begin somewhere.

Gary Taylor was never charged in the killing of Irene Waters, nor in the case of Mrs. Betty Goodrich, strangled and stabbed the week before. Initially, at least, the police didn't think the two cases were related. Three years later, in 1975, Taylor's picture appeared in the Detroit papers after two women's bodies were discovered buried in Jerry Smeenge's backyard in Onsted, Michigan, and then the Lansing police suggested his possible connection with these deaths.

I set the folder aside, in the nightstand drawer, set the alarm for early in the morning, and snap out the light. Why, I wonder, as I settle under the sheet, do I not have nightmares about that face?

The devil doesn't have a face. There's only the lie he leaves behind. What you don't know won't hurt you. What you ignore goes away.

I stumble to my coffee the next morning, a long walk from my bedroom after the alarm wakes me too early, and once I am clear-headed, I spend a few hours getting reacquainted with my apartment. I always know it better after I've had to look for something, this morning, a photograph from Weegee's New York, Evans's Appalachia, one of Cartier-Bresson's wars, something implicitly narrative, something real I can give my students for their first writing assignment of the term. Maybe I'm the kind of teacher a mother worries about. But it's good exercise for them: from a true picture, they can imagine a plot, if they're not still too soft in the brain.

I've come to much of my story, what I can't know or didn't observe myself, through photographs, which I have learned to read, imaginatively, like a text. A photograph is the next best thing to being there, and the next best thing to a photograph is a good description of one. I have one photograph of Sandra Horwath from the Ann Arbor paper, but I have not seen the other picture, the one the police officer described, because it is buried in an evidentiary file to which the ordinary citizen has no access. Engaged no doubt by a theory of his own, the detective described the picture in detail for the reporters, who took the details down and recorded them in the newspaper for me to read.

The two women in the picture worked together briefly in the same real estate office in Ann Arbor, Michigan. They both had long brown hair, full around their faces, fair skin, dark eyes, fine, pretty features. In fact, as the police detective later pointed out, they looked enough alike to have been sisters.

I don't know how sharp or practiced that detective's eye is. Perhaps all women look alike to him. Perhaps Sandra Horwath and Gary Taylor's wife resembled each other like sisters. It is enough for me to feel in Sandra Horwath's features, the long, dark hair, the fair skin, the dark eyes, the shock of her resemblance to Lee.

He has seen the picture of them together, these uncanny lookalikes, Sandra Horwath and Gary Taylor's wife. They smile happily for the camera. The picture was taken shortly before Taylor married, and before he tied that knot, Sandra, divorced, the mother of three children, working hard to make it on her own, had gone out with him a few times herself.

On Monday, October 1, 1973, Sandra Horwath put her kids to bed about ten. One of the children remembered that, because the hour was later than usual. She was sitting in the living room of her apartment, reading a magazine and waiting for Johnny Carson to come on, when the telephone rang. Another child thinks she remembers that, though given the noise of the television, the telephone might have been a dream.

The newspapers put it this way: the house showed no sign of disturbance, the door locked tight, no windows broken or locks jimmied, no lamps overturned, no magazines strewn across the floor. Her car was left, untouched, where she always parked it. The kids were asleep upstairs. So it must have been something like this:

The phone rings. A voice on the other end of the line, a voice Sandra knows, or remembers and trusts, announces an emergency of some kind, asks her to come, promises it won't take long. She is no doubt reluctant at first, but what else can you do when a friend needs you, when someone you know calls and says come? She grabs her purse and her sweater, locks the door carefully behind her, and stands by the curb, where her own car is parked and locked, to wait for her ride.

She hates going off and leaving the kids alone, but you can't get a sitter on such short notice at this hour, and besides, the kids are sleeping. They sleep soundly now, all through the night, if she keeps them up late enough. The voice on the other end of the telephone line said she won't be away long, an hour at the most. She'll be back before the kids miss her.

A car rounds the corner onto Braeburn Circle, a car she recognizes, just about the time she convinces herself that the kids won't even know she's gone out.

But Sandra Horwath doesn't come home that night, or the next, or the next. A year and a half later, workers in bandana face masks hired by the Lenawee County Sheriff's office will tear up Jerry Smeenge's backyard looking for her, but her body is never found.

Four months after Sandra Horwath disappeared, in January 1974, Lee ran off from the Fletchers' care, but she didn't go far. She settled herself into an apartment on East Broadway in Toledo, Ohio, an hour's drive from Ann Arbor, her old haunts, the seedy bars and street corners a few blocks off.

She might have liked to have gone further. From her rooms on the edge of the city, overlooking the river, she tried to imagine Canada. All she could see she got from the movies. Men wrapped in bearskins, their horses trudging along through endless expanses of snow. Nelson Eddy and Jeanette MacDonald calling *"you-oo-oo-oo-oo-oo-oo"* over the gape of a canyon. Indians and snowshoes and people speaking French. A bunch of phony Technicolor postcards of places where people couldn't possibly live.

Of course that wasn't right. There were cities in Canada, people living in apartment buildings and going to work like everywhere else in the world.

Lee had done just about everything, but she'd never been anywhere. She didn't have a passport, and now that she was a convicted felon on parole, she couldn't get one. Distances had closed in on her. She couldn't see more than a few blocks at a time. When she tried to picture Canada, she couldn't get past Windsor, Ontario, and it looked just like Detroit.

For the time being, she needed the familiar space of a small apartment in a neighborhood she had some experience with. She was too tired to imagine another life for herself just now. But one of these days, she told herself, she'd take off.

For starters, Lee cut herself off from people she'd known in her life before. She let Eric know where she was, because he would have worried, and might have tried to find her, even though he wouldn't have much chance of it from prison, unless he sent his parents after her. She didn't want calls from his parents, and insisted to Eric that she was all right, doing just fine on her own. She sent her brother Geoff her address, and wrote him occasionally. She put the rest behind her and was ready to make new friends. She knew how to do that: you go to bars.

She had her probation officer to check in with, resented the regularity of that, having to show up for her appointments. If she wasn't careful, he could make trouble for her. But she could handle that, at least for a while, and when she couldn't take it anymore, she could slip through a crack in the world, lose herself in a vast country full of women on their own, people starting over, and nobody would miss her for a good while.

In the meantime, late in January of 1974, Lee found a runaway to keep her company, a seventeen-year-old girl she rescued from the streets. Now there were two of them, on their own together, sharing her little apartment, looking out for each other, waiting for whatever came their way.

I find the photograph I've been looking for all morning, Weegee's record of the death of a gambler in a Brooklyn street. You do not see the body in the picture. You read its presence in the faces of the children gathered to look.

This is a man who lived by his nickname. They called him Weegee, and it stuck, became his signature, a transliteration of Ouija, the magical board that vibrates with the mysteries of the future. An uncanny instinct, like vision, led him to scenes of violence in the streets of New York in the forties, almost before the incidents occurred. The police took to following him around, convinced that where Weegee went, something horrible was bound to happen. Some of them thought it more logical to assume Weegee himself an accomplice, who would do anything for his art, who arranged the crimes in advance so he could get the pictures that would make him famous.

I look now at the faces of the children before me. One winces at what she sees, another grins like a monkey at the camera, indifferent to everything but the show he creates. The adult face in the middle of the picture collapses into tears. Learned, imitated from the violence they witness, violence has already erupted among them. A bare arm, connected to a body I cannot find in the crowd, cuts horizontally across the picture, the fist reaching out to yank on a girl's hair, or to shove a boy from his place. Other hands, tough and restraining, reach into the confusion, eager to stop what will soon be a fight. A woman in the picture, a mother perhaps, looks on with a scold in her face.

But in the back, a boy cranes his neck, stretches as tall as he can make himself, greedy to see over the heads of the children in front of him, oblivious to the camera, oblivious to the melee in his midst, his eyes fixed on the street, on the body I cannot see.

I read the future in these faces. This one will have nightmares for weeks. That one will meet a similar end, perhaps, on a neighborhood street. This one will sit, steady and calm, in the basement, until the ghost story comes to an end. He has learned already there are no bargains to be had. He'll make no deals with the devil. He won't trade away truth, he won't give up knowing, for safety, or pleasure, or comfort, his own or someone else's. Weegee is his hero. He'll take pictures of his own one day.

My mother's voice sounds in my head. "What is this morbid fascination? Why do you want to look?" And I think of Lee, who did so much and saw so little, who, trapped by anger or sorrow or blame, blinded, finally, to her own possibilities, couldn't imagine herself out of the life imposed on her; who tried to see Canada, and decided it looked like Detroit.

I wonder: which one in the picture is she?

Throughout 1973, Gary Taylor had been living in southern Michigan, working erratically at the GM plant, frequenting bars in nearby Toledo, Ohio. In the spring of 1974, he abruptly left his house in Onsted, and moved to Washington State. Perhaps he thought he could lose himself there, live as he pleased, where the newspaper accounts of "Ted" provided a cover.

For about a year now, over the course of 1973 and into 1974, the city of Seattle had been terrorized by a wily killer whose victims were all young women. Some of them had disappeared without a trace, one a young woman who shared an apartment in Burien, the South Seattle suburb where Vonnie Stuth lived with her new husband Todd. As recently as July, two women had apparently been abducted from Lake Sammamish State Park by a man witnesses identified as "Ted." The newspapers domesticated him, turned him into a sportsman, a fisherman who trailed a baited line behind his lazy boat. "Ted the Troller," the papers called him, and they ran pictures of his handsome face on the front page.

In early September, the remains of several bodies were unearthed a few miles away from the state park. By October 1974 it had been almost three months without a killing or disappearance, and things were beginning to calm down.

At 10:20 P.M. on November 27, 1974, the telephone in the kitchen rang. Vonnie Stuth was in the middle of making her holiday salad, a favorite from her childhood, cream cheese balls rolled in chopped walnuts, floated in lime Jell-O. She appreciated the chore, now that her husband was working the night shift, and the evenings were long and boring.

Her mother still insisted on fixing the turkey and the stuffing and the mashed potatoes herself, the most work at the last minute, and it was the least she could do, to bring the salad. The girls had trouble getting their mother to stop doing everything, even though they were all married themselves now.

It was her sister Alicia on the phone. Alicia was bringing candied yams.

"What can I call this salad?" Vonnie asked.

"Why do you have to call it anything? We're just going to eat it."

"It ought to have a name, something with 'pearls' in it, maybe."

Her mother had always called it cream cheese balls in lime Jell-O.

"That's pretty," Alicia says. "But you don't want it confused with tapioca."

"Can you hang on a minute?" Vonnie said. "I think there's someone at the door."

The television was on in the other room. She wasn't sure she'd heard a knock.

"Don't open the door to a stranger," Alicia said.

Over the course of these months, women had learned caution, and they weren't going to set it by yet.

When Vonnie looked through the window, she saw the dark-rimmed glasses, the broad forehead, and the sweep of brown hair she recognized as a man from the neighborhood. She opened the door a crack, but kept the chain on.

"What was that all about?" Alicia asked when her sister returned to the phone.

"The guy from across the street has a stray puppy he thought we'd be interested in."

"Will Todd let you have a dog?"

"I'm home alone so much. I'd have plenty of time to train it and everything."

"They are a lot of company," Alicia said, encouraging.

"I told him I'd have to ask my husband. He said he'd come back later, tomorrow maybe."

Vonnie was watching the eleven o'clock news, waiting for the salad to congeal so she could fold in the cream cheese pearls, when the man came back to the door.

"I have that puppy in my van right now," he said. "You want to have a look?"

"I know," Vonnie said. "You think I'll fall in love with it before I check with my husband."

"You girls are so soft-hearted," he said.

"Just a minute," she said. "I'll get my coat."

She grabbed her gray jacket, the one with the torn pocket. She'd dropped Todd plenty of hints that she wanted a new one for Christmas.

Todd came home from the foundry, tired, shortly after 1:00 A.M. The front door was unlocked, the television was still on, cream cheese balls softened against waxed paper, and the Jell-O had gone stiff in the refrigerator. Vonnie wasn't there, and Todd called the police.

"She never goes off without her purse," Todd said. "Her cigarettes are in her purse."

"How long have you two been married?" the officer asked.

"A little over six months."

"You have a fight maybe, earlier today?"

"We don't have fights," Todd said.

"These young wives, they get crazy notions. Walk off in the middle of the night for reasons unbeknownst to us men. I remember once my wife . . ."

"Vonnie wouldn't have gone to the mailbox by herself after dark. Not these days."

"Now, don't panic," the officer said, back to his immediate duties. "That kook is probably locked up somewhere. You check around, call us back in an hour if your wife don't turn up."

Todd called his in-laws, Ken and Lola. They hadn't seen their daughter, and worried with him. He woke up several of her friends. He called the Youth Service Center where she volunteered a couple of times a week, thinking maybe some teenager had a heartbreak and Vonnie went to fix it. That would have been just like her, though he was sure she would have left a note.

About 3:30 A.M. he called the police again. He went through the whole story, and the officer wrote everything down.

"It's probably nothing to worry about," the policeman said. "No signs of forced entry, no signs of violence."

"Yeah, well, there haven't been any signs of violence when all those other girls disappeared either."

Most of them had disappeared from public places, and a few had vanished as if into thin air. No sign of struggle, no fingerprints on air.

The police station sent an officer around on Thanksgiving morning, and a detective the next day. Todd gave them all the same details: she was wearing her blue swabbies, he said, and a work shirt, probably. Ankle-length boots, fashionable that fall, but sensible. She didn't have any identification on her, and she couldn't have had much cash, since she left her wallet full of the household money, about $150, at home. Vonnie was nineteen years old, five feet six, had golden-blond hair and hazel eyes. Todd had plenty of copies of her high school graduation picture, not much more than a year old.

"You guys watch it that you don't futz around until it's too late," Todd said.

He waited through the weekend. Sergeant Leonard returned his call on Sunday evening, and showed up at the house shortly thereafter.

He assured Todd that they were working on it. A neighbor had seen the van at the house, and the police were checking vehicle registrations. They examined the house across the street where the man who owned the van lived. Had lived, they discovered. The house had recently been vacated, emptied out except for a few desk drawers. There they found photographs of nude women contorted into impossible positions, some of them believed to have been the man's wife.

Todd Stuth sat in the police station for four hours on Monday. His boss at the foundry had given him time off to devote to finding his wife. When he wasn't at the police station, he sat at home, playing chess, imagining the moves his wife would make if she were there. For weeks, then months, Todd waited and the local police worked.

By early December, the police had traced the Stuths' former neighbor to his next residence, a house near Enumclaw, south of the Seattle area. It was a pretty piece of property, a bit isolated, a creek running behind the house. The detective nosed around a while, but they didn't find anything suspicious. Still, they wanted to talk to the owner. On Friday, December 6, a week after the detective had made the first full report of the missing woman, a policeman knocked on Gary Taylor's door.

Taylor accompanied the officer to the station downtown. They wanted to ask him some questions, routine, they said. Taylor chatted comfortably in the car, but once they got to the station and Detective Bailey let Taylor know he was under suspicion for murder, advised Taylor fully of his rights, the man clammed up.

"I'm allowed a lawyer here," he said.

"We're not charging you with any crime yet," the detective said. "We just want to ask some questions."

"I'm not telling you anything without a lawyer here. You got any evidence of a crime?"

"No physical evidence, no," Bailey said. "But the girl's been missing a week. With all these other murders in the area, we need to check any lead."

"Well," Taylor said.

"You ever seen her before?" Bailey set Vonnie Stuth's picture out on the table.

"I might, I might not. I told you I'm not saying anything."

The officer knew he couldn't hold the guy without some specific evidence of a crime, but he didn't much like Taylor's looks, thought he seemed nervous, and wanted to get some information out of him.

"Would you be willing to come back tomorrow, Mr. Taylor, for a polygraph test?"

Taylor leaned into the back of his chair, pushed the two front legs off the floor.

"Sure," he said. "I can do that."

They set up the appointment for the next morning at ten.

That afternoon, the King County authorities ran Taylor's name through the national crime computer. It turned up no information.

Meanwhile, Taylor consulted with Peter Berzins of the Public Defender's Office, and the next morning he failed to show for the polygraph. When the police went by his house to bring him in, the place was empty and the van gone.

Todd Stuth was first disappointed, then angry. Detective Bailey explained that they couldn't hold the man, because they didn't have any clear evidence against him, and besides, when they checked, the computer came up empty.

"Computers," Todd said. "What do they know?"

"Computers keep track of these things," the detective said.

On January 3, 1975, Lieutenant Richard Kraske, of the King County Sheriff's Office, received a telephone call from authorities in Michigan who wished to issue an "escape complaint" against Gary Taylor. He hadn't broken out of jail, but he'd walked away from a convalescent leave at the Ypsilanti Forensic Center in the fall of 1973, a little over a year before. The State of Michigan started listing him as "officially" missing a full year after he walked, on November 6, 1974, a few weeks before Vonnie Smith disappeared, on November 27. They hadn't entered his name in the national crime computer until shortly after Christmas. Some kind of clerical oversight, they said.

By mid-January 1975, police across the country launched a nationwide search for Taylor. Seattle police checked the area around Taylor's former home for possible grave sites, and found nothing. They located his parents, living in Tucson, Arizona, and Taylor's wife was there, getting a grip on herself since she and her husband had started having trouble the previous fall. They also found his car, a '73 Chrysler, and his dog, a boxer, but they couldn't put their hands on the man himself. By late January, friends and neighbors of Vonnie's family started a fund to help defray the cost of a private investigation, hiring Sal Dena to help find her. Todd had been laid off from work at the foundry, cutbacks all over, and was drawing unemployment.

On Valentine's Day, 1975, Sal Dena located Gary Taylor's van in Portland, Oregon, abandoned and repossessed. Police were scouring it for clues, but they still had no trace of Taylor himself. Later that month, police in Aspen, Colorado, started asking questions about Taylor in connection with the murder of a Michigan woman, Caryn Campbell, whose body was found buried in the snow along the slopes. She had disappeared in mid-January 1975. On March 15 of that year, Julie

Cunningham, a ski instructor at Vail, also disappeared, and police thought Taylor might be involved in that one, too. After the computer foul-up, somebody had been doing his homework. Somebody had heard about Taylor's murderous fascination with women skiers.

Caryn Campbell had not been shot with a high-powered rifle. She was killed by blows to the head with a blunt instrument. Ted Bundy, the "Ted" whose picture had appeared in the Seattle papers, was eventually charged with her murder. Julie Cunningham's body was never found.

On April 25, Seattle papers ran a photograph of Todd Stuth, his long hair cut squarely across his eyebrows, his mustache drooping at the corners of his mouth. He looks sadly at the top tier of his wedding cake, frozen and held back in his mother-in-law's freezer to have for dessert on their first anniversary. The plastic bride holds the coattails of the plastic groom, grinning like he was about to get away with something.

C. A. Rosenquest remembered him as an intelligent man who kept to himself mostly, didn't mess with the neighbors.

That's what they always say when television reporters, eager for a story, thrust microphones in their faces. "He was such a nice boy, quiet, polite, kept to himself mostly. Who'd have thought he could do something like this?"

Rosenquest's tenant, a man about forty, had come by on the evening of April 23, 1975, on some business about the duplex he rented, a leaking faucet, a loose tile in the bathroom, a closet door warped so it wouldn't close. The landlord said he'd take care of the problem. The tenant didn't seem the least bit distressed.

Earlier that day, however, a few hours before Taylor dropped in on his landlord, Diana Shuler had stumbled into a phone booth on the other side of Houston and called the police.

"Come get me right away," she said. "A man raped me. I'm afraid he'll come back."

Later, down at the office of the City Homicide Unit of the Houston Police, which also handled cases of sexual assault, Diana told her story.

"When he finished with me," she said, "he fell asleep, and I snuck out."

Falling asleep had been his second mistake.

"He told me he'd kill me if I didn't," she said. "He had a gun."

"Could you identify the man?" the police officer asked.

"Yes," Diana said. "Sure."

Diana Shuler was sixteen years old, still legally a child herself by Texas law, and she was pregnant. The man picked her up in a two-tone '73 Chrysler and drove her to a motel, where he wrote down his license plate num-

ber, NMC 553, from the State of Michigan, on the registration form.
That was his first mistake.

Detectives at the Homicide Unit of the Houston Police checked out
the vehicle registration. The car belonged to Gary Addison Taylor, once
of Michigan, more recently of parts unknown.

The description Diana Shuler provided of her assailant—a man
about six feet tall, weighing two hundred pounds, with brown hair going
gray, hazel eyes, a broad forehead, and heavy, dark-rimmed glasses—
matched the pictures created by several other Houston women who had
been sexually assaulted in the past month. In early March, Carla Baird,
an apartment house manager, had been forced under threat of death or
bodily injury to fellate a man fitting that description, and had reported
the incident immediately. A little over a week later, Paula Tunning, who
also managed an apartment house, had filed a similar charge. On the
same day, Irma Hobbs had narrowly escaped being raped. Yet another
woman had filed a complaint of aggravated sexual assault. By May 1,
three of the five women, including Diana Shuler, had identified Taylor's
picture in a photographic line-up, and a warrant was issued for his arrest.

By this time, the computers had gotten it straight. Since January,
Taylor had been listed as escaped from a Michigan mental hospital, a
known sex offender.

*They didn't know about the killings yet. And to me, reading this record in the Harris
County files, it seems oddly regressive, a reversion to an older mode. They calmed him,
perhaps, after the blood, these acts of aggravated assault, torments of their own kind, to
be sure, but much less final than death.*

The Texas authorities didn't find him right away. Once Diana Shuler
left the motel room, Taylor knew better than to keep regular hours at
his job or his duplex. Instead, he hid out, went itinerant, and Texas was
a big state. That's what they used to do in the old days. Lawmen wrote
GTT across the wanted posters of outlaws they'd lost track of: Gone
to Texas.

Taylor may have taken himself as far as Sherman, a small town near
the Oklahoma border, about three hundred miles north of Houston. On
the night of May 16, along Route 75, a gunman took aim from an
overpass, and fired shots at the tires and windows of buses and trucks
going by underneath him. He kept up the attacks for about two hours,
and then disappeared before police could apprehend him. A phantom,

with a very solid .22 caliber rifle. In one incident, a fifteen-year-old girl, a passenger in a bus, was injured slightly when fragmenting bullets or glass struck her behind the ear.

By the end of May, authorities in Sherman knew Taylor had been absent from his job in Houston during the week of the sniping attacks, and, knowing enough about his history to be suspicious, they wanted to ask the man some questions.

By the end of May, they had to wait in line.

On May 20, at 3:00 A.M., Gary Taylor was arrested back in Houston, driving his Michigan car to work. The arresting officers pulled the car over, approached it cautiously, with a gun. Taylor had been listed as armed and dangerous. He got out, rattled and confused. The officers searched the car on probable cause, and found a .22 caliber rifle in the trunk. Officer R. L. LoBue read Taylor his Miranda rights, and that seemed to calm him down.

He read over the warrants briefly, and returned them to the detective.

"Do you understand why you're being arrested?" Detective Ray Trimble asked.

"Yes," Taylor said.

"Well, then, let's go."

They then took him down to the Houston City Jail, where he was booked on five counts representing three separate charges of rape, attempted rape, and aggravated sexual assault. He had $359 and small change in his pockets.

Six hours after his arrest, at 9:00 A.M., May 20, Gary Taylor appeared before Judge Michael Breen for the judicial warning required by Texas law. The judge reviewed the charges for Taylor, and asked if he had any questions.

"I have a right to an attorney," Taylor said. "I want to see somebody from the Public Defender's Office."

"We don't have public defenders here," the judge explained. "But if you can't afford your own lawyer, the court will appoint one for you."

"How am I going to find a lawyer?" Taylor asked.

"The officers will allow you free access to the telephone. You can call the Lawyer Referral Service."

The judge also reminded him that he needn't say anything at all about the cases under investigation, or his part in them, without having an attorney present.

Back at the city jail, Taylor made several telephone calls, among them to the Legal Referral Service and the Houston Legal Foundation Judge Breen had suggested. He probably called his parents, then living in Tucson, Arizona, and his estranged wife, Helen Mueller Taylor, in San Diego.

With the legal services office, Taylor was brisk and peremptory.

"They got me down here on some cracked-up rape charges," he said. "I'm broke and I need a lawyer."

The person on the other end asked a few questions.

"I want somebody to get me a writ to get me out of jail," Taylor said. "And I want a lawyer to come for the show-up."

When he'd hung up the phone, he turned to the officer watching over him.

"You got a cigarette?" he said.

"Anything you want, buddy," the officer said.

The next morning, Wednesday, May 21, at approximately ten o'clock, Detectives Maddox and Garner, of the Harris County Sheriff's Office, checked Taylor out of the city jail and transported him to the homicide office. They wanted to take some full-length photographs of the suspect, and they may also have asked him some questions. In late March, Suzanne Jackson, a topless go-go dancer who worked in a roadside bar beyond the Houston city limits, had been killed, shot through the head. Taylor was their best suspect.

"Sure," Garner recalled Taylor saying. "Anytime a girl gets killed, somebody comes knocking on my door." The statement may have been in response to a question, or it may have been volunteered. Garner couldn't remember for sure. Taylor tended to get caught up in his own story, and couldn't stop talking. That afternoon, however, Taylor refused the opportunity to use the telephone when it was offered to him.

At about the same time that morning, Detective Carol Stephenson, of the City Homicide Unit, was, in fact, knocking on Taylor's door. Having obtained the proper search warrants, she went to poke around Taylor's apartment. A thirteen-year veteran of the force, Detective Stephenson was in charge of the investigations of the rape and sexual assaults for which Taylor had been arrested. She didn't know that Taylor was a suspect in a murder case, as well. She worked in the city unit. The murder was under the jurisdiction of unincorporated Harris County.

Among Taylor's possessions, Stephenson found copies of *The Portable Nietzsche*, dog-eared and heavily underlined, and Camus's *The Rebel: An Essay on Man in Revolt*. Scribbled commentary in pencil littered the margins. Under the phrase "absolute nihilism," two penciled lines, and a note in the near margin: "absolute indifference to life, permitting suicide and logical murder." At another point, Stephenson read: "The unity of the world, which was not achieved with God, will henceforth be attempted in defiance of God."

The night of May 20, 1975, Helen Taylor didn't sleep much. Gary had been arrested in Houston on rape and assault charges, and she was beginning to put things together. She'd been living scared for a long time now. She felt a little safer with Gary behind bars and so many miles away, but she knew as well there was something she had to do, and she didn't quite know how to do it. She called in sick at work the next morning, May 21, spent a couple of hours pacing around in her apartment, and finally picked up the phone to call Frederick A. Meiser, a lawyer who'd been recommended by a friend.

"I think I need a lawyer," she said.

"What's the problem?" Meiser asked.

"Well, I think my husband—actually we're separated, we've been living apart since last fall—but I think my husband murdered a bunch of people. And I think I knew about it."

"Why don't you come down to the office, and we'll talk," Meiser said.

She made the appointment for later that afternoon. She was anxious to get all this off her chest. She dressed carefully, something simple and understated. She'd had her share of working around lawyers, and knew what made the right kind of impression. She arrived promptly at Meiser's office, somewhat harried by the California traffic, which she never would get used to, but ready to tell her story.

"Why don't you begin at the beginning," Meiser suggested.

Helen rehearsed the whole sorry business, how she'd known Taylor through the lawyer for whom she worked, the lawyer who had represented him back in 1967, how she felt she knew the man better than the facts did, or at least knew him differently. He'd been good to her at first, polite, gentle. She just couldn't believe all those things other people said about him, the crazy things.

Besides, she said, a man can change—sick people can get better. He was smart, fun, exciting.

"The doctors said he'd be fine," she said, "as long as he took his medicine."

"When did you start to suspect things were going bad?" Meiser asked.

"I'm not sure I ever did, really," Helen said. "At least not until he got arrested in Seattle. That was when I left."

"And there'd been no trouble before then?"

"Well, he had started drinking again, used to come home loud and obnoxious sometimes."

"When was that?"

"The winter of '74," she said. "About the time we moved to a house in Onsted. We didn't live there long, only a few months. January, February, March, maybe. Gary was into real estate. Liked to buy and sell, move around a lot."

"What happened there?" the lawyer asked.

"I came home one night, kind of late, and he was drunk. I'd never seen him so bad. I asked him what was going on, and he said he'd had a party. He said he'd killed a bunch of people in the basement, and buried them in the backyard. Just like that, 'I killed a bunch of people in the basement and buried them in the backyard.' "

"And you did nothing about it?"

"I thought he was putting me on, all talk. Gary's a big talker. Or maybe he was trying to scare me, I don't know. I put it out of my mind. I started to get a little scared when we up and moved so quickly after that. But like I said, Gary was into real estate."

"Do you know who these people might have been?"

"He said three women and a man. I don't have any idea who the women were, and the only man he ever mentioned was somebody he worked with at the GM plant. Bill Parks, Bill Parker, something like that."

By this time, Helen was frantically searching her pocketbook for a Kleenex. Meiser pulled one from the box on his desk and walked around to Helen's chair to give it to her.

"They'll think it was my fault," she said.

"You were afraid for your own life," Meiser said.

She dabbed at her eyes with the tissue, and her shoulders jerked involuntarily.

"I'll call the authorities in Michigan," he said, "once I've taken down all your information, dates, places, as well as you can remember them."

"What if they put me in jail?" she said.

"They won't," the lawyer said. "It may not be anything at all, like you first thought. But it's best to check these things out. And you won't have to say anything to anybody. I'll do the talking."

Helen Taylor felt relieved. She went back over her information with Meiser, then stood to leave. He shook her hand, slipped his arm around her shoulder.

"Don't you worry," he said. "And don't answer questions for anybody. Not even on the phone."

At 9:08 P.M. on Thursday, May 22, Carol Stephenson had Taylor brought to the office of the City Homicide Unit for questioning about the rape and assault cases. It was the first time she confronted him. Right away, she advised him of his rights to remain silent and have an attorney present.

"You understand what you've been charged with?" she asked.

"Yeah," Taylor said. "How long is this going to take?"

"You mean the questioning?"

"No, the whole shebang."

"Well," Stephenson said. "That depends on how congested the courts are. Probably six months to a year."

"Figures," Taylor said.

"Have you hired an attorney yet?" Stephenson asked.

"I talked to some people," Taylor said. "But I'm not going to waste my money on it. I been in this much trouble before, down in Florida. No lawyer ever did me that much good."

"I think you're going to need one," Stephenson said. She had several eyewitnesses, the victims of assault and rape, who could identify Taylor absolutely.

"So if I need one, I'll get a public defender. I told you, I'm not going to waste my own money."

"There is no public defender here," Stephenson reminded him. "The court will have to appoint a lawyer if you can't afford one."

"Yeah, well, who can afford one?"

Taylor had $359 in his pocket when he was arrested, and he claimed his own indigence throughout the proceedings. Yet he worked fairly regularly, as a machinist, on an assembly line. He had the money for cars, and to buy or rent two different homes in the Seattle area. He must have lived on a narrow margin, from what he accumulated, buying and selling as he moved around. He must have carried what he had.

"Are you ready to make a statement about these charges?"

"Nope," Taylor said. "Not right now."

Stephenson sent the man back to his cell. If he wouldn't talk about it, she couldn't ask. That was the law.

Her usual working hours were 6:00 P.M. to 2:00 A.M., but tonight, Carol Stephenson was working overtime. She finished with the paperwork on the assault charges, and now was working with Detective Trimble on the homicide cases. They had word from the State of Washington that Taylor may have been involved in the disappearance of a young woman from Seattle. They heard also from Michigan authorities, operating on the tip provided by Helen Taylor, that two bodies had been recovered from the yard of a home Taylor once owned. They still had the Suzanne Jackson case to work on, and felt pretty sure Taylor was responsible for that one, too.

At 2:15 A.M. on Saturday, May 24, Carol Stephenson had Taylor brought to the homicide office for questioning. She had shared with Ray Trimble what she'd found in Taylor's apartment. Detective Trimble was interested in Nazi Germany himself, was quite well informed about its history, and the two of them thought that subject could be their lead-in. It might get Taylor talking, at least keep him awake. He looked pretty sleepy when they brought him in.

"You don't have to talk to us," Stephenson began, "without your lawyer present."

"I know that," Taylor said.

"Anything we can get for you?" Trimble offered.

"Coffee," Taylor said. "And some cigarettes."

They called out for what he wanted, and then settled in for what might be a long night.

"I understand you've got some interest in the SS," Trimble began.

"That's right," Taylor said. "What of it?"

"Just curious," Trimble said. "I've done a lot of reading on that subject myself. I bet you could tell me a thing or two."

"Probably," Taylor said.

"So who's your favorite Nazi?"

"I always admired that SS colonel," Taylor said, "who parachuted into Italy in 1943, to rescue Mussolini for Hitler."

"It doesn't take brains to follow orders."

"None of them made decisions on their own. Hitler knew about everything."

"Hitler said he didn't know anything about Hess's mission into Britain."

"Sure he knew. He wanted to get rid of Hess. Hess was a weakling. He sat out the war in prison."

"They captured him."

"Sometimes suicide is the better choice."

"Like Goering at Nuremberg?"

"Yeah," Taylor said. "Like Goering."

"They all confessed, though. Your heroes all confessed."

"Anybody can *say* they did something."

"But it takes a man to really do it, huh?"

"That's right," Taylor said.

"Like that guy who killed the dancer outside of town here."

"Logical murder," Taylor said.

"She was earning a living," Stephenson offered. "She didn't deserve to die for that."

"Women weren't made for that," Taylor said. "They exist for three reasons. To breed, to serve the state, and to make men happy."

"It made you happy to kill her," Trimble said, taking the chance.

"That's right," Taylor said. "It made me happy to kill her."

Within forty-five minutes, the detectives elicited a verbal confession from Taylor on the murder of Suzanne Jackson. By 4:20, his confession was reduced to writing, and Taylor signed it. By then, Carol Stephenson needed a break. She hadn't expected it to be this bad. She excused herself, and left the room.

"So that's the way it is with women," Trimble continued.

"Yeah," Taylor said.

"And you don't feel bad about it?"

"No."

"You want to kill all women?"

"All of them."

"Even Detective Stephenson? If you had the chance, you'd kill Detective Stephenson?"

"Especially Detective Stephenson."

"You don't go after men?"

"I never killed a man."

It was a ruse, a cover of some kind, Taylor's confessing to his wife that he'd killed a man in Michigan. It must have been quite a shock to Bill Parker, when, a few days after Helen Taylor mentioned his name to her lawyer, the police knocked on his door. It makes an almost comical scene in the newspapers.

"We have some information that you might be dead."

"Well, as you can see, I'm very much alive."

I could have told the police not to bother with that visit.

"Does it get easier?" the detective wanted to know. "Was it hard the first time?"

"The more you do it," Taylor said, "the easier it gets."

When Carol Stephenson returned to the interrogation room, the conversation shifted to the missing woman in Washington. They didn't have many details on the case, but what the Seattle police sent them was enough to start with.

At first Taylor didn't have anything to say. Trimble tried working on his sympathies, suggesting that the family of the missing woman wanted to know where she was, wanted to give her a proper funeral. Once Stephenson suggested that the officials in Washington actually had some evidence against Taylor, he started to talk.

Between 4:40 and 5:40 A.M., Detectives Trimble and Stephenson elicited a signed confession from Taylor on the murder of Vonnie Stuth. He lured her from her home on the promise of a puppy. He took her to his place in Enumclaw, where he tied her up, smashed her breasts with the butt of a rifle, cut out the nipples, then shot her and buried the body in the backyard.

The information was relayed immediately to the authorities in Washington State. When by 12:50 that afternoon they still hadn't found Vonnie's body, King County Police called Houston, asked to speak to Taylor personally. He was advised of his rights, then agreed to talk to them. "I'm glad this is over," he said. He told the police in Washington where to dig.

At six o'clock on the morning of May 24, after nearly four hours of questioning, Taylor said he was hungry. The detectives sent out to the all-night burger joint around the corner for a hamburger and french fries and three cups of coffee.

It took two more hours to get all the information they wanted out of Taylor. Shortly after six, they got him talking about his past in Michigan.

"They think you're crazy in Michigan," Trimble began.

"My lawyer forced me to plead insanity," Taylor said. "I would have chosen prison if I'd known."

"Like Rudolph Hess?"

"You never get out if you're crazy," Taylor said.

Within a few minutes, he had confessed orally to killing two women in Michigan.

"Who were they?" Stephenson asked.

"Who remembers names," Taylor said.

"How did you know them?"

"I picked them up in a bar, a couple of whores."

It's there in the record of the Harris County file, a simple confession. He met two women in a bar in Toledo, Ohio, took them home to Onsted, killed them, buried them in the backyard. He doesn't remember the details, or chooses not to provide them. And the detectives don't bother with dragging out of him a full written confession this time. The State of Michigan has already judged that the guy's crazy anyway. And with everything else they have to deal with, having the record of two more murders in writing won't make much difference to anybody.

"So how many women is that?" Trimble asked.

Taylor grinned.

"You mean there are more?"

"Maybe," Taylor said.

Betty Goodrich? Irene Waters? Sandra Horwath?

"You want to tell us about it?" Stephenson asked.

"No," Taylor said.

"You have anything more to say?" Trimble asked.

"Yeah," Taylor said. "These are lousy french fries."

When Detective Terry Pierce came to work that morning, she found Taylor and Trimble talking amicably about the Nazis and real estate and Taylor complaining about the quality of the french fries. Carol Stephenson was exhausted, and went home to bed.

On the morning of May 27, just before he was booked in unincorporated Harris County for the murder of Suzanne Jackson, Gary Taylor had a cup of coffee with Detective Jay Evans of the County Sheriff's Office, who again advised Taylor of his rights. During the booking procedure, the two of them were having a little chat about weightlifting, man talk, when Stuart Kinnard arrived and introduced himself. He had been appointed Taylor's attorney by Justice of the Peace Lawrence Wayne.

"I'd like to see my client privately," he said.

Evans walked them to an examination room where they could confer, and then left.

"There's probably not much I can do here," Kinnard said. "You signed all these confessions."

"They obtained those confessions under duress," Taylor said.

"What do you mean, duress?" Kinnard was used to his clients having a grip on legal jargon, but had long since learned they didn't always know what they were talking about.

"They got the confessions forcibly," Taylor said. "I wouldn't have signed otherwise."

Taylor proceeded to tell his attorney that seventy-two hours after he was brought into the Houston City Jail, he was taken out again by several officers whose names he couldn't remember and driven to the Arboretum in Memorial Park, where he was beaten severely and threatened with death if he did not confess. In fact, Taylor said, for a period of days he was tortured, and confessed finally only when the police officers put a gun to his head.

Kinnard made an exact record of the times and dates Taylor mentioned. The police log, of course, told a different story.

"It probably won't fly," Kinnard said, "but we can slow things down a bit. Just a few more questions."

"Shoot," Taylor said.

"Were you fully advised of your rights to counsel?"

"No," Taylor said. "I kept asking for a lawyer, and they kept right on asking me questions. The third degree."

"Did the officers ever cease questioning because you didn't want to talk?"

"They stopped talking when they got good and ready. It didn't matter what I said."

"You should have kept your mouth shut," Kinnard said. "And you should have had your lawyer present when you made those confessions."

"I know," Taylor said, and smiled. "What took you so long?"

The motion Kinnard filed a few days later wasn't enough to keep Taylor in Texas forever, but it was enough, as the lawyer had predicted, to slow things down. Taylor won an appeal of his extradition order, originally scheduled for June 30, and was granted a new hearing at a later date. At that time, in March of 1976, nearly a year after his arrest in Houston, he was again ordered to be returned to the State of Washington to stand trial for the murder of Vonnie Stuth.

The allegations he made—that he was beaten into signing his confession—didn't stand up under scrutiny. The court declared that Taylor's rights had not been violated, that he'd known all along what was happening to him. Repeatedly, the investigating officers had admonished him of his rights, he'd had access to an attorney, and at least once said he didn't want one. When he said he didn't want to talk, the officers had not pursued that line of questioning. Considerable legal precedent defined cases of reinterrogation over the course of several days, and the procedures followed in the questioning of Taylor fell within those guidelines.

The hint of irregularities in the proceedings, however, made the district attorney in King County, Washington, nervous. That office reduced the charges against Taylor in the State of Washington to second-degree murder in the case of Vonnie Stuth. In return, Taylor pleaded guilty to the reduced charge and thus saved the state the expense of an elaborate trial by jury that might well have been thrown out of court on a technicality.

At Taylor's sentencing for the Stuth murder in Seattle, Judge William C. Goodloe apologized to Vonnie's family for having to put into grim words what must have been the facts of the young woman's death, the final, terrifying moments of her life. So grim was the crime, the judge recommended that Taylor never be paroled. Assured of his conviction in the State of Washington, authorities in Texas and Michigan agreed

not to prosecute Taylor for the crimes with which he had been connected in those states.

So, no lawyers ever pieced together what happened in that basement
room in Onsted, Michigan, because as far as the authorities were concerned, the Michigan murders were a legal redundancy. They had his
oral confession, what there was of it. His memory remained fuzzy, or
he refused to say anything beyond the basic facts. He picked up two
women in a bar in Toledo, Ohio. He killed them. He couldn't remember
their names.

1 9 7 4

Her name is Lee Snavely, and I'm looking for her.

I have before me a photograph on loan from someone who knew Lee when I didn't. The cardboard sign propped up in the front row reads FIFTH GRADE, SOUTH MAIN SCHOOL, 1960. *I hesitate a moment before I look.*

The boys in the back row have not yet overtaken Mrs. Banks, the teacher, still the tallest person in the picture. Her gray hair sweeps back into a bun; she wears a silk bouquet, old-fashioned even then, at her belt. Her charges (she is proud of most of them) line up in rows, poised for the ritual of the class photograph. They grin shyly into the camera. A gangly boy stands at the end of the row, his plaid shirt coming untucked, his eyes caught shut in the moment the camera clicked. A girl in braids sits cross-legged in the front row, her hands carefully folded, her skirt carefully arranged, the toes of her scuffed shoes showing from under its folds. Near the center of the middle row is the face I'm looking for. I was foolish to think I might not recognize her right away, the child I have to piece together from someone else's pictures.

Her head tilts to the side, and she avoids the camera, the only face in the picture turned slightly away. Her smile, too, or the hint of it, sits a little off center. Her eyes, unmistakably dark, peer out from a fringe of hair, shorter than I ever saw it in life. I, too, had the pixie cut that year, and I cried all the way home from the beauty parlor at the loss of my braids. My mother felt my grief. She still keeps my hair wrapped in Saran in the buffet drawer.

When I turn the photograph over, I find all the names, written with a fat lead pencil. My finger pauses on each signature, counting the places in the middle row. There is the graceful loop of the L. There are no i's to dot with hearts or circles or smiling faces, but she adds a curl to the S, like a treble clef sign. In their individuated shapes, the letters slant perfectly, like letters above a blackboard, but the whole name slopes rapidly downward, and runs off its imaginary line into the row beneath.

I turn the picture back to the faces again, and the ghost of someone else's memory, as sure as if it were my own, steps out of the photograph. She takes her place in front of the class.

This is a big day for a fifth grader: Lee's science project is due. She's been working on it for weeks. The posters, cheerful blues and reds, are neatly printed in block letters. Her father helped her with the photographs, from his files, perhaps, enlarged now to reveal the detail clearly, arranged in order to demonstrate the progress of the disease. She has glued the pictures carefully to the posterboard so the smear of the rubber cement doesn't show. The posters line up, proud of themselves, on the chalk tray.

Suddenly self-conscious in front of the class, her skirt too long and her blouse a little too tight, Lee takes a deep breath and begins. Once she has entered the science of it, she is calm again. She has borrowed the white pointer Mrs. Banks uses in the geography lessons, and now she traces it across the pictures in her display.

"Here we see evidence of the problem in its first stages," she says. She points to an odd angle in the bone, the hip joint out of place.

The gangly boy in the plaid shirt and the girl in braids exchange a worried glance across the aisle between them. This is pretty weird, even for a science report.

"And here is the dysplasia fully developed," Lee continues with another picture. "See where the bones spread out so much?" She moves the pointer back, and brings it to rest along what used to be the hindquarters of what used to be a dog.

"This disease is common in big dogs with long legs," she says. "This one was a German shepherd."

Now it is an enlarged photograph of the skeleton, the disease she examines bred in the bone.

"When it gets to this point," she says, "it's very painful, and the dog has to be put down."

The other children shift uncomfortably in thier seats. They have dogs at home that romp in their backyards, sleep in their beds, bark when strangers come to the door. They have dogs named Tigger and Smidgen and Scamp.

"It happens all the time." Lee shrugs.

Mrs. Banks doesn't let the moment pass. She assumes her place as the tallest person in the room, walks up the aisle quickly, nodding as she goes, saying, my how interesting, wasn't that interesting, class? Then she leafs through her papers, looking for names, and calls on Janine, the inspiration of a seasoned teacher who knows her students well, knows who to count on when the moment counts.

Janine plugs a hot plate into the outlet under the blackboard. Her project is called The Physics of Popcorn. She's going to explain why it pops.

"We can eat it when I'm done," she says.

The class erupts in hungry applause.

Whatever pain Lee spoke from, cleverly disguised as a precocious student ("almost brilliant," her nervous teacher said), whatever vision she managed from a clinical perspective, whatever pain she voiced, went on unnoticed, uncared for, or denied. Caught up in somebody else's bargain, she waited for someone to look.

When I glanced back, when I turned around, I found myself waiting there, a child too, in the shadows. Lee, I think, waits there still.

Lee found Debbie Henneman one night on the street, like a dropped nickel. She took her home to her apartment on East Broadway and doctored the cut above her eye with peroxide, showed her how to smooth make-up over the bruise. The two of them set up house together. Lee gave Debbie coffee in the morning, and lessons in survival at night; she was the older girl letting her in on the rules.

"Don't carry much money on you," Lee told her. "Money can get you into trouble."

Rule #1 was easy. Debbie didn't have much money.

"And don't take any more I.D. than you need to get yourself served in a bar."

Rule #2 presented a problem. Debbie's driver's license, newly acquired so she could buy a beat-up car, clearly showed she was under-age.

"You have anything else?" Lee asked.

"Well," Debbie said, tentative. "I got a library card."

They had a laugh over that one.

"The places we go aren't going to check too carefully," Debbie suggested.

"Sure," Lee said. "A library card will do."

Then Lee went on to the next rule.

"Keep it simple," she said. "If you can't do it with whatever you've got here," she tapped the front of her shirt, "don't."

"You mean, if my heart isn't in it?"

"This business doesn't involve the heart," Lee said. "Don't do a gig that requires a change of clothes."

There is still an innocence to it, as if the world hadn't fallen out of Eden a million years ago. Rule #1: Keep your knees together at all times. Rule #2: Always walk up the middle of the stairs. Follow the rules and you'll be safe. Follow the rules, and bad things won't happen.

Two and a half years before Lee took Debbie in, the girl's mother had given up on her and turned her over to the courts. The Ohio Youth Commission took charge of her then, and as required by law, she did time at the Diagnostic Center in Columbus. A year and a half before Lee found her, in August 1972, the authorities released Debbie to a series of foster homes in Toledo. Twice thereafter she was reported as a runaway. By February 1974, she was discharged altogether from the rolls of the Youth Commission, officially AWOL, whereabouts unknown.

She wasn't lost or missing, at least not yet. She was sharing the life with Lee.

The two of them had a lot in common, motherless daughters, both on their own. In the daytime, Debbie padded around the apartment like a puppy, and in her own way, Lee watched out for her. Sometimes, late at night, Debbie cried, and Lee took her in her arms on the sofa that served as a bed, held her, rocked her, told her everything would be all right. Come on now, she said. Chin up. Don't be a baby.

Lee hated babies. Babies were soft in the brain.

I imagine Debbie's life before Lee met her from my sister's reports. She was about my sister's age, thirteen in 1970, when she first ran into trouble with the law. Social life must have been harder then. My sister remembers parties in junior high where the kids got wildly drunk, trashed, potted like plants, ripped, smashed, blitzed, bombed, a violent vocabulary I didn't learn until I went to college. My sister remembers parties where lots of them got stoned, tripped out, wasted. In fact, when she was in high school, the principal started chaining the doors shut every morning, to lock the kids in and the sellers of certain pharmaceuticals out.

She remembers kids driving around the high school parking lot, seeing how fast they could go, then bailing out, opening the doors and jumping or falling or sky-diving into the gravel, just for kicks. (One of them was Lee's youngest brother, Bruce.) She remembers plenty of girls who didn't graduate from junior high because they were pregnant. And lots of them had good mothers.

Only ten years before, I'd been in junior high myself, and I didn't know I knew anybody who had trouble like that.

"It's easy," I hear Lee say. "You just stick out your thumb and go."

I don't know about it when it happens; I pick up foggy rumors from my friends a few years later, and gather the details years after that, from Eric, and from Lee's brother, Geoff.

Lee has had it with her stepmother who, she thinks, plans to dump her anyway. She has relatives in Cleveland who might help her and her brothers out. She knows she has a mother in Cleveland.

Lee rises early, before six, on a Saturday, and feeds the dogs before she goes. It is February, still dark at that hour. A thick fog hovers across the fields of stubble all around her. She walks a mile or so, hugging the brink of the ditch along the road so as not to lose her way or risk walking too close to the cars that lurch like drunken ghosts in and out of the fog. Napoleon Road brings her to the Golden Lily, an old truck stop that marks the intersection with Route 6. She has charted her course on the map. Route 6 will take her to the turnpike, and the turnpike unfolds all the way to Cleveland.

She bums a ride with a trucker who has a daughter about her age, thirteen or so. He buys her a cup of coffee, heavy on the cream, and lets her fiddle with the radio dial all she wants. She tunes in WLS, from Chicago, the Tower of Power in the Midwest.

That's where the trucker is heading, CHICAGO AND WEST, the sign says, so he lets her off at the turnpike entrance where she can catch a ride going east. She doesn't wait long. A big car eases onto the shoulder where she stands, her own arms around herself against the cold, and the front door opens. She climbs in beside an older man with a bald head and a pocket protector; the back seat is full of sample cases. He's going to Youngstown, and can take her the whole way.

At first he wants to make conversation, but she resists. It's either that, or lie, because the less he knows about her the better. "Aw, come on, honey," he says. "I want to pick your brain, find out what makes a kid like you tick."

She looks at him like where does he come from anyway?

Eventually he gives up.

She stares out the window, her breath making fog on the glass, counts the exits, passes the signs for places she's never been. One sign announces the birthplace of Rutherford B. Hayes, One of Ohio's Eight Presidents. (All the presidents nobody ever heard of came from Ohio.) Then there's the birthplace of Thomas Alva Edison, American Genius. Sandusky. Put-in-Bay. Cedar Point. Elyria. She's always liked the sound of that word. Elyria might be a nice place to visit, but there's no off ramp at 8A. You can get out of Elyria, but you can't get in.

She hitches another ride at the ramp for Exit Ten, so she can get through the toll booth. That car lets her out at the first sign of civilization, a shopping center near the airport, *where she calls a cab. She's brought enough money with her to pay a cab to take her to her mother's door.*

Slowly, as the cab winds through suburban Cleveland, the roads stop looking like highways and more like streets. She recognizes her mother's street the minute the car turns there, and has the driver let her out a block away. She'll have an easier time of it if her mother doesn't see her coming, isn't alarmed by the cab.

She knocks on the door and waits, takes a few deep breaths, practices. She has a lot of faces to save here, and the first words have to be right.

"Hi, Mom," she says when the door opens. It's all she can think of to say. And then she remembers. "Happy Birthday."

The woman on the other side of the door looks through the screen and sees the face of her dead husband looking back at her in the features of a thirteen-year-old girl.

"What are you doing here?"

Lee shrugs. "I was in the neighborhood."

The mother looks anxiously toward the driveway, the street, and doesn't ask the obvious question. Awkwardly, she invites the girl in.

Once they are seated in the living room, the daughter opts for the direct request.

"I'd like to live here with you now," she says.

The mother has a line of excuses she's been rehearsing in her head for it seems years now, although it is probably less than two since she returned the three children to the welfare office and their stepmother. Her father is sick, she says, probably dying. She has a good job now, a life of her own. She's put the past behind her and wants to move on. There's no place here for her children.

"All those bedrooms," Lee says.

"That's not what I mean," the mother says.

Lee pulls back immediately and tries another ploy. "I'm all right, really," she says. "I'm not asking for me. But the boys. The boys can't take it anymore."

Her mother can't help that. You've made your bed, she almost says, then collects herself, speaks more calmly. She thinks everyone will be better off with an arrangement that's already well under way.

In the end, Lee is returned to Bowling Green in a highway patrol car, the smoothest ride of her life.

A vague memory of my own floats out of the fog that hovers over the winter fields along Route 6. I sit, as I often did, at the kitchen table in my mother's house. She works at the counter between us. Through the space between the counter and the cabinets that hang down from the ceiling I see only her torso and her hands, chopping celery for apple salad, mixing batter for a cake, doing motherly things. I am perhaps fifteen, still caught between needing my mother's help and wanting to know for myself.

Maggie has said something about it at school, and I want my mother to tell me it didn't happen, that Lee didn't hitchhike all the way to Cleveland, that her family didn't turn her away. Had I known then it was her mother, I might have voiced my fear: Could a mother do that? Could any mother do that? Could you do that? My faceless mother, her head lost behind the cabinets, answers, vague as the memory itself. It seems to me, she says, puzzled, searching, we heard something about that trip.

I can't be sure that the memory predates the story. I may have imagined it, the way I remember my earliest life, from having heard about it, or seen photographs. But now that I have the picture in mind, the middle of my mother glimpsed between the cabinet and the counter, the way I saw her so often as a child, I leave my chair at the kitchen table and walk around the end of the cabinet. I step easily into the picture I imagine.

I can see my mother's face now, as I couldn't have seen it then, and she's crying. She feels for Lee, and for her mother, too, freely. Here, there is nothing but sorrow to weigh. She and I were never tested like that. We saw pieces of each other from behind the kitchen counter, but I know: my mother was always there.

Lee's last winter wore on into the dull cold of February. On Valentine's Day, to break the monotony, to pick up some cash, she dolled herself up. Plenty of lonely guys out there, she thought, hoping for a sweetheart. One they had to pay for would do. That night, on February 14, 1974, Lee was arrested for solicitation. When she got home in the middle of the night, she probably told Debbie Rule #4: Do as I say, honey, not as I do.

Lee started out in her new life pretty well, checking in every two weeks with her probation officer, but lately she'd gotten lazy. Now, with this most recent arrest, she had violated the conditions of her parole. If she didn't work it out with the man in the office, he'd tighten the screws, make life impossible for her. She prepared to set things right.

"I need a real job," she told him. "Life on the streets isn't worth it."

"We can get you something," he said. "You've waitressed before, right?"

"That's right."

"It won't be much at first," he said. "But it can get you going. As long as your paycheck doesn't go up in a needle."

"I'm working on it," Lee said.

"I'll want some evidence of that," he said. "And I'll need to see you again," he checked his calendar, counted the days, "on March 6."

On her way out of the building, Lee stepped into the bathroom. Coming out of the stall, she caught a glimpse of a stranger in the mirror.

Her long hair, cut once at uneven lengths, came full around her face at the ears, tangled curls falling well below her shoulders. Her mouth made a sullen line across her face. She wore a yellow pullover, the turtleneck rumpled and uneven. The mirror cut the woman off at the middle, like a mug shot. She wasn't wearing a bra, and her nipples showed clearly through her shirt, the cloth bunched up around her breasts.

Lee closed her eyes and stood there for a good five minutes. Someone walking into the bathroom might have thought she had fallen asleep. She might have been dreaming.

I have a picture of that woman in the mirror. It is a mug shot, taken at the time of Lee's arrest on February 14, a little more than a week after her twenty-fourth birthday. It shocks me to see it, the weight in her sleepy eyes, the tangle in her hair, and though I can't know for certain, I imagine that the face in the mirror pulled her up short, too.

It looks like she had every intention of fixing her life, of turning whatever dreams she had for the woman in the mirror into something hard and real. Lee missed her appointment with the probation officer on March 6, but a little over a week later, on Friday, March 15, she checked in with a drug rehabilitation center in Toledo for an initial consultation. They took her name down on a clipboard, recorded an address and a telephone number. She signed her own name on the dotted line of a rebirth certificate. Every indication in the official record suggests that she made that appointment on her own.

She called her probation officer from the rehab center and he rescheduled their next meeting for April 3.

She had done it before, come to a juncture, taken a look at herself, pulled herself together with every intention she could muster, tried to start over. I'll go to college, she said in 1968, get my life back on track, make something of this mess, down there where nobody knows me. She lasted at Ohio State less than a year. I'll get a job, she said. I'll get married. I'll get myself straight. I'll move in with Eric's parents. But every time, the memories she couldn't make something of (I made her out of mine) pulled her back into the life she knew best, the life she was accustomed to, the life, perhaps, she thought she deserved. Every time, she came home to the places she knew.

But this time, perhaps, something else stopped her before her memories could. She didn't keep the appointment with her probation officer on April 3, because by then she was dead. Except for a couple of phone calls recorded in a police log, that piece of paper at the drug rehabilitation center, dated Friday, March 15, 1974, is the last official record of Lee in life.

It had been a cold winter, and Lee and Debbie had gotten on each other's nerves, day after day of gray and wind and chill. The weather settled into the bone like an ache. The apartment was small, dingy, like the day. From her bedroom window, she looked out to the railroad tracks below her, where the same few cars went back and forth, back and forth all day. The tracks stretched on forever, through the vast Midwest, cutting across country roads, the trains whistling past one small town after another, freight trains, not meant for passengers. It was a coupling yard down there, where connections were made, where engines were traded, tracks switched and redirected, and pieces of trains sent out into the world. From where she stood, Lee could read the black and white sign on the far side of the yard. No HUMPING, it said. She wanted to steal it for her bedroom wall.

Beyond the rail yard the smelly old Maumee River sludged by. Barges loaded with tons of chipped glass came into the city on that river. The shards glinted in the afternoon sun, what there was of it, heaps of them, to be remelted, reformed, reshaped into coffee jars, fruit juice jars, drinking glasses, by Libby-Owens, or Owens-Illinois. Lee lived in the Glass Capital of the World. Every city, every little town, wanted to be the capital of something. Ohio was full of them, places trying to live up to their pretensions, from the Rubber Capital in Akron to the Radish Capital in McClure.

Standing there at her window, Lee had a sudden imagination of rivers, the connections they made, the borders they formed, the journeys they took across a landscape she'd never seen. Two mighty rivers in Pittsburgh met to make the Ohio that flowed to the Mississippi that flowed to the sea. The Maumee River out there, below her window, hooked up with the St. Lawrence and sent boats all the way to the huge Atlantic Ocean. Then Lee's mind drifted back to the south again, along the path of rivers, from the Maumee to the Poe, homing like a bird.

The little Poe River that ran past the farm on the outskirts of Bowling Green met up somewhere with the Maumee. There at the farm, the Poe, as big as a creek, at least, would just about now be free of the winter ice on which she had skated as a child. Across town the Poe trickled down to nothing, Poe Ditch, they called it. Lee laughed to think of it: water flowing backwards, from the ocean to the seaway to the river to the creek to the ditch.

Standing there at her window, Lee may have imagined the rivers she knew as a child.

I have this picture of the child from Lee's brother, living before memory himself, but it's one of those family stories he's heard over and over. He thinks he remembers.

Lee isn't more than five years old, because this is before all the troubles. They are living in Waterville, on the banks of the Maumee River. A year later, her father will buy Kaskaden Farms, and they'll move to Bowling Green, where the river is the Poe, and much smaller.

It is July. She wears seersucker overalls and a white T-shirt. Her half brother, William Greggory, called Bill, has come to stay with them for the summer. He is fifteen, and handsome, old enough to get her into trouble, old enough to give her fun.

A few weeks earlier, they visit someone at a lake, somewhere nearby. She doesn't have to go to the bathroom until they get there, so they can't have driven far. When they arrive, everybody hugs everybody. They pinch her cheek and pat her behind and tell her how much she's grown. You've grown, too, she says, but she can't remember if she's seen them before.

After they swim, they eat, and then the grown-ups sit around and talk a lot of boring talk and make jokes she doesn't understand. From across the room, Bill winks at her, and jerks his thumb toward the door.

Outside, on the porch, she takes his hand. They watch the fireflies blink on and off, little lights that dance in the sky like eyes opening and shutting again. When they all sit on the same bush, Bill says, they blink together, like a Christmas tree.

Then she and Bill walk down to the dock. They listen quietly and the water breathes. All the way across the lake, a light flashes on and off, on and off. Lee says maybe it's a bush full of fireflies, blinking in unison.

You just might be right about that, Bill says.

The people they're visiting have a boat tied to the dock, hoisted now just above the water on a giant canvas swing. Bill whirls a metal wheel around a couple of times, and the boat slips quietly into the breathing water. Let's find out, Bill says. Let's see how far we can get.

Lee claps her hands with delight. We'll follow the light, she laughs. We'll see how far we can go.

The boat pushes the water aside, and they head out, making for the light way off on the other side of the lake.

It isn't a bush full of fireflies at all. It's a fog lamp, burning on and off to warn the boats. But Lee is glad they made the trip anyway. She's glad, even when they run out of gas and have to row the boat most of the way home. She's glad even when they pull up to the dock, practically in the middle of the night, and her father is waiting there.

He yanks Bill out of the boat like a rag doll and wollops him a good one across the face. It comes so fast, and it comes so hard, Bill falls backward into the lake, his legs and arms going every which way. He comes up, spitting water and grinning.

Now it's July and they're back in Waterville where there's a river, but no lake. Bill hauls a huge coil of rope slung over his shoulder, and he has Lee by the hand. They're looking for fun.

They're on the walker's path of the Waterville Bridge, stretched a long way across the Maumee River, which glitters in the sunlight way below, where it dances over rocks and broken trees. The river banks, steep and bumpy, struggle down, down, down to the water's edge.

Not quite halfway across the bridge, they stop, and Bill explains the game. It's called "Dare the Devil," he says, and she gets to be the first "it." He wraps the giant rope around one of the steel girders, and she rolls up the cuffs of her seersucker overalls. Then he makes a big loop, like a noose, with a slip knot, at the other end of the rope.

You sit here, he says, and I lower you over.

Lee looks over the edge of the bridge, down to the dancing water that glistens in the sun. In the air between her and the water, she tries to count how many houses would fit.

She wants to know how the game got its name. She thinks Bill made it up.

Because when you get down there, Bill says, that's what you do. You dare the devil. You stand up to the Old Man. You want me, you come and get me.

Not even the devil makes a trip like that.

Lee clutches the rope above her head (so little rope beneath her), all the way down, until her fingers turn red, then white. Bill lowers her a few feet at a time, and it's scary all the way down, like a roller coaster on the way up. But when there's no more rope to go, when she's almost to the water, it's not so scary any more unless she looks up. So she looks down at the hole in her Keds, down to the water a few feet below her, then gives herself over to flight. She swings back and forth in the summer air, higher and higher, louder and louder. With every sweep of the arc she makes, she takes the courage of the dare.

You want me, she whoops, come and get me. You want me, she shouts, I'm yours. The water dances beneath her. The water laughs back.

On March 23, Debbie decided to party. It was a Saturday night, date night, and she was seventeen.

"Let's go out," she said. "Celebrate something."

"Like what," Lee said. "The weather?"

"Why not?"

"It's as good a reason as any," Lee said.

"We didn't do much for your birthday last month," Debbie suggested.

Lee's twenty-fourth birthday, on February 5, had passed uneventfully. They'd gone to the mall that night, walked around, looked at windows and people, played the style police, imagined making citizens' arrests. They charged one woman with having excessively large hair, teased into a giant nest. A man wearing a shirt that clashed with his pants looked too much like an insurance salesman at a convention in Hawaii. A teen-aged girl shuffled along in a skirt that was way too long and made her legs look like sausages. They pretended they were undercover agents for *Glamour*, snapping candid photographs for the Fashion Do's and Don'ts, catching people at their worst.

"This is an anniversary of sorts," Lee said, giving herself over to Debbie's mood. "Eleven months ago to the day I got sentenced."

They fixed themselves up nice, and headed for their favorite spot downtown, just around the corner from the apartment. They hadn't been sitting at the bar long when a man joined them. He pulled a stool around so it formed a triangle with theirs, climbed on, and slipped an arm around each of them.

"How 'bout if I buy you ladies a drink?"

That was an appropriate question, for starters.

"You from around here?" Lee asked.

"This pipsqueak of a town?" he said.

"What's wrong with Toledo?" Debbie said. "Corporal Maxwell Klinger comes from here."

"I rest my case," the man said. "The jerk wears dresses."

"I don't know why everybody thinks Toledo is a joke," Debbie said. "It's a nice place."

"Sure," the man said, "if you like Jeeps. Where I come from, they make real cars."

"Where's that?" Lee wanted to know.

"Where do you think?" the man said.

"Tokyo, maybe?" Lee offered.

"Detroit," the man said, sullen now. "I'm working for GM myself. That's temporary. I'm investing in real estate. You can really go someplace with real estate."

"You got a quarter?" Debbie asked. "For the jukebox?"

The man dug into his pocket.

"Play me some Motown," he said. He grunted to the rhythm, if not to the tune, of *Dancin' in the Streets.*

"Gladys Knight and the Pips," he said.

"Martha and the Vandellas," Lee said.

"One nigger group's about the same as the next," he said.

Debbie wandered over to the jukebox and dropped the quarter in. Jim Morrison's voice floated over the noise of the bar. She didn't want to give the man the satisfaction of Motown. Los Angeles was as far away from Detroit as she could imagine, and Jim Morrison was a lot farther away than that.

"I got myself a good start," the man said to Lee. "A fancy house in a big subdivision over the border. Five hundred lots they got there, only seven houses so far. The area's booming."

"Sounds nice," Lee said.

"Why don't you and your friend come up? Spend a few days. Go swimming."

"I'll see if we have plans," Lee said.

Debbie had buzzed some guy standing by the jukebox. He was lighting her cigarette. She wanted to get him dancing, but Lee pulled her aside.

"That turkey's not worth your time," she said.

"And that guy at the bar is?"

"He wants us to do a gig at his place for a couple of days," Lee said. "He's got a spread in Michigan."

"You mean break Rule Number Three?" Debbie asked. A few days in Michigan would definitely require a change of clothes.

"This is simple enough," Lee said. "Earn all our money in one place, spend it wherever we want."

"Whatever," Debbie said.

Lee knew what she was doing, and Debbie didn't much care.

Lee came back to the bar, and worked out the details with the man. He wanted their services for a weekend, nothing too heavy, nothing she probably wasn't used to already. All she had to do was say the word, and he'd let her and her friend out. That was what he was after, pushing the game to the limit, to the outermost edge of the possible, to the very verge of control.

Jim Morrison's voice screeched through the air in the bar.

Lee felt high with the possibility. This could mean a lot of money, a new start, a way out. She'd swung on a rope from the Waterville Bridge. She could handle a little light S and M.

"For what you have in mind," Lee said, "I'll have to see some money up front."

"No problem." The man withdrew his wallet and fished out a couple hundred bucks.

"She's pretty young-looking," the man said, nodding toward Debbie. "You sure she can handle this?"

"She's old enough," Lee said.

"You got a car?"

"Yeah," Lee said.

Well, Debbie had a car.

The man explained that he'd have to go home that night. He had a wife waiting there. If she and her friend gave him the chance to get rid of his wife, send her off to visit with her sister or something, the three of them could have a bang-up time.

"I got a party room," he said. "All fixed up."

The whole business was more complicated than she was used to, but the money was good, more than a few months rent, enough, maybe, to lose herself in. A sudden picture came into her head of all the places she'd never seen, beaches and palm trees and glaciers and mountains and little cafés under striped awnings, all arranged on one postcard. And who, she wondered, would she send it to?

"How will we find it?" Lee asked.

"I'll drive down tomorrow and pick you up," he said. "You'll never get there on your own."

Lee tried to tell him her name, but he couldn't hear her over the noise in the bar, the music and the laughter and the television all blaring at once. So she wrote the words down for him, *Lelah Fletcher*, a little phoney, but jazzier than her real one. She cocked her head and squinted at the letters. She'd always had a beautiful hand, a sweep of an L, one smooth motion, clear, graceful, not fussy. Here, all of a sudden, on that little piece of paper, she saw ancient hieroglyphics, Greek, Russian, some alphabet she didn't know.

"Here you go," she said, uncertain.

She named a street corner near her apartment where they should meet. She had long since learned to be wary of giving out her address to the men she picked up in bars.

The next morning, a friend of theirs, Herb Howard, who lived next door, arrived at Lee's apartment, and found the two of them packing their bags.

"Where you making off to?" he asked.

"Lee met a guy last night," Debbie said. "He's rich, and wants us to come for a party at his place."

"Where's that?"

"Somewhere near Adrian," Lee said.

"You sure you want to do this?"

"The guy looks like a retard," Lee said. "What could go wrong?"

"Did you get a load of the glasses?" Debbie said. "Nobody wears those dark frames anymore."

"When should I expect you back?" Herb said.

"Since when do you keep tabs on us?" Lee wanted to know.

"I don't like you going off without knowing where, that's all."

"You're loads of fun, Herb," Lee said. She pulled the zipper closed on her overnight bag.

"You want to give us a hand with these?" Debbie said, handing the friend their bags. On her way out, she grabbed a couple of beers from the fridge, and snapped out the kitchen lights. Then she made her way out to the street, down two flights of darkened stairs.

Lee stood with Herb at the top of the steps and her irritation melted. "Here," she said. "I'll help you with those bags."

On their way down, she told him what she knew of her host for the weekend, his name, where he lived, roughly, in Lenawee County. "It's the usual thing," she said. "A little harmless fun. It's out of town, that's all."

It's one of those family stories significant enough to have earned a name, a title. Lee's younger brothers laughed about this one for years, though I have to be pointed to what's funny.

They are all gathered at the farm for Christmas. Their mother is pregnant with Bruce, who will be born in January. Geoff is three, Lee, six. Some of the half brothers and sisters have come, and so has Aunt Mary, who all the kids think a bossy old schoolmarm from Cleveland. Lee has memorized " 'Twas the Night Before Christmas," and is trying to get someone to hear her recite it, tugging on every shirtsleeve and skirt hem in the room. The father is well into his eggnog. The aunt is complaining about the lights, they're not on straight, they don't cover the gaps in the tree, which is pretty scraggly anyway, where did it come from? The mother is trying to talk Geoff into going to bed, but he is afraid he'll miss the fun.

He doesn't.

The boys don't remember how it happens exactly, but given the mood in the room, any little thing could have set it off. The father says something sharp to Lee, brushes her aside, scolds her for her chatter, and Lee sasses him back. Then before anyone can do anything about it, before the mother can grab his arm or step between them, if she was going to do that, before the aunt can holler, the father has his loafer off his foot. He pulls his arm back and lets go with that shoe, right across Lee's face.

But now, they say, here's the funny part.

Lee doesn't cry. She doesn't even whimper. She looks back at him, steady-eyed, sure of herself. She balls her hands into fists, makes her face into a scowl, and pounds at the air in front of her. Then she steps out of her slippers and turns her back, storms right out of the house. "I'll show you," she shouts over her shoulder.

They all gather around the window, pull the curtains back. There goes Lee, a furious little ghost, punching away at the air, walking barefoot along Durlam Road, her white nightgown soon lost in a swirl of snow.

"She'll be back," her father says, and they pull the curtain closed.

Her brothers call this one, "The Night Daddy Hit Lee with His Shoe."

Maybe all family stories, the ones we disguise as jokes, betray some form of violence. In my family, we don't have any stories quite as bald as that.

The man waited around the corner, as they'd planned, his van pulled up at the curb. He swung himself out of the car when he saw them coming, opened the back for their bags. And then they had a little squabble. Isn't that the way it always is, just before you go on a trip?

"I'll ride with him," Lee said to Debbie. "You follow in your car."

It was the least she could do, since Debbie didn't know yet where they were heading.

"I don't want to drive by myself," Debbie said. "I don't know the way."

"Don't be such a baby," Lee said.

"Don't you be so bossy," Debbie said.

"So we'll both ride in your car."

"Come on," the man said. "You think I want to make the trip without a little company?"

He reached over and gave Debbie's chin a squeeze.

That decided it. Lee, who knew southern Michigan pretty well, who'd gone to high school there, who'd gotten married there, agreed to follow along behind the van in Debbie's car.

On Sunday morning, March 24, the three of them started out from Toledo, driving north on Route 23 caravan-style in a line of two. According to newspaper accounts written over a year later, their friend watched them drive off, Lee in the second car, and Debbie in the van with the man who was driving. Their friend thought maybe he'd been foolish to worry. The man looked harmless enough. In fact, except for the glasses, he looked a lot like Billy Graham.

Despite the little argument at the curb, Lee enjoyed high spirits. She was off for a party on a pretty day for late March, sunny, not a cloud in the sky, no sign of rain or snow. It might even get warm. It was amazing: spring came so suddenly, and yet so predictably every year. Wintry and blustery and unpleasant one day, and then all at once things looked up. And it usually happened one day in March. In like a lion, Lee thought as she moved into the left lane for Route 23.

In like a lion and out like a lamb.

When Lee and Debbie hadn't returned by that night, the man who watched them drive off with Billy Graham got nervous again. The next day, he called the police. People have to be missing longer than one day, they told him, before you can file a report. Call back, they said, if the women haven't returned in a couple of days. On March 26, Herb contacted the sheriff's office near Adrian and spelled out his suspicions. He got more or less the same treatment then. It's not enough reason, they said; there's not enough to go on. A few days later, some men from the sheriff's office drove out to Onsted and checked out Taylor's place. No evidence of foul play, they told him. Relax. They'll come home. You know how women are.

At the end of the month, Herb drove up to Onsted himself. He knew the man's name. He looked him up in the phone book. Then he poked around the yard, pulled the boards off the basement windows, and peeked in. Gadgets littered the floor, he said, like sex toys, but nobody was home. He gave up looking, finally. Maybe Billy Graham had saved their souls.

Around the middle of April, Geoff Snavely made a trip to Toledo. He'd begun to suspect something when he hadn't heard from Lee in a while. He came by her apartment, found the mailbox stuffed full, a light bill, a phone bill, a bunch of envelopes addressed to occupant. From the stack of mail, he guessed that she hadn't come home for at least two weeks. He asked a few questions at the police station. A report had been filed by a friend of theirs, they told him, but they couldn't do much about it. Those women could have gone any place. Where would they start to look? But the girls had been listed as missing with the FBI. Maybe the Feds could turn up something.

Geoff figured they couldn't be bothered spending their time and the good taxpayers' money combing Ohio, Michigan, who knows where, looking for an ex-con hooker and her runaway friend.

He remembered the last letter he had from Lee, dated sometime in early February. She was getting antsy, hated having a parole officer glaring over her shoulder, panting down her neck. She wanted to start over, she said, had high hopes for a new life for herself. The official check-ins and questions and forms to fill out made her nervous, reminded her too much of the old way she wanted to leave behind. Maybe she'd get herself over the border into Canada, lose herself up there, like the draft dodgers used to do, change her name maybe, begin all over. The world was full of cracks a girl could lose herself in, if she had a mind to.

Geoff felt uneasy about it. But if she wanted to be lost, the least he could do as her brother was to stop looking. Until I turned up years later, Geoff was the last person to look.

All the while that Herb and Geoff are trying to find her, I see where Lee is. I have suspended her in time. In my mind, they're still driving along Route 23, the three of them, Gary Taylor and Debbie and Lee, deeper and deeper into Michigan, through Toledo and Sylvania, past Temperance, past Dundee, toward the exit for Tecumseh. Between Tecumseh and the end, the garbage bags, and the cheap jewelry, and the slip of paper with Lelah Fletcher written on it, and the smudged library card, and the blood-stained sheets, and Jerry Smeenge looking out his window at the whole mess, I have no evidence of what happened. It is mine to imagine, what no one can know.

Tecumseh is the last recorded stop. The newspapers tell me that Debbie's car, the car Lee was driving when her friend Herb saw them leave town, was found on May 21, 1974, the tank near empty, abandoned in a parking lot near the Tecumseh exit off Route 23. Lee had been dead over a month by then.

Tecumseh is also the last point on this journey when things might have happened differently. At any point along the way, at any point before Tecumseh, where Lee abandons the car, she could have turned off the highway and gone her own route. Until then, she is driving a car alone, straggling along behind Gary Taylor's van.

But somewhere near Tecumseh, Lee pulls the car into the left lane, steps on the gas, and passes the van in front of her. Then she flips the blinker, signalling to the car behind her now to turn off the highway to the right.

No, I say. Let him pass the exit first. Then you can pull off and go wherever you want. You can lose him that way, on the back roads of Michigan.

Then I remember: Debbie, too, is in the van and I want to give Lee credit. She wouldn't go off and leave Debbie there, alone.

Besides, Lee hasn't learned all my tricks for long-distance drives. She hasn't lived long enough, she's only twenty-four, and she's rarely been as far from home as I've traveled.

So together the two cars pull off at the Tecumseh exit into a shopping center parking lot. It is a Sunday afternoon. In conservative small towns, shopping centers aren't yet open on Sundays, and the lot is practically empty.

"What'd you do that for?" Taylor wants to know.

"I'm about out of gas," Lee says, "and I don't have the cash on me to fill it up."

"Ditch the car here," Taylor shrugs.

"We'll need it to get home," Debbie says.

"I can bring you back here when we're done," Taylor says. "By then you'll have plenty of money for gas."

Lee stands by Debbie's open window, exchanges a few words with her.

"Hop in," Taylor insists. "We haven't got all day." Then he moves around to the driver's side at the front of the van.

Lee reaches for the handle on the side door, and her hand rests there a moment along the broad side of the van.

I have heard that at funerals, the eyes of the mourners fix on the body's hands, folded at the waist, holding a flower, perhaps, or a missal, a Bible, a rosary placed there as a comfort not to the dead but to the living. We can trick ourselves, then, into seeing the fingers play on the beads. So dear are the hands, so close to the being itself, we cannot imagine, we do not let ourselves see a hand that will not move again, a hand that will never raise up in greeting or farewell, never reach out in anger or love, never twitch on a knitting needle or twirl a spoon in a bowl. The unmoving hand estranges the body beyond recognition.

We learn the metaphor from our schoolbooks, the part for the whole, the hand for the person, whoever the person is. All hands on deck, we say. The hand that rocks the cradle. Idle hands are the devil's workshop. And we mean the laboring body. The mother's love. The unbusy soul.

I know Lee's hair, thick, and dark and tangled now. I know her eyes, her fair skin, the beauty mark on her cheek like Elizabeth Taylor's. I know her breasts, too, and I know her body. But I have never looked at Lee's hands.

It's my last chance. Wait, I say. Where's your hand? Let me see your hand.

Lee withdraws her arm from the door of the van, and tugs at the sleeve of her sweater—it is a cool March day, and we stand together in a parking lot in Tecumseh, Michigan, where the wind whips out of the deep Midwest and chills to the bone. She pulls her hand back into the warmth of the sleeve, curls her shoulder with the motion of it. She is embarrassed by my request.

The picture has stopped moving. What happened in that parking lot is over and done with. Lee is dead and gone. But it happens again now, in my mind, where it is only we two, there by the door of the van.

I approach her and reach out my own hand for hers. Her nails, carefully shaped and polished, stretch past the tips of her fingers. I have bitten my nails since childhood, nervously, out of stupid habit, and polish is a foolish exercise for me.

Next to mine, Lee's hand is small and white, the fingers short, rounded at the tips. Her palm is smooth, the skin taut and elastic. The knuckles dimple her hand like a child's.

I have baby hands, she says. She speaks like an apology.

She turns from me then, reaches out again for the handle on the van door, and pulls it open with one steady movement. She steps up, and as she stands there, facing me, framed by the gaping rectangle of the van door, for a moment, I can barely distinguish her dark hair from the shadows behind her.

Don't go, I say. Not yet.

Another picture struggles into place for this one. From the door of the van, or the door of the biology shed behind the junior high, a thirteen-year-old girl in a plaid kilt and saddle shoes speaks again.

I hate babies, she says. Babies are soft in the brain.

Yes, I say. An impression will stay there forever.

Lee pulls her sweater around her middle. It's cold out here, she says. You want to step inside? She gestures into the shadows behind her.

I hear my mother's voice in my head. "Don't," she says.

Lee stands in the cold sunlight, her arms wrapped around herself against the wind. She stamps her feet on the asphalt, as if running in place. She has been patient a long time.

Let's go inside, she says again.

This is what I have been doing all along: listening to other people's stories, and telling my own, about Lee. She lives in the stories, and she isn't a ghost to me.

Sure, I say. I have a story to tell you.

Will it take long? Lee asks. I haven't much time.

We settle in on the bench seat in the back of the van, leave the door open a crack. It's warmer in here, dark and sheltering, in its way. The carpet curls up at the edge near the door, and debris is scattered about, a few empty cigarette packs, a beer can, a map marked by coffee stains.

This story is about a little girl, I say. It's one of many.

Girls or stories? Lee says.

Both, I say. At first she is six, hiding in the dark hallway behind the kitchen door.

You forgot once upon a time, Lee says, and giggles like a child.

I start again. Once upon a time, a dark-haired girl hides in the shadowed hallway behind the kitchen door. She peers through the crack along the hinged edge where the light comes in, so that she sees only a long, thin slice of the room beyond, where all the noise is coming from. The voices, loud and angry, fill up the room and squeeze through where the light comes in. She makes herself smaller to fit where she crouches behind the door. She takes her little brother's hand.

Geoff, Lee says, almost an accusation. You heard this story from Geoff.

Yes, I say. I have this picture from Lee's brother, who told me they used to sit there together behind the kitchen door, drawn by the noise they couldn't stop hearing to the scene of their parents' fights. He said it was like watching TV, fictional strangers reduced to a box on the table and distanced by black and white. It looked like no world they knew.

Ralph and Alice Kramden, Lee says. She makes a fist with one hand, and slams it against her open palm. "One of these days, Alice, one of these days." Some honeymoon, huh?

This picture's in color, I remind her.

Yes, Lee says. So what happens next?

The little girl keeps herself quiet so no one will see her there behind the door, but the noise grows louder all around her, and it lasts a long time. Some days it's in the kitchen, some days in the den, and some days, or at night sometimes, it's upstairs in the room next to hers. And all the time, she grows older and smaller at once, or she grows taller without getting older, although before long she turns eight.

One day, when the noise is upstairs, she hides in her closet until it's quiet again. Then she tiptoes past her parents' room, where her father is stripping the bed. He spots her there in the doorway (there's no place to hide, although she's buried herself as far down as she can), and motions for her to come in.

The spider to the fly, Lee says.

"Help me with these," her father says, casually, as if there were nothing strange about her father stripping the bed.

But there is something strange, Lee says, from a dream.

Yes, I say. When they fold the sheets back together, she sees blood all over them. Maybe she asks, and maybe her father lies, about whose it is and how it got there. But she knows anyway, the way children know, wordlessly, in their bones: All that noise made her mother small, too. It's her mother's blood on the sheets, and her father put it there.

But now he has an errand for her, a favor to ask. Take these things down to the basement, he says. Burn them up in the incinerator, and be quiet about it, so your mother won't know.

But wait, Lee says. She moves quickly to defend him still. She asks the question right away that took me a while to come to. That's silly, she says. If it was the mother's blood, she already knew. Why keep it a secret from her? And if he wanted to hide what he'd done, why show it like that to the child?

Yes, yes, I say. There are gaps in the narrative logic, the details don't quite fit. It would be easy to say that it never happened like that, that the child made it up, or misremembered, that by the time she told the story to Eric, who told the story to me, she was no longer a credible witness to her own history. Or maybe Eric made it up, to corroborate or explain his own story, somehow.

Sometimes the truth is that simple, Lee says.

And sometimes it's not, I say. Sometimes, out of details that don't make sense, details that beggar reason every time, in instance after distorted instance, the truth shows a more complicated face.

But you're right in one way, I tell her. He doesn't have to hide the evidence of the deed itself. His wife already knows. And besides, other people, a whole community of them, judges and lawyers and teachers and ministers and social workers, bargain makers all of them, agree to hide the evidence for him, too challenged in their comfortable lives to allow that husbands can do such things. They build a wall around their Eden, they say it can't happen here.

But still, he shares his secret with a child.

Because he cannot prevent himself from laying hands on her mother, and the impulse spills over to her. But here he can stop it just short of the use of his hand. Because here is a person he can shape without touching, here is a woman not yet born from the child, here is the intimacy he wants but cannot have with a grown person who's more troublesome to control. And to make the child's innocence complicit blesses his choice somehow. She isn't angry at him. She loves him, depends upon him, needs his attention. She wants to be seen, and he seems to be looking. All she can say is yes.

Lee turns from me, looks out the window, stares toward the highway where a car heads north in slow motion. It honks its horn for no apparent reason—there's not another car in sight—a long, slow wail. Lee sits there, quietly, folds her hands in her lap.

She's not mad at her father, Lee says. She's mad at her mother, instead.

I think it's the story of our lives, whether fathers make silence or noise.

She knows now that her mother can't protect her, and she's angry at that. Besides, she's heard it before: "Your mother doesn't love you. I love you." She's only eight years old, and her father stands there, telling her he loves her, trusts her, wants her.

No wonder the mother takes off, Lee says.

That wasn't the child's fault. Children don't deal with the devil. They deal with their parents, and when they have parents like this, making deals of their own and using the child as a chip in the bargain . . .

She should have refused, Lee says.

No. Her father made sure she saw it, the hand behind the stain on the sheet. He left the print of his hand not on her body but on her mind. She was always, always, always his child.

We have fogged up the window with our talk. Lee reaches over, doodles a tic-tac-toe board there, and places an X in the middle. Then she swipes at the window, smears the drawing away.

So how did you get so smart? she says. College and all?

College and all helped, I say. But mainly, you taught me. Remembering you taught me.

So I was good for something after all?

I drop my head and smile. You were good for me, I say. Back then, when we were kids, you took all those giant steps. At least they looked like giant steps to me. And they were, at a certain age, in a certain context.

Back then, Lee says, you were pretty dumb.

Yeah, I laugh. I was pretty dumb. My world was so narrow. Remember "Stan, Bayou Man"?

Lee sits up straight, at attention in her seat, and speaks in crisply enunciated syllables. If you ask me, she says, Christ figure or not, Billy Budd had an erection like everybody else.

We collapse into giggles, and Lee almost slips from the seat. Don't make me laugh, she says. I have to pee.

I'm inventing all this, I say, with a grand sweep of my hand through the air around me. I'll make it go away.

I don't think so, Lee says, suddenly serious.

My mood shifts back into hers. My memory of the steps you took, I tell her, or the steps I thought you took, taught me to make steps of my own, taught me to look at the world, to look at myself, to see my parents, to see myself separate from them. You helped me grow up.

I guess I fooled you, Lee says. They were just baby steps, all the time.

Yes, I think, though I don't say it out loud. You grew old without growing up. The part of you that mattered most stayed eight years old, and you lived out of that child's fear and uncertainty, burying her deeper and deeper, hiding her behind your precocious intelligence, your developed body, your wit, your cynicism, your seemingly adult behavior, way ahead of its time, all the while hoping that someone would see.

The sun hasn't moved in the sky. The van sits in the parking lot. The motor's not running. I don't have to hurry. We have all day if we want it. I lean into the seat, stretch out, throw my head back, and breathe in the dusty air.

So tell me what happens, Lee says, to the child in your story, to this little girl of yours.

I have seen her through it all. The child, I say, learns to equate love with a nameless power that can hurt her unless she says yes. She marries as her mother married, and her own blood seeps into their sheets. She says yes to her husband's schemes.

No, Lee says. She was clever, smarter, probably, than he was. She thought them up herself, those schemes.

Perhaps, I say. But perhaps she just gave him what he wanted before he asked. How then could all his power fall back on her? But it did, and she ended up in the prison of his addiction.

She wanted it too, Lee says. She knew what she was doing. She liked small spaces.

By then she did, yes, I say. She had already made herself small, fit herself to the space she'd been given.

And later, after her husband went to prison, when she was on her own, she thought she could trade places with the power that ruled her. She was holding the cards, she worked out the scam. She had the man in her bedroom, she had the film in her hands. She could make him do what she wanted.

But he had all the room in the world, Lee says. When she said, "Do it," he could say no.

Yes, I say. It takes all the power, all that space in the world to say no. So she trusted herself to the only other power in the room. And when the gun went off, when the man's blood this time seeped into the sheets, she went to prison, again.

Like you said, Lee shrugs. She was used to small spaces.

She looks around her, pushes her toe at an empty pack of cigarettes on the floor of the van. And now, she says, here we are.

I pull at a tuft of stuffing that erupts from a tear in the seat. I don't want to say what comes next.

Don't be a baby, Lee says. It happens all the time.

Yes, all the time. Who cares about the death of a prostitute, anyway? A prostitute is a murder victim waiting to happen. Someone voices the insidious question: Didn't she ask for it? Didn't she get what she deserved?

Lee reaches into the back of the van behind her and brings out her purse. Inside, she finds her blush and some lipstick. She cranes her head forward, to see into the rearview mirror above the dash, and puts on her make-up. Then she looks at her watch. It's ticking again.

It was good to see you, she says, after all this time. But I have to be going now.

Yes, I say. It's time to go.

She looks at me, then smiles and raises her hand. It flutters into a wave.

No, I say. I'm going with you.

There's not a thing you can do about it, she says.

I know, I say.

But I don't want her to go by herself. My mother would go with me.

Lee reaches across my lap in the back seat of the van, gives the door a good push, and it slams shut.

It's about time, the driver growls from the front seat. I thought you girls would never stop gabbing.

Oh, shut up, I tell him. And he starts the engine without another word.

Taylor heads the van out of the parking lot, and eases back onto the highway. We ride in silence for a few minutes, watching southern Michigan blur past the windows. Route 223 turns and twists through the Irish Hills. It's too close to winter, it isn't green yet, but the trees have all budded. Cattails shoot up at the berm, and tiger lilies, orange trumpets streaked with black, open out to the sun. Lee grows more and more thoughtful as we ride. We pass a stand of daffodils growing wild along the roadside, and she slips her arm through mine, snuggles up, close.

What happens to Eric? she asks.

I give her the comfort I have. He learns to stay the power of his own hand, I tell her. Eric is fine.

I thought so, she sighs. The last time I saw him, he already seemed like a stranger to me.

The van speeds on, Gary and Debbie chattering to each other in the front seat. We pass through Hillsdale and Adrian. I follow the road signs, the juncture of this little highway with that, a turn-off here, a hidden drive there. I see Onsted coming, and I would protect Lee if I could. I draw my arm out from hers, slip it around her shoulder, and pull her as close as I can. But Lee, sly as ever, reaches out for my hand. It's her turn to comfort me.

I'm already dead, remember? she says.

Everything happened a long time ago. Now it's only ink on paper, words on a page, images that linger on in the mind. I take solace in that. It isn't her pain anymore. It's mine.

We drive into Onsted about noon on March 24, taking a spin around Loch Erin for a few minutes, so Gary Taylor can show off the neighborhood he's so proud to live in.

"Look at that house," Debbie says. "That's the kind of place I want to live someday."

I've seen it all before, but not like this, practically empty, isolated, seven houses on countless acres, a place where, cut off from his neighbors (but not from their later report), Gary Taylor can spend hours in his own backyard, shooting one of his many guns into the woods behind his house. The neighbors don't think much of it. That's what privacy like this is for.

We pull into the driveway of the brick house where Taylor lives and pile out of the van. Debbie cracks open a few beers once we're into the kitchen. She's not yet of drinking age, officially, and avoids opening cans in the car. She finds the radio and turns the volume up loud. It's a Golden Oldies weekend on one of the Detroit stations, and Debbie has fun with that.

"Hey," she says. "What are you, Gary, forty? How about that, Lee? We all know different oldies."

"Where's the bathroom?" Lee says. "I really have to pee."

Taylor waves his arm toward the end of the hall.

I follow along behind Lee as she heads the way he pointed. Once inside the bathroom, she closes the door after us.

I almost didn't make it the last twenty miles, she laughs.

I try to laugh back. So I couldn't make it disappear after all, I say.

And then I realize: she's talking to herself. I'm not even here. I can't do anything for her now except keep her in sight.

Lee looks in the mirror, rubs a little lipstick into her cheeks for the color. The music from the radio drifts in through the locked door. It's the Isley Brothers, and Lee sings along. You know you make me want to shout, oooooh, kick my heels up and shout. She nods at herself in the mirror (I hear her say, "You be the boy") and raises her empty arms in the gesture of a dance. She spins herself a few times around the tiny bathroom, then smiles and shakes her head before she breezes back out the door.

"Who wants to dance?" she announces to the kitchen.

Taylor looks at her as if he'd just as soon shoot somebody.

"Oh, come on," Debbie says. "Be a sport."

But Taylor only shrugs and goes into the other room. Debbie takes up Lee's offer, steps into her waiting arms, and the two of them move there in the middle of the kitchen, swaying, turning, dipping to the music.

When Taylor returns to the kitchen, he stands there a moment, watching them, then snaps the radio off.

"What'd you do that for?" Debbie asks.

He raises a gun in their direction, then pokes the muzzle toward the basement door, as if to say, the fun's down there.

Debbie's arms drop from Lee's shoulders. Lee's arms drop from Debbie's waist. They step back from each other. Debbie's forehead wrinkles into a question, and Lee turns up her palms in a shrug.

"Some creeps get their kicks this way," she says. "He wants you to act scared."

"That'll be easy," Debbie says.

"Do what the man tells you," Lee says. It's her best advice.

We clatter down the stairs into the basement. Debbie goes first, a little unsteadily in her wedgy shoes. Lee follows her, Taylor's gun at her back. The stairs empty into a large open room.

So this is the basement to which I have come, where I have agreed to keep my place, to wait it out until the ghost story's done. I scan the room quickly, take it all in with a sweep of the eye. The bare walls breathe. The few windows stare. A bucket and a mop stand outside a closet door. A clothesline stretches across the corner at the far end of the room. A beat-up sofa against one wall. A few chairs, one of them set upside down.

A noise, like the fall of a key in a lock, startles me, and I turn in its direction. No, it's only the furnace clicking on behind me somewhere. I turn again, back the other way, my eye caught for an irrational instant by something moving, a body, a hand, a patch of color. I blink hard, and look again. It's only an empty blouse hanging on the clothesline, moving, yes, moving so slightly, as if in a breeze I can't see.

But there's no one else here. It is only these three: Gary Taylor, Debbie Henneman, and Lee.

Taylor motions the two women into a smaller room at the left, where in somebody else's basement we might find a washer and dryer. The walls are thick with padded insulation. Two chairs wait in the center of the room.

Taylor rummages around in a box near the furnace, and brings out a length of electrical cord, a coil of rope, a pair of handcuffs, and a white sheet he spreads out under the chairs. He pushes them clumsily nearer one wall.

While he works, Lee's dark eyes move quickly about the room. Beyond the door, on the other side of the basement, light comes through a window where Lee can just see a fringe of brown grass. She glances at Debbie, then back to the window, and Debbie lurches in the direction of the light. But Taylor anticipates her move, and without even looking up at her, bars her path with the shotgun he holds. Then he turns the gun on both of them and orders them to undress.

It has begun now, what I've come here to see. The picture wavers in front of me, then refracts, bends. Two images, four images, eight images split into a hundred pieces that spin around the center, as if I look through a dragonfly lens. I press my fingers into my eyelids, shake my head, and look again. They are still here, the two, the three of them.

Taylor motions for Debbie to have a seat in one chair. He pulls her feet together, wraps the electrical cord several times around her ankles, then jerks it up across her stomach and binds her hands together behind the chair. She is locked in.

He traces a finger upwards from her wrist to her shoulder, then brings his hand around her throat and strokes there. He moves his other hand down to her breast, and pinches hard at the nipple. Debbie's stomach pulls in quickly, and the chair jerks back. She brings her knees together, tight. He wedges his open palm between them, then makes a fist, and shoves it up toward her crotch.

"Stop that," she shouts.

He glares at her in awful silence.

Then he motions for Lee to take the other seat. He forces her knees wide apart, so she straddles the chair, bends each leg back at the knee, and ties her feet with the rope to the back chair leg. He ties her hands together behind the chair, and clicks the handcuffs in place over the rope.

He paces back and forth in front of them, his heels clipping against the linoleum. He accuses them of crimes against the state. They are women, women, women, and they make too much noise.

Shut up, shut up, shut up, I hear him say.

A flashlight swings from a short cord in his hands. Occasionally he lifts it, and shines the light down into their eyes.

Debbie starts to cry.

Shut up, I hear him say. I hate it when you make noise.

This is what you get, I hear him say.

His words echo in the empty room. They sound in my ear like a pulse.

And then, it starts, a dull hum at first, from the edges of the room, growing steadier, more intense, more certain, as one voice tumbles in on another and then another until the words themselves shimmer into something else. This is what we get.

I look up, I look around me, and they are all here. The basement is full of ghosts. They stand in a solemn line around the edges of the room, their hands at their sides, their eyes open, their mouths moving together with the words. Lawyers and doctors and ministers and social workers and psychiatrists and teachers and parents. Everyone who looked the other way. Everyone who studied only deductive patterns and statistics, and missed the stories they told, which is the same as not looking at all. All the people who refused to see what was right in front of them.

They are not called to a docket (this is not a docket, it is a basement room where women are dying). They are not here for expiation, or to be punished themselves, although this is what they get, a summons they cannot refuse. They are here because they must be, because they are in the act they witness now. They belong to the complicated pattern that will not end here unless they can see themselves in it, unless they can look on these human faces before them, more substantial than the ghosts they are, and say no.

The vision fades, the hum around me subsides, the ghosts drift away, and it is just these three. Gary Taylor, and Debbie Henneman, and Lee.

Taylor paces in front of them, reaches out with a wrench or a knife or a razor, slashes at the air, raises a welt on the shoulder, draws a red line down an arm or a leg. His agitation increases, his speech slurs, his movements jerk and twitch. He takes in air by gulps. It whistles into his heaving chest.

I stand beside Lee now, my hand on her shoulder, and together we see the end coming.

Debbie sees it, too. She screams once, and Taylor slaps her face. The sound collapses into a whimper and a jumble of words. No, no, no. Please. I'll do anything you say. Please. Let me out of here.

Taylor pulls off his T-shirt and stuffs it in Debbie's mouth.

No, I say for her. Make all the noise you can.

Lee stares for a moment, as if fascinated, where the man carves a swastika in Debbie's left breast.

She shuts her eyes tight, and I can hear in her head the sound of something that pleases. The breath of Eric's love in her hair. The water in the river, sweeping along and alive, dancing beneath her feet. An old snatch of a piano tune her father used to play in happier times, eight to the bar. The steady tick of the metronome on top of the old upright at the farm, the accidental she couldn't get right in the fifth measure of "Gertrude's Waltz." She hears her mother upstairs making the bed. The snap of clean white sheets in the air, the drift of white settling down like snow on the bed.

The snap of clean sheets and the drift of white, and then a noise comes to her, muffled, as if it traveled a great distance to reach her ear, through miles of pillow. Lee turns her head, slowly it seems, toward Debbie. She can't quite focus on the picture. Debbie's chin is gone. How can that be, a girl without a chin. And then another muffled sound. A blazing star appears suddenly on Debbie's forehead, just there, between her eyes. What does it mean? What does it stand for, that special mark, a star, a comet, between that woman's eyes?

And then Lee knows. That woman is dead.

Now a man stands in front of her. His breathing whistles in and out. The noise fills up the room.

I have taken his voice away.

He seems to be shouting. She sees his lips move, but she cannot hear his words.

They ring in my ears now. Shut up, I hear him say.

No, I say. I'll make all the noise I can.

I look around me again. The walls breathe. The window stares. A motion catches my eye. A hand, a body, a patch of color. No, it is an empty blouse hanging on the clothesline, swinging in a breeze I cannot see. No, it is the walls moving. It is the whistle of his breath. It is the furnace clicking on somewhere behind me.

No, it is a ghost fading through the wall. It is a voice coming from behind the sofa, up through the floor, down from the top of the stairs, in from the window, around the corner, down the street, through the trees, into the sky itself. One voice tumbles in on another, a distant hum, louder and louder, a rhythm, a building chord, a song.

No, they say. Make all the noise you can.

They are all here. Pearl Washburn. Rhonda Olson. Pauline Leggett. Imogen Crosby. Beth Ann Drake. Mona Hopkins. Myra Fosdick. Cathy Estabar. Sheila Evers. Annie Rippon. Bonnie Strauss. Diana Shuler. Carla Baird. Paula Tunning. Irma Hobbs.

They pass through the walls. They slip out from the corners. They sweep in through the windows. They pool up like blood from the floor.

They have come here from bus stops, padded barefoot across their own living room carpets behind picture windows, they have risen from their sofas. They wear housedresses and bathrobes and mini-skirts. They have curlers in their hair. They come from their kitchens and their classrooms, they have come—who knows how many of them—from the streets of Boston, or Baltimore, or Detroit.

I do not know all their names, but someone knows them, and they are all here, joined now by the people who loved them. Husbands and fathers, and sisters and brothers and mothers, and lovers and friends. All the people who wrote their names every year on birthday cards, who called their names across the partition in an office, or spoke them across the dinner table, or whispered them in love. Who speak them still, like a litany for the dead. Betty Goodrich. Irene Waters. Sandra Horwath. Vonnie Smith. Suzanne Jackson. Debbie Henneman. And Lee.

No, they say. Make all the noise you can.

They stand around me in a ghostly circle in the center of this room. They are here to touch their hands and raise their voices. They are here to witness and to mourn. They are here to speak this "no," one voice, then another, but they cannot stay the power of one hand.

It happened a long time ago, and all these words echo in an empty room.

Lee feels a twinge of pain at the back of her head.

I take her hand, and whisper a lullabye in her ear. Hush, little baby, don't say a word. Mama's going to buy you a mockingbird.

It's only a little pinch of pain, and Lee blinks against the light of it.

A bird beats its wings in my heart. It swoops and chatters in the frenzied air, without its bearings, unable to find the way out. Here, Lee, I say. The window is here. I wave my arms in the air.

The sky is a wide and terrible place. I open my heart, and she flies.

Epilogue

Given the power that someone like Gary Taylor has to alter a life, to ruin it, to reduce by one at a time the number of people gathered for the family portrait on the next wedding anniversary or birthday party, the survivors may have trouble saying whose life has more significance for them, the one they lost, or the one who took her away.

Given the power that a person like Gary Taylor has. He has that power only if we give it to him, only if we let him take over our memories and our dreams, only if we subordinate the loss to the cause of it, only if we say the life he took, by some indecent standard, doesn't count.

Who cares about the death of a prostitute, anyway?

Lee Snavely's remains were cremated and buried in the Oak Grove Cemetery in Bowling Green, next to her father's grave.

Lee's stepmother sells real estate in northwest Ohio. Her mother still lives in Cleveland.

Geoff Snavely was graduated from high school in 1971. He lived an itinerant life for a while, first in California and later in Minnesota, where he settled down into a construction business. In his middle thirties, he returned to Bowling Green to go to college. In all that time, he had no significant relationships. He speaks to his mother, on the phone, on holidays, and sees her occasionally. She is always pleasant, but they don't know each other very well. He knows now they never will and has all but given up trying.

Bruce Snavely stopped throwing himself out of cars spinning in parking lots and threw himself into a ministry in a small town in Canada, bringing Jesus into the lives of his parishioners. In Christ, he says, he has found the family he always wanted. After nine years in the mission field, he has returned to the United States with his wife and four children to raise support for his next missionary effort.

William Greggory Snavely, called Bill, abandoned a promising career in astrophysics, I am told, and moved to the American Southwest, where he lives by subsistence farming. He shares his life with three women. Among them, he has eight children.

In 1981, Eric Fletcher married Holly Ashworth. In 1984, they became the parents of a blond-headed boy, Ethan. Today, Eric is completing an advanced degree in counselling and family ecology. He intends to commit his practice to the rehabilitation of neglected and abused children.

Vonnie Stuth's family sued Dr. Ames Robey, charging him with gross negligence in permitting Gary Taylor to leave the Ypsilanti Forensic Center.

Gary Taylor pleaded guilty to a charge of second-degree murder in the case of Vonnie Stuth. On the recommendation of the judge and the prosecution, the typical sentence for second-degree murder (five to twenty years) was increased in this case to up-to-life in prison in the penitentiary at Walla Walla, Washington. In 1984, Taylor was transferred from that prison to the state penitentiary in Rawlins, Wyoming, where he remains under the conditions of his original sentence.

I have petitioned the state of Washington for the right to be informed of any changes in his status.

Acknowledgments

To Jerry and Ellen Brimcombe, Deborah Retterer Chapman, Christine Anders Claflin, Jan Dimick, John Dunipace, Michael Halleck, Ron June, Karl Lowell, Edward C. Preston, Bruce Snavely, Fred and Elizabeth Uhlman, for sharing their memories with me. To Geoffrey Snavely and Eric Fletcher for their full cooperation and support. To my brother Greer Imbrie, my sisters Charity Imbrie and Catherine Imbrie Milligan, for helping me reconstruct the social history, and especially to my parents for their patience and help.

For their assistance in helping me track down documentary evidence: Anne E. Bartlett (St. Petersburg); Arthur Claflin, Ann Rule, Max and Christine Woolslayer (Seattle); Andy Lewis (Houston); Paul W. Jones (Bowling Green). To the reference staffs of the Wood County Public Library, the Bowling Green State University Library, and the Ann Arbor Public Library. To the county clerks of Lucas and Wood Counties (Ohio); Ionia, Oakland, and Washtenaw Counties (Michigan); Pinellas County (Florida); Harris County (Texas); King County (Washington). To David Stoll, of Simpson, Thatcher and Bartlett (New York City), for his legal expertise. To Mary Beth Caschetta, for the simile, the balloons, and the fact checking. To Lori Lehrer for sparing me *The New York Times* on microfilm. And to Vassar College for funds to support some of the research.

To generous friends and colleagues, consistent in their encouragement and advice: Mark and Marie Cooper, Eileen Dunn, Eryc W. Eyl, Archie Gresham, Gregory Hrbek, Thomas Mallon, Susan McCloskey and David Kelley, Robert Pounder, and Pat Wright. Special thanks, for good ears and good sense, to Beverly Coyle and Paul Russell; to Carole DeSanti, for easing my way; to my agents, Regula Noetzli and Charlotte Sheedy; and to my editor, Pat Mulcahy.

Author's Note

This work of nonfiction depends on several sources identified in the narrative itself: my own memory, the accounts other people provided of actual events they witnessed and participated in, and documentary evidence in the form of newspaper accounts, certified court records, depositions, other forms of sworn testimony, and trial transcripts, collected over several years. With the exceptions noted here, names appear in this book as they do in the public record. To ensure their privacy, I have changed the names of Gary Taylor's living victims, and the names of those persons I call Connie Humphrey, Tommy Matson, and Carl Woodman.

In recounting events from the private record, I have changed the names of persons playing supporting roles, using invented first names alone wherever appropriate, and have altered other identifying details. The following are also fictitious names: Phil Donovan, Mr. Hilton, the various Holdens, Maggie Howell, Mrs. Leonard, Pam Robbins, and Mr. Warren. Where the narrative relies on the personal recollections of people who agreed to be interviewed for this book, I have made conscientious efforts to corroborate their accounts.